Bayesian Methods
for Hackers

   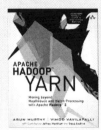 

 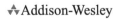

Bayesian Methods for Hackers

Probabilistic Programming and Bayesian Inference

Cameron Davidson-Pilon

✦✦Addison-Wesley

New York • Boston • Indianapolis • San Francisco
Toronto • Montreal • London • Munich • Paris • Madrid
Capetown • Sydney • Tokyo • Singapore • Mexico City

Many of the designations used by manufacturers and sellers to distinguish their products are claimed as trademarks. Where those designations appear in this book, and the publisher was aware of a trademark claim, the designations have been printed with initial capital letters or in all capitals.

The author and publisher have taken care in the preparation of this book, but make no expressed or implied warranty of any kind and assume no responsibility for errors or omissions. No liability is assumed for incidental or consequential damages in connection with or arising out of the use of the information or programs contained herein.

For information about buying this title in bulk quantities, or for special sales opportunities (which may include electronic versions; custom cover designs; and content particular to your business, training goals, marketing focus, or branding interests), please contact our corporate sales department at corpsales@pearsoned.com or (800) 382-3419.

For government sales inquiries, please contact governmentsales@pearsoned.com.

For questions about sales outside the United States, please contact international@pearsoned.com.

Visit us on the Web: informit.com/aw

Library of Congress Cataloging-in-Publication Data

Davidson-Pilon, Cameron.
  Bayesian methods for hackers : probabilistic programming and bayesian inference / Cameron Davidson-Pilon.
    pages cm
  Includes bibliographical references and index.
  ISBN 978-0-13-390283-9 (pbk.: alk. paper)
  1. Penetration testing (Computer security)–Mathematics. 2. Bayesian statistical decision theory.
  3. Soft computing. I. Title.
  QA76.9.A25D376 2015
  006.3–dc23

                                                                                        2015017249

ISBN-13: 978-0-13-390283-9
ISBN-10: 0-13-390283-8
Text printed in the United States on recycled paper at RR Donnelley in Crawfordsville, Indiana.
First printing, October 2015

❖

This book is dedicated to many important relationships: my parents, my brothers, and my closest friends. Second to them, it is devoted to the open-source community, whose work we consume every day without knowing.

❖

Contents

Foreword

Bayesian methods are one of many in a modern data scientist's toolkit. They can be used to solve problems in prediction, classification, spam detection, ranking, inference, and many other tasks. However, most of the material out there on Bayesian statistics and inference focuses on the mathematical details while giving little attention to the more pragmatic engineering considerations. That's why I'm very pleased to have this book joining the series, bringing a much needed introduction to Bayesian methods targeted at practitioners.

Cameron's knowledge of the topic and his focus on tying things back to tangible examples make this book a great introduction for data scientists or regular programmers looking to learn about Bayesian methods. This book is filled with examples, figures, and working Python code that make it easy to get started solving actual problems. If you're new to data science, Bayesian methods, or new to data science with Python, this book will be an invaluable resource to get you started.

—Paul Dix
Series Editor

Preface

The Bayesian method is the natural approach to inference, yet it is hidden from readers behind chapters of slow, mathematical analysis. The typical text on Bayesian inference involves two to three chapters on probability theory, then enters into what Bayesian inference is. Unfortunately, due to the mathematical intractability of most Bayesian models, the reader is only shown simple, artificial examples. This can leave the user with a "So what?" feeling about Bayesian inference. In fact, this was my own prior opinion.

After some recent success of Bayesian methods in machine-learning competitions, I decided to investigate the subject again. Even with my mathematical background, it took me three straight days of reading examples and trying to put the pieces together to understand the methods. There was simply not enough literature bridging theory to practice. The problem with my misunderstanding was the disconnect between Bayesian mathematics and probabilistic programming. That being said, I suffered then so the reader would not have to now. This book attempts to bridge the gap.

If Bayesian inference is the destination, then mathematical analysis is a particular path toward it. On the other hand, computing power is cheap enough that we can afford to take an alternate route via probabilistic programming. The latter path is much more useful, as it denies the necessity of mathematical intervention at each step; that is, we remove often intractable mathematical analysis as a prerequisite to Bayesian inference. Simply put, this latter computational path proceeds via small, intermediate jumps from beginning to end, whereas the first path proceeds by enormous leaps, often landing far away from our target. Furthermore, without a strong mathematical background, the analysis required by the first path cannot even take place.

Bayesian Methods for Hackers is designed as an introduction to Bayesian inference from a computational/understanding first, and mathematics second, point of view. Of course, as an introductory book, we can only leave it at that: an introductory book. For the mathematically trained, the curiosity this text generates may be cured by other texts designed with mathematical analysis in mind. For the enthusiast with a less mathematical background, or one who is not interested in the mathematics but simply the practice of Bayesian methods, this text should be sufficient and entertaining.

The choice of PyMC as the probabilistic programming language is twofold. First, as of this writing, there is currently no central resource for examples and explanations in the PyMC universe. The official documentation assumes prior knowledge of Bayesian inference and probabilistic programming. We hope this book encourages users at every level to look at PyMC. Second, with recent core developments and popularity of the scientific stack in Python, PyMC is likely to become a core component soon enough.

PyMC does have dependencies to run, namely NumPy and (optionally) SciPy. To not limit the user, the examples in this book will rely only on PyMC, NumPy, SciPy, and matplotlib.

The progression of the book is as follows. Chapter 1 introduces Bayesian inference and its comparison to other inference techniques. We also see, build, and train our first Bayesian model. Chapter 2 focuses on building models with PyMC, with a strong emphasis on examples. Chapter 3 introduces Markov Chain Monte Carlo, a powerful algorithm behind computational inference, and some techniques on debugging your Bayesian model. In Chapter 4, we detour and again visit the issue of sample sizes in inference and explain why understanding sample size is so important. Chapter 5 introduces the powerful idea of loss functions, where we have not a model but a function that connects inference to real-world problems. We revisit the idea of Bayesian priors in Chapter 6, and give good heuristics to picking good priors. Finally, in Chapter 7, we explore how Bayesian inference can be used in A/B testing.

All the datasets used in this text are available online at `https://github.com/CamDavidsonPilon/Probabilistic-Programming-and-Bayesian-Methods-for-Hackers`.

Acknowledgments

I would like to acknowledge the many people involved in this book. First and foremost, I'd like to acknowledge the contributors to the online version of *Bayesian Methods for Hackers*. Many of these authors submitted contributions (code, ideas, and text) that helped round out this book. Second, I would like to thank the reviewers of this book, Robert Mauriello and Tobi Bosede, for sacrificing their time to peel through the difficult abstractions I can make and for narrowing the contents down for a much more enjoyable read. Finally, I would like to acknowledge my friends and colleagues, who supported me throughout the process.

About the Author

Cameron Davidson-Pilon has seen many fields of applied mathematics, from evolutionary dynamics of genes and diseases to stochastic modeling of financial prices. His main contributions to the open-source community include *Bayesian Methods for Hackers* and lifelines. Cameron was raised in Guelph, Ontario, but was educated at the University of Waterloo and Independent University of Moscow. He currently lives in Ottawa, Ontario, working with the online commerce leader Shopify.

The Philosophy of Bayesian Inference

1.1 Introduction

You are a skilled programmer, but bugs still slip into your code. After a particularly difficult implementation of an algorithm, you decide to test your code on a trivial example. It passes. You test the code on a harder problem. It passes once again. And it passes the next, *even more difficult*, test too! You are starting to believe that there may be no bugs in this code...

If you think this way, then congratulations: You already are thinking Bayesian! Bayesian inference is simply updating your beliefs after considering new evidence. A Bayesian can rarely be certain about a result, but he or she can be very confident. Just like in the example above, we can never be 100% sure that our code is bug-free unless we test it on every possible problem, something rarely possible in practice. Instead, we can test it on a large number of problems, and if it succeeds, we can feel more *confident* about our code, but still not certain. Bayesian inference works identically: We update our beliefs about an outcome, but rarely can we be absolutely sure unless we rule out all other alternatives.

1.1.1 The Bayesian State of Mind

Bayesian inference differs from more traditional statistical inference by preserving *uncertainty*. At first, this sounds like a bad statistical technique. Isn't statistics all about deriving *certainty* from randomness? To reconcile this, we need to start thinking like Bayesians.

The Bayesian worldview interprets probability as measure of *believability in an event*—that is, how confident we are in an event occurring. In fact, we will see in a moment that this is the natural interpretation of probability.

For this to be clearer, we consider an alternative interpretation of probability: **Frequentists**, who ascribe to the more classical version of statistics, assume that probability is the long-run frequency of events (hence the name). For example, the *probability of plane accidents* under a frequentist philosophy is interpreted as the *long-term* *frequency of plane accidents.* This makes logical sense for many probabilities of events, but becomes more difficult to understand when events have no long-term frequency of occurrences. Consider: We often assign probabilities to outcomes of presidential elections, but the election itself only happens once! Frequentists get around this by invoking alternative realities and saying that across all these realities, the frequency of occurrences defines the probability.

Bayesians, on the other hand, have a more intuitive approach. Bayesians interpret a probability as the measure of belief, or confidence, in an event occurring. Simply, a probability is a summary of an opinion. An individual who assigns a belief of 0 to an event believes with absolute certainty that the event will *not* occur; conversely, assigning a belief of 1 implies that the individual is absolutely certain that the event *will* occur. Beliefs between 0 and 1 allow for weightings of other outcomes. This definition agrees with the example of the probability of a plane accident occurring, for having observed the frequency of plane accidents, an individual's belief should be equal to that frequency, excluding any outside information. Similarly, under this definition of probability being equal to beliefs, it is meaningful to speak about probabilities (beliefs) of presidential election outcomes: How confident are you that candidate A will win?

Notice that in the preceding paragraph, I assigned the belief (probability) measure to an *individual*, not to nature. This is very interesting, as this definition leaves room for conflicting beliefs between individuals. Again, this is analogous to what naturally occurs: Different individuals have different beliefs of events occurring because they possess different information about the world. The existence of different beliefs does not imply that anyone is wrong. Consider the following examples demonstrating the relationship between individual beliefs and probabilities.

1. I flip a coin, and we both guess the result. We would both agree, assuming the coin is fair, that the probability of heads is 0.5. Assume, then, that I peek at the coin. Now I know for certain what the result is, and I assign probability 1.0 to either heads or tails (whichever it is). Now what is *your* belief that the coin is heads? My knowledge of the outcome has not changed the coin's results. Thus we assign different probabilities to the result.

2. Your code either has a bug in it or doesn't, but we do not know for certain which is true, though we have a belief about the presence or absence of a bug.

3. A medical patient is exhibiting symptoms x, y, and z. There are a number of diseases that could be causing all of them, but only a single disease is present. A doctor has beliefs about which disease, but a second doctor may have slightly different beliefs.

This philosophy of treating beliefs as probability is natural to humans. We employ it constantly as we interact with the world; we only see partial truths, but gather evidence to form beliefs. Alternatively, you have to be trained to think like a frequentist.

To align ourselves with traditional probability notation, we denote our belief about event A as $P(A)$. We call this quantity the **prior probability**.

John Maynard Keynes, a great economist and thinker, is often quoted (perhaps apocryphally) as saying, "When the facts change, I change my mind. What do you do, sir?" This quotation reflects the way a Bayesian updates his or her beliefs after seeing evidence. Even—especially—if the evidence is counter to what was initially believed, the evidence cannot be ignored. We denote our updated belief as $P(A|X)$, interpreted as the probability of A given the evidence X. We call the updated belief the **posterior probability** so as to contrast it with the prior probability. For example, consider the posterior probabilities (read: posterior beliefs) of the preceding examples, after observing some evidence X.

1. $P(A)$: The coin has a 50% chance of being heads. $P(A|X)$: You look at the coin, observe it is heads, denote this information X, and assign probability 1.0 to heads and 0.0 to tails.

2. $P(A)$: This big, complex code likely has a bug in it. $P(A|X)$: The code passed all X tests; there still might be a bug, but its presence is less likely now.

3. $P(A)$: The patient could have any number of diseases. $P(A|X)$: Performing a blood test generated evidence X, ruling out some of the possible diseases from consideration.

It's clear that in each example we did not completely discard the prior belief after seeing new evidence X, but we *re-weighted the prior* to incorporate the new evidence (i.e., we put more weight, or confidence, on some beliefs versus others).

By introducing prior uncertainty about events, we are already admitting that any guess we make is potentially very wrong. After observing data, evidence, or other information, we update our beliefs, and our guess becomes *less wrong*. This is the alternate side of the prediction coin, where typically we try to be *more right*.

1.1.2 Bayesian Inference in Practice

If frequentist and Bayesian inference were programming functions, with inputs being statistical problems, then the two would be different in what they return to the user. The frequentist inference function would return a number, representing an estimate (typically a summary statistic like the sample average), whereas the Bayesian function would return *probabilities*.

For example, in our debugging problem, calling the frequentist function with the argument "My code passed all X tests; is my code bug-free?" would return a *YES*. On the other hand, asking our Bayesian function "Often my code has bugs. My code passed all X tests; is my code bug-free?" would return something very different: probabilities of *YES* and *NO*. The function might return

YES, with probability 0.8; *NO*, with probability 0.2

This is very different from the answer the frequentist function returned. Notice that the Bayesian function accepted an additional argument: "Often my code has bugs." This parameter is the prior. By including the prior parameter, we are telling the Bayesian function to include our belief about the situation. Technically, this parameter in the Bayesian function is optional, but we will see that excluding it has its own consequences.

Incorporating Evidence   As we acquire more and more instances of evidence, our prior belief is "washed out" by the new evidence. This is to be expected. For example, if your prior belief is something ridiculous like "I expect the sun to explode today," and each day you are proved wrong, you would hope that any inference would correct you, or at least align your beliefs better. Bayesian inference will correct this belief.

Denote N as the number of instances of evidence we possess. As we gather an *infinite* amount of evidence, say as $N \to \infty$, our Bayesian results (often) align with frequentist results. Hence for large N, statistical inference is more or less objective. On the other hand, for small N, inference is much more *unstable*; frequentist estimates have more variance and larger confidence intervals. This is where Bayesian analysis excels. By introducing a prior, and returning probabilities (instead of a scalar estimate), we *preserve the uncertainty* that reflects the instability of statistical inference of a small-N dataset.

One may think that for large N, one can be indifferent between the two techniques since they offer similar inference, and might lean toward the computationally simpler frequentist methods. An individual in this position should consider the following quotation by Andrew Gelman (2005)[1] before making such a decision:

> Sample sizes are never large. If N is too small to get a sufficiently-precise estimate, you need to get more data (or make more assumptions). But once N is "large enough," you can start subdividing the data to learn more (for example, in a public opinion poll, once you have a good estimate for the entire country, you can estimate among men and women, northerners and southerners, different age groups, etc). N is never enough because if it were "enough" you'd already be on to the next problem for which you need more data.

1.1.3   Are Frequentist Methods Incorrect?

No. Frequentist methods are still useful or state-of-the-art in many areas. Tools such as least squares linear regression, LASSO regression, and expectation-maximization algorithms are all powerful and fast. Bayesian methods complement these techniques by solving problems that these approaches cannot, or by illuminating the underlying system with more flexible modeling.

1.1.4   A Note on "Big Data"

Paradoxically, the predictive analytic problems of "big data" are actually solved by relatively simple algorithms.[2][3] Thus we can argue that big data's prediction difficulty does not lie in the algorithm used, but instead in the computational difficulties of storage and execution on big data. (One should also consider Gelman's aforementioned quote about sample sizes and ask, "Do I really have big data?")

The much more difficult analytic problems involve *medium data* and—especially troublesome—*really small data*. Using an argument similar to Gelman's, if big-data problems are big enough to be readily solved, then we should be more interested in the *not-quite-big-enough* datasets.

1.2 Our Bayesian Framework

We are interested in beliefs, which can be interpreted as probabilities by thinking Bayesian. We have a prior belief in event A—for example, our prior belief about bugs being in our code before performing tests.

Next, we observe our evidence. To continue our buggy-code example: If our code passes X tests, we want to update our belief to incorporate this. We call this new belief the *posterior probability*. Updating our belief is done via the following equation, known as Bayes' Theorem, after its discoverer Thomas Bayes:

$$P(A|X) = \frac{P(X|A)P(A)}{P(X)}$$
$$\propto P(X|A)P(A) \quad (\propto \text{ means "is proportional to")}$$

This formula is not unique to Bayesian inference; it is a mathematical fact with uses outside Bayesian inference. Bayesian inference merely uses it to connect the prior probability $P(A)$ with an updated posterior probability $P(A|X)$.

1.2.1 Example: Mandatory Coin-Flip

Every statistics text must contain a coin-flipping example, so I'll use it here to get it out of the way. Suppose, naively, that you are unsure about the probability of heads in a coin flip. (Spoiler alert: It's 50%.) You believe that there is some true underlying ratio—call it p—but have no prior opinion of what p might be.

We begin to flip a coin, and record the observations of either heads or tails. This is our observed data. An interesting question to ask is,

How does our inference of p change as we observe more and more coin flips?

More specifically, what do our posterior probabilities look like when we have little data versus when we have lots of data? Next, we plot a sequence of incrementally updated posterior probabilities as we observe increasing amounts of data (coin flips).

The posterior probabilities are represented by the curves, and our uncertainty is proportional to the width of the curve. As Figure 1.2.1 shows, as we start to observe data, our posterior probabilities start to shift and move around. Eventually, as we observe more and more data (coin flips), our probabilities will tighten more and more closely around the true value of $p = 0.5$ (marked by a dashed line).

Notice that the plots are *not always* peaked at 0.5. There is no reason that they should be; you will recall that we assumed we did not have a prior opinion of what p is. In fact, if we observe quite extreme data—say, 8 flips and only 1 observed heads—our distribution would look very biased *away* from lumping around 0.5. (With no prior opinion, how confident would you feel betting on a fair coin after observing 8 tails and 1 head?) As more data accumulates, we would see more and more probability being assigned at $p = 0.5$, though never all of it.

The next example is a simple demonstration of the mathematics of Bayesian inference.

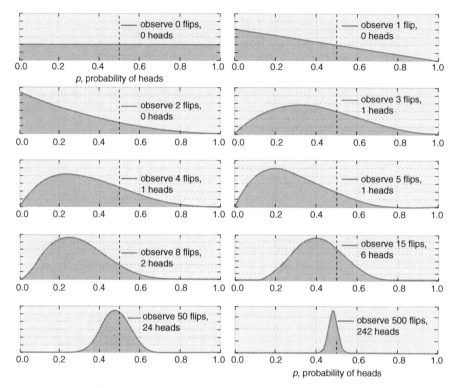

Figure 1.2.1: Bayesian updating of posterior probabilities

1.2.2   Example: Librarian or Farmer?

Consider the following story, inspired by *Thinking, Fast and Slow* by Daniel Kahneman (2011).[4] Steve is described as a shy individual, very helpful, but he has little interest in other people. He likes things in their proper order, and is very detailed about his work. Do you think Steve is more likely to be a librarian or a farmer? It may seem that Steve is more likely to be a librarian, and most people would agree with this conclusion, but that's ignoring the background distribution of librarians and farmers: The ratio of male farmers to male librarians is 20:1. Steve is *statistically* more likely to be a farmer!

How can we correct this error? Is Steve actually more likely to be a farmer or librarian now? To make this simpler, suppose that there are only two professions, librarians and farmers, and there are indeed 20 times more farmers than librarians.

Let A denote the event that Steve is a librarian. If we have no information about Steve, then $P(A) = 1/21 = 0.047$. This is our prior. Now suppose we are given the information about his personality by his neighbor; we'll call this information X. We are interested in $P(A|X)$. Recall Bayes' Theorem:

$$P(A|X) = \frac{P(X|A)P(A)}{P(X)}$$

We know $P(A)$, but what is $P(X|A)$? This quantity can be defined as the probability of this neighbor's description *given* Steve is a librarian—that is, how likely the neighbor would be to describe Steve in this way if he is in fact a librarian. This is probably pretty close to 1.0. Let's just say it is 95%, or 0.95.

Next is $P(X)$, which is the chance of someone—anyone—being described in the way the neighbor described Steve. This is pretty difficult to estimate in its current form, but we can apply some logical refactoring:

$$P(X) = P(X \text{ and } A) + P(X \text{ and } \sim A)$$
$$= P(X|A)P(A) + P(X| \sim A)P(\sim A)$$

where $\sim A$ means that Steve is *not* a librarian, and thus is a farmer. So we know $P(X|A)$ and $P(A)$, and $P(\sim A) = 1 - P(A) = 20/21$. Now we just need $P(X| \sim A)$, the probability of a neighbor describing Steve as X, given he's a farmer. Let's say this is 0.5; thus, $P(X) = 0.95 * (1/21) + (0.5) * (20/21) = 0.52$.

Combining everything:

$$P(A|X) = \frac{0.951/21}{0.52} = 0.087$$

That's not very high, but considering how many more farmers there are than librarians, it does seem logical. In Figure 1.2.2, we compare the prior and posterior probabilities of Steve being a librarian and Steve being a farmer.

```
%matplotlib inline
from IPython.core.pylabtools import figsize
import numpy as np
from matplotlib import pyplot as plt
figsize(12.5, 4)
plt.rcParams['savefig.dpi'] = 300
plt.rcParams['figure.dpi'] = 300

colors = ["#348ABD", "#A60628"]
prior = [1/21., 20/21.]
posterior = [0.087,1-0.087]
plt.bar([0, .7], prior, alpha=0.70, width=0.25,
        color=colors[0], label="prior distribution",
        lw="3", edgecolor="#348ABD")

plt.bar([0+0.25, .7+0.25], posterior, alpha=0.7,
        width=0.25, color=colors[1],
        label="posterior distribution",
        lw="3", edgecolor="#A60628")

plt.xticks([0.20, 0.95], ["Librarian", "Farmer"])
plt.title("Prior and posterior probabilities of Steve's\
        occupation")
plt.ylabel("Probability")
plt.legend(loc="upper left");
```

Notice that after we observed X, the probability of Steve being a librarian increased, though not by much—it is still overwhelmingly likely that Steve is a farmer.

This was a very simple example of Bayesian inference and Bayes' rule. Unfortunately, the mathematics necessary to perform more complicated Bayesian inference only becomes more difficult, except for artificially constructed cases. We will later see that this type of mathematical analysis is actually unnecessary. First we must broaden our modeling tools. The next section deals with *probability distributions*. If you are already familiar with them, feel free to skip (or at least skim) it, but for the less familiar the next section is essential.

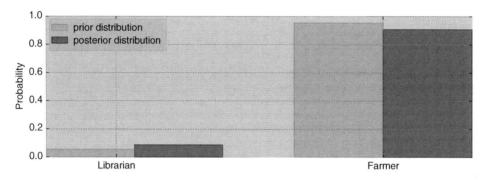

Figure 1.2.2: Prior and posterior probabilities of Steve's occupation

1.3   Probability Distributions

Let's first define some Greek letters, so we have a common vocabulary:

$$\alpha = \text{alpha}$$
$$\beta = \text{beta}$$
$$\lambda = \text{lambda}$$
$$\mu = \text{mu}$$
$$\sigma = \text{sigma}$$
$$\tau = \text{tau}$$

Great. Let's move on to probability distributions. Let's quickly recall what a probability distribution is. Let Z be some random variable. Then associated with Z is a *probability distribution function* that assigns probabilities to the different outcomes Z can take.

We can divide random variables into three classifications:

- Z is **discrete**. Discrete random variables may only assume values on a specified list. Things like currency, movie ratings, and number of votes are all discrete random variables. Discrete random variables become more clear when we contrast them with. . .

- Z is **continuous**. Continuous random variables can take on arbitrarily exact values. For example, temperature, speed, and time are all modeled as continuous variables because you can progressively make the values more and more precise.

- Z is **mixed**. Mixed random variables assign probabilities to both discrete and continuous random variables; that is, they are a combination of the first two categories.

1.3.1 Discrete Case

If Z is discrete, then its distribution is called a *probability mass function*, which measures the probability that Z takes on the value k, denoted $P(Z = k)$. Note that the probability mass function completely describes the random variable Z; that is, if we know the mass function, we know how Z should behave. There are popular probability mass functions that consistently appear; we will introduce them as needed, but let's introduce the first very useful probability mass function. We say that Z is *Poisson*-distributed if:

$$P(Z = k) = \frac{\lambda^k e^{-\lambda}}{k!}, \quad k = 0, 1, 2, \ldots$$

λ is called a parameter of the distribution, and it controls the distribution's shape. For the Poisson distribution, λ can be any positive number. By increasing λ, we add more probability to larger values; conversely, by decreasing λ, we add more probability to smaller values. One can describe λ as the *intensity* of the Poisson distribution.

Unlike λ, which can be any positive number, the value k in the preceding formula must be a non-negative integer—that is, k must take on values 0, 1, 2, and so on. This is very important, because if you want to model a population, you cannot make sense of populations with 4.25 or 5.612 members.

If a random variable Z has a Poisson mass distribution, we denote this by writing

$$Z \sim \text{Poi}(\lambda)$$

One useful property of the Poisson distribution is that its expected value is equal to its parameter. That is,

$$E[Z|\lambda] = \lambda$$

We will use this property often, so it's useful to remember. In Figure 1.3.1, we plot the probability mass distribution for different λ values. The first thing to notice is that by increasing λ, we add more probability of larger values occurring. Second, notice that although the x axis ends at 15, the distributions do not. They assign positive probability to every non-negative integer.

```
figsize(12.5, 4)

import scipy.stats as stats
a = np.arange(16)
```

(*Continues*)

(Continued)

```
poi = stats.poisson
lambda_ = [1.5, 4.25]
colors = ["#348ABD", "#A60628"]

plt.bar(a, poi.pmf(a, lambda_[0]), color=colors[0],
        label="$\lambda = %.1f$" % lambda_[0], alpha=0.60,
        edgecolor=colors[0], lw="3")

plt.bar(a, poi.pmf(a, lambda_[1]), color=colors[1],
        label="$\lambda = %.1f$" % lambda_[1], alpha=0.60,
        edgecolor=colors[1], lw="3")

plt.xticks(a + 0.4, a)
plt.legend()
plt.ylabel("Probability of $k$")
plt.xlabel("$k$")
plt.title("Probability mass function of a Poisson random variable,\
        differing \$\lambda$ values");
```

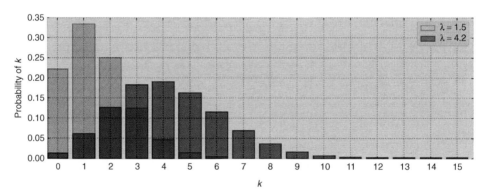

Figure 1.3.1: Probability mass function of a Poisson random variable, differing λ values

1.3.2   Continuous Case

Instead of a probability mass function, a continuous random variable has a *probability density function*. This might seem like unnecessary nomenclature, but the density function and the mass function are very different creatures. An example of a continuous random variable is a random variable with *exponential density*. The density function for an exponential random variable looks like this:

$$f_Z(z|\lambda) = \lambda e^{-\lambda z}, \ \ z \geq 0$$

Like a Poisson random variable, an exponential random variable can take on only non-negative values. But unlike a Poisson variable, the exponential can take on *any* non-negative values, including non-integral values such as 4.25 or 5.612401. This property makes it a poor choice for count data, which must be an integer, but a great choice for time data, temperature data (measured in Kelvins, of course), or any other precise *and positive* variable. Figure 1.3.2 shows two probability density functions with different λ values.

When a random variable Z has an exponential distribution with parameter λ, we say Z *is exponential* and write

$$Z \sim \text{Exp}(\lambda)$$

Given a specific λ, the expected value of an exponential random variable is equal to the inverse of λ. That is,

$$E[Z|\lambda] = \frac{1}{\lambda}$$

```
a = np.linspace(0, 4, 100)
expo = stats.expon
lambda_ = [0.5, 1]

for l, c in zip(lambda_, colors):
    plt.plot(a, expo.pdf(a, scale=1./l), lw=3,
            color=c, label="$\lambda = %.1f$" % l)
    plt.fill_between(a, expo.pdf(a, scale=1./l), color=c, alpha=.33)

plt.legend()
plt.ylabel("Probability density function at $z$")
plt.xlabel("$z$")
plt.ylim(0,1.2)
plt.title("Probability density function of an exponential random\
          variable, differing $\lambda$ values");
```

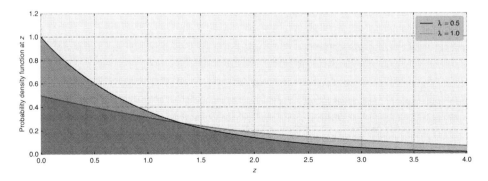

Figure 1.3.2: Probability density function of an exponential random variable, differing λ values

It's important to know that the value of the probability density function at a point does *not* equal the *probability* of that point. This will come up a bit later, but if you want to dive in now, try this discussion: http://stats.stackexchange.com /questions/4220/a-probability-distribution-value-exceeding-1-is-ok

1.3.3   But What Is λ?

This question is what motivates statistics. In the real world, λ is hidden from us. We see only Z, and must work backward to try to determine λ. The problem is difficult because there is no one-to-one mapping from Z to λ. Many different methods have been created to solve the problem of estimating λ, but since λ is never actually observed, no one can say for certain which method is best!

Bayesian inference is concerned with *beliefs* about what λ might be. Rather than trying to guess λ exactly, we can only talk about what λ is likely to be by assigning a probability distribution to λ.

This might seem odd at first. After all, λ is fixed; it is not (necessarily) random! How can we assign probabilities to values of a non-random variable? Uh-oh; we have fallen for our old, frequentist way of thinking. Recall that under Bayesian philosophy, we *can* assign probabilities if we interpret them as beliefs. And it is entirely acceptable to have *beliefs* about the parameter λ.

1.4   Using Computers to Perform Bayesian Inference for Us

Let's try to model a more interesting example, one that concerns the rate at which a user sends and receives text messages.

1.4.1   Example: Inferring Behavior from Text-Message Data

You are given a series of daily text-message counts from a user of your system. The data, plotted over time, appears in Figure 1.4.1. You are curious to know if the user's text-messaging habits have changed over time, either gradually or suddenly. How can you model this? (This is in fact my own text-message data. Judge my popularity as you wish.)

```
figsize(12.5, 3.5)
count_data = np.loadtxt("data/txtdata.csv")
n_count_data = len(count_data)
plt.bar(np.arange(n_count_data), count_data, color="#348ABD")
plt.xlabel("Time (days)")
plt.ylabel("Text messages received")
plt.title("Did the user's texting habits change over time?")
plt.xlim(0, n_count_data);
```

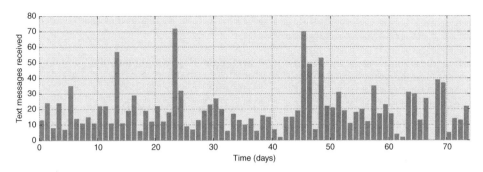

Figure 1.4.1: Did the user's texting habits change over time?

Before we start modeling, see what you can figure out just by looking at Figure 1.4.1. Would you say there was a change in behavior during this time period?

How can we start to model this? Well, as we have conveniently already seen, a Poisson random variable is a very appropriate model for this type of *count* data. Denoting day i's text-message count by C_i,

$$C_i \sim \text{Poi}(\lambda)$$

We are not sure what the value of the λ parameter really is, however. Looking at Figure 1.4.1, it appears that the rate might become higher late in the observation period, which is equivalent to saying that λ increases at some point during the observations. (Recall that a higher value of λ assigns more probability to larger outcomes. That is, there is a higher probability of many text messages having been sent on a given day.)

How can we represent this observation mathematically? Let's assume that on some day during the observation period (call it τ), the parameter λ suddenly jumps to a higher value. So we really have two λ parameters: one for the period before τ, and one for the rest of the observation period. In the literature, a sudden transition like this would be called a *switchpoint*:

$$\lambda = \begin{cases} \lambda_1 & \text{if } t < \tau \\ \lambda_2 & \text{if } t \geq \tau \end{cases}$$

If, in reality, no sudden change occurred and indeed $\lambda_1 = \lambda_2$, then the λs' posterior distributions should look about equal.

We are interested in inferring the unknown λs. To use Bayesian inference, we need to assign prior probabilities to the different possible values of λ. What would be good prior probability distributions for λ_1 and λ_2? Recall that λ can be any positive number. As we saw earlier, the *exponential* distribution provides a continuous density function for positive numbers, so it might be a good choice for modeling λ_i. But recall that the exponential distribution takes a parameter of its own, so we'll need to include that parameter in our model. Let's call that parameter α.

$$\lambda_1 \sim \text{Exp}(\alpha)$$
$$\lambda_2 \sim \text{Exp}(\alpha)$$

α is called a *hyperparameter* or *parent variable*. In literal terms, it is a parameter that influences other parameters. Our initial guess at α does not influence the model too strongly, so we have some flexibility in our choice. In our model, we don't want to be too opinionated with this parameter. I suggest setting it to the inverse of the sample average of the count data. Why? Since we're modeling λ using an exponential distribution, we can use the expected value identity shown earlier to get:

$$\frac{1}{N}\sum_{i=0}^{N} C_i \approx E[\lambda|\alpha] = \frac{1}{\alpha}$$

By using this value, we are not being very opinonated in our prior, and this minimizes the influence of this hyperparameter. An alternative option, and something I encourage the reader to try, would be to have two priors, one for each λ_i. Creating two exponential distributions with different α values reflects our prior belief that the rate changed at some point during the observations.

What about τ? Because of the noisiness of the data, it's difficult to pick out a prior when τ might have occurred. Instead, we can assign a *uniform prior belief* to every possible day. This is equivalent to saying:

$$\tau \sim \text{DiscreteUniform}(1,70)$$
$$\Rightarrow P(\tau = k) = \frac{1}{70}$$

So after all this, what does our overall prior distribution for the unknown variables look like? Frankly, *it doesn't matter*. What we should understand is that it's an ugly, complicated mess involving symbols only a mathematician could love. And things will only get uglier the more complicated our models become. Regardless, all we really care about is the posterior distribution.

We next turn to PyMC, a Python library for performing Bayesian analysis that is undaunted by the mathematical monster we have created.

1.4.2   Introducing Our First Hammer: PyMC

PyMC is a Python library for programming Bayesian analysis.[5] It is a fast, well-maintained library. The only unfortunate part is that its documentation is lacking in certain areas, especially those that bridge the gap between beginner and hacker. One of this book's main goals is to solve that problem, and also to demonstrate why PyMC is so cool.

We will model this problem using PyMC. This type of programming is called *probabilistic programming*, an unfortunate misnomer that invokes ideas of randomly generated code and has likely confused and frightened users away from this field. The code is not random; it is probabilistic in the sense that we create probability models using programming variables as the model's components. Model components are first-class primitives within the PyMC framework.

Cronin[6] has a very motivating description of probabilistic programming:

> Another way of thinking about this: unlike a traditional program, which only runs in the forward directions, a probabilistic program is run in both the forward and backward direction. It runs forward to compute the consequences of the assumptions it contains about the world (i.e., the model space it represents), but it also runs backward from the data to constrain the possible explanations. In practice, many probabilistic programming systems will cleverly interleave these forward and backward operations to efficiently home in on the best explanations.

Because of the confusion engendered by the term *probabilistic programming*, I'll refrain from using it. Instead, I'll simply say *programming*, since that's what it really is.

PyMC code is easy to read. The only novel thing should be the syntax, and I will interrupt the code to explain individual sections. Simply remember that we are representing the model's components $(\tau, \lambda_1, \lambda_2)$ as variables:

```
import pymc as pm

alpha = 1.0/count_data.mean()   # Recall that count_data is the
                                # variable that holds our text counts.
lambda_1 = pm.Exponential("lambda_1", alpha)
lambda_2 = pm.Exponential("lambda_2", alpha)

tau = pm.DiscreteUniform("tau", lower=0, upper=n_count_data)
```

In this code, we create the PyMC variables corresponding to λ_1 and λ_2. We assign them to PyMC's *stochastic variables*, so called because they are treated by the back end as random number generators. We can demonstrate this fact by calling their built-in `random()` methods. During the training step, we will find better values for `tau`.

```
print "Random output:", tau.random(), tau.random(), tau.random()
```

```
[Output]:

Random output: 53 21 42
```

```
@pm.deterministic
def lambda_(tau=tau, lambda_1=lambda_1, lambda_2=lambda_2):
    out = np.zeros(n_count_data) # number of data points
    out[:tau] = lambda_1  # lambda before tau is lambda_1
    out[tau:] = lambda_2  # lambda after (and including) tau is
                          # lambda_2
    return out
```

This code creates a new function `lambda_`, but really we can think of it as a random variable—the random variable λ from before. Note that because `lambda_1`, `lambda_2`, and `tau` are random, `lambda_` will be random. We are *not* fixing any variables yet.

`@pm.deterministic` is a decorator that tells PyMC this is a deterministic function. That is, if the arguments were deterministic (which they are not), the output would be deterministic as well.

```
observation = pm.Poisson("obs", lambda_, value=count_data,
                         observed=True)

model = pm.Model([observation, lambda_1, lambda_2, tau])
```

The variable `observation` combines our data, `count_data`, with our proposed data-generation scheme, given by the variable `lambda_`, through the `value` keyword. We also set `observed = True` to tell PyMC that this should stay fixed in our analysis. Finally, PyMC wants us to collect all the variables of interest and create a `Model` instance out of them. This makes our life easier when we retrieve the results.

The following code will be explained in Chapter 3, but I show it here so you can see where our results come from. One can think of it as a *learning* step. The machinery being employed is called *Markov Chain Monte Carlo* (MCMC), which I will explain in Chapter 3. This technique returns thousands of random variables from the posterior distributions of λ_1, λ_2, and τ. We can plot a histogram of the random variables to see what the posterior distributions look like. Next, we collect the samples (called *traces* in the MCMC literature) into histograms. The results are shown in Figure 1.4.2.

```
# Mysterious code to be explained in Chapter 3. Suffice it to say,
# we will get
# 30,000 (40,000 minus 10,000) samples back.
mcmc = pm.MCMC(model)
mcmc.sample(40000, 10000)
```

```
[Output]:

[----------------100%----------------] 40000 of 40000 complete
    in 9.6 sec
```

```
lambda_1_samples = mcmc.trace('lambda_1')[:]
lambda_2_samples = mcmc.trace('lambda_2')[:]
tau_samples = mcmc.trace('tau')[:]

figsize(14.5, 10)
# histogram of the samples

ax = plt.subplot(311)
ax.set_autoscaley_on(False)

plt.hist(lambda_1_samples, histtype='stepfilled', bins=30, alpha=0.85,
         label="posterior of $\lambda_1$", color="#A60628", normed=True)
plt.legend(loc="upper left")
```

```
plt.title(r"""Posterior distributions of the parameters\
          $\lambda_1,\;\lambda_2,\;\tau$""")
plt.xlim([15, 30])
plt.xlabel("$\lambda_1$ value")
plt.ylabel("Density")

ax = plt.subplot(312)
ax.set_autoscaley_on(False)
plt.hist(lambda_2_samples, histtype='stepfilled', bins=30, alpha=0.85,
         label="posterior of $\lambda_2$", color="#7A68A6", normed=True)
plt.legend(loc="upper left")
plt.xlim([15, 30])
plt.xlabel("$\lambda_2$ value")
plt.ylabel("Density")

plt.subplot(313)
w = 1.0 / tau_samples.shape[0] * np.ones_like(tau_samples)
plt.hist(tau_samples, bins=n_count_data, alpha=1,
         label=r"posterior of $\tau$", color="#467821",
         weights=w, rwidth=2.)
plt.xticks(np.arange(n_count_data))
plt.legend(loc="upper left")
plt.ylim([0, .75])
plt.xlim([35, len(count_data)-20])
plt.xlabel(r"$\tau$ (in days)")
plt.ylabel("Probability");
```

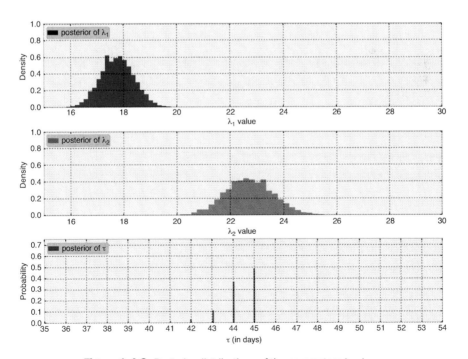

Figure 1.4.2: Posterior distributions of the parameters $\lambda_1, \lambda_2, \tau$

1.4.3   Interpretation

Recall that Bayesian methodology returns a *distribution*. Hence we now have distributions to describe the unknown λs and τ. What have we gained? Immediately, we can see the uncertainty in our estimates: The wider the distribution, the less certain our posterior belief should be. We can also see what the plausible values for the parameters are: λ_1 is around 18 and λ_2 is around 23. The posterior distributions of the two λs are clearly distinct, indicating that it is indeed likely that there was a change in the user's text-message behavior. (See Appendix 1.6 for a more formal argument.)

What other observations can you make? If you look at the original data again, do these results seem reasonable?

Notice also that the posterior distributions for the λs do not look like exponential distributions, even though our priors for these variables were exponential. In fact, the posterior distributions are not really of any form that we recognize from the original model. But that's okay! This is one of the benefits of taking a computational point of view. If we had instead done this analysis using mathematical approaches, we would have been stuck with an analytically intractable (and messy) distribution. Our use of a computational approach makes us indifferent to mathematical tractability.

Our analysis also returned a distribution for τ. Its posterior distribution looks a little different from the other two because it is a discrete random variable, so it doesn't assign probabilities to intervals. We can see that near day 45, there was a 50% chance that the user's behavior changed. Had no change occurred, or had the change been gradual over time, the posterior distribution of τ would have been more spread out, reflecting that many days were plausible candidates for τ. By contrast, in the actual results we see that only three or four days make any sense as potential switchpoints.

1.4.4   What Good Are Samples from the Posterior, Anyway?

We will deal with this question for the remainder of the book, and it is an understatement to say that it will lead us to some powerful results. For now, let's end this chapter with one more example.

We'll use the posterior samples to answer the following question: What is the expected number of texts at day t, $0 \leq t \leq 70$? Recall that the expected value of a Poisson variable is equal to its parameter λ. Therefore, the question is equivalent to, What is the expected value of λ at time t?

In the following code, let i index samples from the posterior distributions. Given a day t, we average over all possible λ_i for that day t, using $\lambda_i = \lambda_{1,i}$ if $t < \tau_i$ (that is, if the behavior change has not yet occurred), else we use $\lambda_i = \lambda_{2,i}$.

```
figsize(12.5, 5)
# tau_samples, lambda_1_samples, lambda_2_samples contain
# N samples from the corresponding posterior distribution.
N = tau_samples.shape[0]
expected_texts_per_day = np.zeros(n_count_data) # number of data points
for day in range(0, n_count_data):
```

```
# ix is a bool index of all tau samples corresponding to
# the switchpoint occurring prior to value of "day."
ix = day < tau_samples
# Each posterior sample corresponds to a value for tau.
# For each day, that value of tau indicates whether we're
# "before"
# (in the lambda_1 "regime") or
# "after" (in the lambda_2 "regime") the switchpoint.
# By taking the posterior sample of lambda_1/2 accordingly,
# we can average
# over all samples to get an expected value for lambda on that day.
# As explained, the "message count" random variable is
# Poisson-distributed,
# and therefore lambda (the Poisson parameter) is the expected
# value of
# "message count."
expected_texts_per_day[day] = (lambda_1_samples[ix].sum()\
                              + lambda_2_samples[~ix].sum()) / N

plt.plot(range(n_count_data), expected_texts_per_day, lw=4,
         color="#E24A33", label="Expected number of text messages\
         received")
plt.xlim(0, n_count_data)
plt.xlabel("Day")
plt.ylabel("Number of text messages")
plt.title("Number of text messages received versus expected number\
          received")
plt.ylim(0, 60)
plt.bar(np.arange(len(count_data)), count_data, color="#348ABD",
        alpha=0.65, label="Observed text messages per day")
plt.legend(loc="upper left")
print expected_texts_per_day
```

```
[Output]:

[ 17.7707  17.7707  17.7707  17.7707  17.7707  17.7707  17.7707  17.7707
  17.7707  17.7707  17.7707  17.7707  17.7707  17.7707  17.7707  17.7707
  17.7707  17.7707  17.7707  17.7707  17.7707  17.7707  17.7707  17.7707
  17.7707  17.7707  17.7707  17.7707  17.7707  17.7707  17.7707  17.7707
  17.7707  17.7707  17.7707  17.7708  17.7708  17.7712  17.7717  17.7722
  17.7726  17.7767  17.9207  18.4265  20.1932  22.7116  22.7117  22.7117
  22.7117  22.7117  22.7117  22.7117  22.7117  22.7117  22.7117  22.7117
  22.7117  22.7117  22.7117  22.7117  22.7117  22.7117  22.7117  22.7117
  22.7117  22.7117  22.7117  22.7117  22.7117  22.7117  22.7117  22.7117
  22.7117  22.7117]
```

The results, illustrated in Figure 1.4.3, strongly demonstrate the influence of the switchpoint. We should view this cautiously, though; from this view, there is no

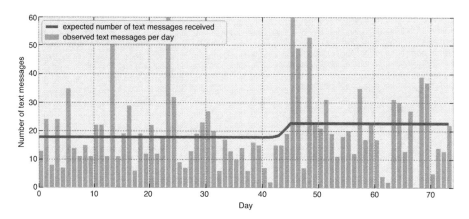

Figure 1.4.3: Number of text messages received versus expected number received

uncertainty in the "expected number of text messages" line, which is something we'd probably like to see. Our analysis shows strong support for believing the user's behavior did change (λ_1 would have been close in value to λ_2 had this not been true), and that the change was sudden rather than gradual (as demonstrated by τ's strongly peaked posterior distribution). We can speculate what might have caused this: a cheaper text-message rate, a recent weather-to-text subscription, or perhaps a new relationship.

1.5   Conclusion

This chapter introduced the difference between the frequentist and the Bayesian interpretation of probabilities. We also learned about two important probability distributions: the Poisson distribution and the exponential distribution. These are two building blocks that we will use to constuct more Bayesian models, like we did with the text messaging example previously. In Chapter 2, we will explore some more modeling and PyMC strategies.

1.6   Appendix

1.6.1   Determining Statistically if the Two λs Are Indeed Different?

In the text-messaging example, we visually inspected the posteriors of λ_1 and λ_2 to declare them different. This was fair, as the general locations of the posteriors were very far apart. What if this were not true? What if the distributions partially overlapped? How can we make this decision more formal?

One way is to compute $P(\lambda_1 < \lambda_2 \mid \text{data})$; that is, what is the probability that the true value of λ_1 is smaller than λ_2, given the data we observed? If this number is close to 50%, no better than flipping a coin, then we can't be certain they are indeed different. If this number is close to 100%, then we can be very confident that the two true values are very different. Using samples from the posteriors, this computation is very simple—we compute the fraction of times that a sample from the posterior of λ_1 is less than one from λ_2:

```
print (lambda_1_samples < lambda_2_samples)
# Boolean array: True if lambda_1 is less than lambda_2.
```

```
[Output]:

[ True True True True ..., True True True True]
```

```
# How often does this happen?
print (lambda_1_samples < lambda_2_samples).sum()

# How many samples are there?
print lambda_1_samples.shape[0]
```

```
[Output]:

29994
30000
```

```
# The ratio is the probability. Or, we can just use .mean:
print (lambda_1_samples < lambda_2_samples).mean()
```

```
[Output]:

0.9998
```

So, there is virtually a 100% chance, and we can be very confident the two values are different.

We can ask more complicated things, too, like "What is the probability that the values differ by at least 1? 2? 5? 10?"

```
# The vector abs(lambda_1_samples - lambda_2_samples) > 1 is a boolean,
# True if the values are  more than 1 apart, False otherwise.
# How often does this happen? Use .mean()
for d in [1,2,5,10]:
    v = (abs(lambda_1_samples - lambda_2_samples) >= d).mean()
    print "What is the probability the difference is larger than %d\
        ? %.2f"%(d,v)
```

```
[Output]:

What is the probability the difference is larger than 1? 1.00
What is the probability the difference is larger than 2? 1.00
What is the probability the difference is larger than 5? 0.49
What is the probability the difference is larger than 10? 0.00
```

1.6.2 Extending to Two Switchpoints

Readers might be interested in how the previous model can be extended to more than a single switchpoint, or may question the assumption of only one switchpoint. We'll start with extending the model to consider two switchpoints (which implies three λ_i parameters). The model looks very similar to the previous:

$$\lambda = \begin{cases} \lambda_1 & \text{if } t < \tau_1 \\ \lambda_2 & \text{if } \tau_1 \le t < \tau_2 \\ \lambda_3 & \text{if } t \ge \tau_2 \end{cases}$$

where

$$\lambda_1 \sim \text{Exp}(\alpha)$$
$$\lambda_2 \sim \text{Exp}(\alpha)$$
$$\lambda_3 \sim \text{Exp}(\alpha)$$

and

$$\tau_1 \sim \text{DiscreteUniform}(1,69)$$
$$\tau_2 \sim \text{DiscreteUniform}(\tau_1,70)$$

Let's code this model up, which looks very similar to our previous code:

```
lambda_1 = pm.Exponential("lambda_1", alpha)
lambda_2 = pm.Exponential("lambda_2", alpha)
lambda_3 = pm.Exponential("lambda_3", alpha)


tau_1 = pm.DiscreteUniform("tau_1", lower=0, upper=n_count_data-1)
tau_2 = pm.DiscreteUniform("tau_2", lower=tau_1, upper=n_count_data)

@pm.deterministic
def lambda_(tau_1=tau_1, tau_2=tau_2,
            lambda_1=lambda_1, lambda_2=lambda_2, lambda_3 = lambda_3):
    out = np.zeros(n_count_data) # number of data points
    out[:tau_1] = lambda_1  # lambda before tau is lambda_1
    out[tau_1:tau_2] = lambda_2
    out[tau_2:] = lambda_3  # lambda after (and including) tau
                            # is lambda_2
    return out
observation = pm.Poisson("obs", lambda_, value=count_data,
```

```
                    observed=True)
model = pm.Model([observation, lambda_1, lambda_2, lambda_3, tau_1,
                  tau_2])
mcmc = pm.MCMC(model)
mcmc.sample(40000, 10000)
```

```
[Output]:

[-----------------100%-----------------] 40000 of 40000 complete
    in 19.5 sec
```

In Figure 1.6.1, we display the posteriors of the five unknowns. We can see that the model has discovered switchpoints at day 45 and 47. What do you think of this? Has the model overfit our data?

Indeed, we probably have suggestions about how many switchpoints there may be in the data. For example, I think one switchpoint is more likely than two, which is more likely than three, and so on. This suggests we should create a *prior* distribution about how many switchpoints there may be and let the model decide! After training our model, it may decide that yes, one switchpoint is most likely. The code to do this is beyond the scope of this chapter; I simply wanted to introduce the idea of viewing our model with the same skepticism with which we view our data.

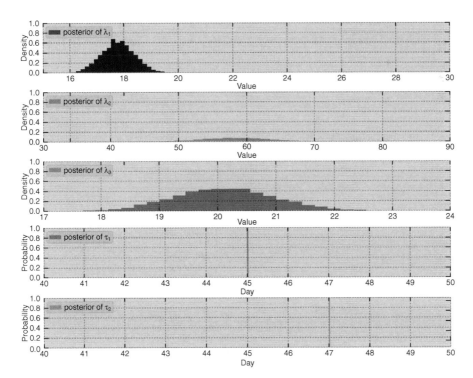

Figure 1.6.1: Posterior distributions of the five unknown parameters in the extended text-message model

1.7   Exercises

1. Using `lambda_1_samples` and `lambda_2_samples`, what is the mean of the posterior distributions of λ_1 and λ_2?

2. What is the expected percentage increase in text-message rates? `Hint`: Compute the mean of `(lambda_2_samples-lambda_1_samples)/ lambda_1_samples`. Note that this quantity is very different from `(lambda_2_samples.mean()-lambda_1_samples.mean())/ lambda_1_samples.mean()`.

3. What is the mean of λ_1 *given* that we know τ is less than 45. That is, suppose we have been given new information that the change in behavior occurred prior to day 45. What is the expected value of λ_1 now? (You do not need to redo the PyMC part. Just consider all instances where `tau_samples < 45`.)

1.7.1   Answers

1. To compute the mean of the posteriors (which is the same as the expected value of the posteriors), we just need the samples and a `.mean` function.

```
print lambda_1_samples.mean()
print lambda_2_samples.mean()
```

2. Given two numbers, a and b, the relative increase is given by $(a - b)/b$. In our example, we do not know with certainty what λ_1 and λ_2 are. When we compute

```
(lambda_2_samples-lambda_1_samples)/lambda_1_samples
```

we get back another vector, representing the *posterior of the relative increase*. For example, see Figure 1.7.1:

```
relative_increase_samples = (lambda_2_samples-lambda_1_samples)
                                /lambda_1_samples
print relative_increase_samples
```

```
[Output]:

[ 0.263 0.263 0.263 0.263 ..., 0.1622 0.1898 0.1883 0.1883]
```

```
figsize(12.5,4)
plt.hist(relative_increase_samples, histtype='stepfilled',
        bins=30, alpha=0.85, color="#7A68A6", normed=True,
        label='posterior of relative increase')
plt.xlabel("Relative increase")
plt.ylabel("Density of relative increase")
plt.title("Posterior of relative increase")
plt.legend();
```

To compute the mean, we just need this new vector's mean value:

```
print relative_increase_samples.mean()
```

```
[Output]:

0.280845247899
```

3. If we know $\tau < 45$, then all samples need to be conditioned on that:

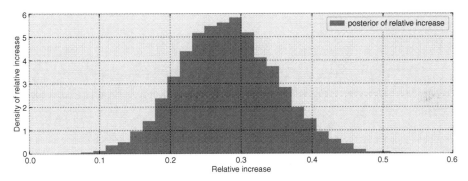

Figure 1.7.1: Posterior of relative increase

```
ix = tau_samples < 45
print lambda_1_samples[ix].mean()
```

```
[Output]:

17.7484086925
```

1.8 **References**

1. Gelman, Andrew. "N Is Never Large," Statistical Modeling, Causal Inference, and Social Science, last modified July 31, 2005, http://andrewgelman.com/2005/07/31/n_is_never_larg/.

2. Halevy, Alon, Peter Norvig, and Fernando Pereira. "The Unreasonable Effectiveness of Data," *IEEE Intelligent Systems* 24, no. 2 (March/April 2009): 8-12.

3. Lin, Jimmy, and Alek Kolcz. "Large-Scale Machine Learning at Twitter." In Proceedings of the 2012 ACM SIGMOD International Conference on Management of Data (Scottsdale, AZ: May 2012), 793–804.

4. Kahneman, Daniel. *Thinking, Fast and Slow*. New York: Farrar, Straus and Giroux, 2011.

5. Patil, Anand, David Huard, and Christopher J. Fonnesbeck. "PyMC: Bayesian Stochastic Modelling in Python," *Journal of Statistical Software* 35, no. 4 (2010): 1–81.

6. Cronin, Beau. "Why Probabilistic Programming Matters," last modified March 24, 2013, `https://plus.google.com/u/0/107971134877020469960/posts/KpeRdJKR6Z1`.

2

A Little More on PyMC

2.1 Introduction

This chapter introduces more PyMC syntax and design patterns, and ways to think about how to model a system from a Bayesian perspective. It also contains tips and data visualization techniques for assessing goodness of fit for your Bayesian model.

2.1.1 Parent and Child Relationships

To assist with describing Bayesian relationships and to be consistent with PyMC's documentation, we introduce *parent* and *child* variables.

- **Parent variables** are variables that influence another variable.
- **Child variables** are variables that are affected by other variables—that is, are the subject of parent variables.

A variable can be both a parent and child. For example, consider the following PyMC code.

```
import pymc as pm

lambda_ = pm.Exponential("poisson_param", 1)
# used in the call to the next variable...
data_generator = pm.Poisson("data_generator", lambda_)

data_plus_one = data_generator + 1
```

`lambda_` controls the parameter of `data_generator`, hence influences its values. The former is a parent of the latter. By symmetry, `data_generator` is a child of `lambda_`.

Likewise, `data_generator` is a parent to the variable `data_plus_one` (hence making `data_generator` both a parent and child variable). Although it does not look like one, `data_plus_one` should be treated as a PyMC variable as it is a *function* of another PyMC variable, hence is a child variable to `data_generator`.

This nomenclature is introduced to help us describe relationships in PyMC modeling. You can access a variable's children and parent variables using the `children` and `parents` attributes attached to variables.

```
print "Children of 'lambda_': "
print lambda_.children
print "\nParents of 'data_generator': "
print data_generator.parents
print "\nChildren of 'data_generator': "
print data_generator.children
```

```
[Output]:

Children of 'lambda_':
set([<pymc.distributions.Poisson 'data_generator' at 0x10e093490>])

Parents of 'data_generator':
{'mu': <pymc.distributions.Exponential 'poisson_param' at 0x10e093610>}

Children of 'data_generator':
set([<pymc.PyMCObjects.Deterministic '(data_generator_add_1)'
    at 0x10e093150>])
```

Of course, a child can have more than one parent, and a parent can have one or more children.

2.1.2 PyMC Variables

All PyMC variables expose a `value` property. This property produces the *current* (possibly random) internal value of the variable. If the variable is a child variable, its value changes given the variable's parents' values. Using the same variables from before:

```
print "lambda_.value =", lambda_.value
print "data_generator.value =", data_generator.value
print "data_plus_one.value =", data_plus_one.value
```

```
[Output]:

lambda_.value = 1.0354800596
data_generator.value = 4
data_plus_one.value = 5
```

PyMC is concerned with two types of programming variables: `Stochastic` and `deterministic`.

- **Stochastic variables** are variables that are not deterministic, i.e., even if you knew all the values of the variables' parents (if it even has any parents), it would still be random. Included in this category are instances of classes `Poisson`, `DiscreteUniform`, and `Exponential`.

- **Deterministic variables** are variables that are not random if the variables' parents are known. This might be confusing at first; a quick mental check is *if I knew all of variable foo's parent variables' values, I could determine exactly what foo's value is.*

Initializing Stochastic Variables The first argument in initializing a stochastic variable is a string that represents the name of the variable. After that are additional arguments that are class-specific. For example:

```
some_variable = pm.DiscreteUniform("discrete_uni_var",0,4)
```

where 0, 4 are the `DiscreteUniform`-specific lower and upper bound on the random variable. The PyMC docs (`http://pymc-devs.github.com/pymc/distributions.html`) contain the specific parameters for stochastic variables. (Or use `??` if you are using IPython!)

The name argument is used to retrieve the posterior distribution later in the analysis, so it is best to use a descriptive name. Typically, I use the Python variable's name.

For multivariable problems, rather than creating a Python array of stochastic variables, setting the `size` keyword in the call to a `Stochastic` variable creates an array of (independent) stochastic variables. The array behaves like a NumPy array when used like one, and references to its `value` attribute return NumPy arrays.

The `size` argument also solves the annoying case where you may have many variables β_i, $i = 1, ..., N$ you wish to model. Instead of creating arbitrary names and variables for each one, like:

```
beta_1 = pm.Uniform("beta_1", 0, 1)
beta_2 = pm.Uniform("beta_2", 0, 1)
...
```

we can instead wrap them into a single variable:

```
betas = pm.Uniform("betas", 0, 1, size=N)
```

Calling `random()` We can also call on a stochastic variable's `random()` method, which (given the parent values) will generate a new, random value. We demonstrate this using the texting example from Chapter 1.

```
lambda_1 = pm.Exponential("lambda_1", 1)  # prior on first behavior
lambda_2 = pm.Exponential("lambda_2", 1)  # prior on second behavior
tau = pm.DiscreteUniform("tau", lower=0, upper=10)
                                          # prior on behavior change

print "Initialized values..."
print "lambda_1.value: %.3f" % lambda_1.value
print "lambda_2.value: %.3f" % lambda_2.value
print "tau.value: %.3f" % tau.value
print
```

(Continues)

(Continued)

```
lambda_1.random(), lambda_2.random(), tau.random()

print "After calling random() on the variables..."
print "lambda_1.value: %.3f" % lambda_1.value
print "lambda_2.value: %.3f" % lambda_2.value
print "tau.value: %.3f" % tau.value
```

```
[Output]:

Initialized values...
lambda_1.value: 0.813
lambda_2.value: 0.246
tau.value: 10.000

After calling random() on the variables...
lambda_1.value: 2.029
lambda_2.value: 0.211
tau.value: 4.000
```

The call to `random` stores a new value into the variable's `value` attribute.

Deterministic Variables   Since most variables you will be modeling are stochastic, we distinguish deterministic variables with a `pymc.deterministic` wrapper. (If you are unfamiliar with Python wrappers—also called *decorators*—that's no problem. Just prepend the `pymc.deterministic` decorator before the variable declaration and you're good to go.) The declaration of a deterministic variable uses a Python function:

```
@pm.deterministic
def some_deterministic_var(v1=v1,):
    #jelly goes here.
```

For all purposes, we treat the object `some_deterministic_var` as a variable and not a Python function.

Prepending with the wrapper is the easiest way, but not the only way, to create deterministic variables. Elementary operations, like addition, exponentials, and so forth implicitly create deterministic variables. For example, the following returns a deterministic variable:

```
type(lambda_1 + lambda_2)
```

```
[Output]:

pymc.PyMCObjects.Deterministic
```

The use of the `deterministic` wrapper was seen in Chapter 1's text-message example. Recall that the model for λ looked like:

$$\lambda = \begin{cases} \lambda_1 & \text{if } t < \tau \\ \lambda_2 & \text{if } t \geq \tau \end{cases}$$

And in PyMC code:

```
import numpy as np
n_data_points = 5  # in Chapter 1 we had ~70 data points

@pm.deterministic
def lambda_(tau=tau, lambda_1=lambda_1, lambda_2=lambda_2):
    out = np.zeros(n_data_points)
    out[:tau] = lambda_1  # lambda before tau is lambda_1
    out[tau:] = lambda_2  # lambda after tau is lambda_2
    return out
```

Clearly, if τ, λ_1, and λ_2 are known, then λ is known completely; hence, it is a deterministic variable.

Inside the deterministic decorator, the `Stochastic` variables passed in behave like scalars or NumPy arrays (if multivariable), and *not* like `Stochastic` variables. For example, running the following:

```
@pm.deterministic
def some_deterministic(stoch=some_stochastic_var):
    return stoch.value**2
```

will return an `AttributeError` detailing that `stoch` does not have a `value` attribute. It simply needs to be `stoch**2`. During the learning phase, it's the variable's `value` that is repeatedly passed in, not the actual stochastic variable.

Notice that in the creation of the deterministic function that we use keyword arguments for each variable used in the function. This is a necessary step, and all variables *must* be specified with keyword arguments.

2.1.3 Including Observations in the Model

At this point, it may not look like it, but we have fully specified our priors. For example, we can ask and answer questions like, "What does my prior distribution of λ_1 look like?", as demonstrated in Figure 2.1.1.

```
%matplotlib inline
from IPython.core.pylabtools import figsize
from matplotlib import pyplot as plt
figsize(12.5, 4)
plt.rcParams['savefig.dpi'] = 300
plt.rcParams['figure.dpi'] = 300
```

(*Continues*)

(Continued)

```
samples = [lambda_1.random() for i in range(20000)]
plt.hist(samples, bins=70, normed=True, histtype="stepfilled")
plt.title("Prior distribution for $\lambda_1$")
plt.xlabel("Value")
plt.ylabel("Density")
plt.xlim(0, 8);
```

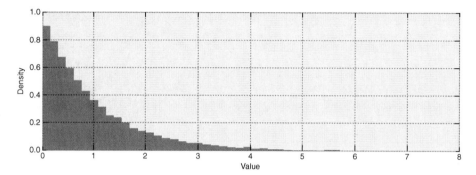

Figure 2.1.1: Prior distribution for λ_1

To frame this in the notation of Chapter 1, though this is a slight abuse of notation, we have specified $P(A)$. Our next goal is to include data/evidence/observations X into our model. We model this next.

PyMC stochastic variables have an additional keyword argument observed which accepts a boolean (False by default). The keyword observed has a very simple role: fix the variable's current value. That is, it makes value immutable. We have to specify an initial value in the variable's creation, equal to the observations we wish to include, typically an array (and it should be a NumPy array for speed). For example:

```
data = np.array([10, 5])
fixed_variable = pm.Poisson("fxd", 1, value=data, observed=True)
print "value: ", fixed_variable.value
print "calling .random()"
fixed_variable.random()
print "value: ", fixed_variable.value
```

```
[Output]:

value:  [10  5]
calling .random()
value:  [10  5]
```

This is how we include data into our models: initializing a stochastic variable to have a *fixed value*.

To complete our text-message example, we fix the PyMC variable `observations` to the observed dataset.

```
# We're using some fake data here.
data = np.array([10, 25, 15, 20, 35])
obs = pm.Poisson("obs", lambda_, value=data, observed=True)
print obs.value
```

```
[Output]:

[10 25 15 20 35]
```

2.1.4   Finally...

We wrap all the created variables into a `pm.Model` class. With this `Model` class, we can analyze the variables as a single unit. This is an optional step, as the fitting algorithms can be sent an array of the variables rather than a `Model` class. I may or may not perform this step in all future examples.

```
model = pm.Model([obs, lambda_, lambda_1, lambda_2, tau])
```

See the example in Chapter 1, section 1.4.1 for the output of this model.

2.2   Modeling Approaches

A good starting thought to Bayesian modeling is to think about *how your data might have been generated*. Position yourself as an omniscient controller, and try to imagine how *you* would recreate the dataset.

In Chapter 1, we investigated text-message data. We began by asking how our observations may have been generated.

1. We started by thinking, "What is the best random variable to describe this count data?" A Poisson random variable is a good candidate because it can represent count data well. So we model the number of text messages received as sampled from a Poisson distribution.

2. Next, we think, "Okay, assuming text messages are Poisson-distributed, what do I need for the Poisson distribution?" Well, the Poisson distribution has a parameter λ.

3. Do we know λ? No. In fact, we have a suspicion that there are *two* λ values, one for earlier behavior and one for later behavior. We don't know when the behavior switches, though, but call the switchpoint τ.

4. What is a good distribution for the two λs? The exponential is good, as it assigns probabilities to positive real numbers. Well, the exponential distribution has a parameter too—call it α.

5. Do we know what the parameter α might be? No. At this point, we could continue and assign a distribution to α, but it's better to stop once we reach a set level of ignorance; whereas we have a prior belief about λ ("It probably changes over time," "It's likely between 10 and 30," etc.), we don't really have any strong beliefs about α. So it's best to stop modeling here.

What is a good value for α, then? We think that the λs are between 10 and 30, so if we set α really low (which corresponds to larger probability on high values) we are not reflecting our prior well. Similarly, a too-high α misses our prior belief as well. A good idea for α to reflect our beliefs about λ is to set the value so that the mean of λ, given α, is equal to our observed mean. This was shown in Chapter 1.

6. We have no expert opinion of when τ might have occurred. So we will suppose τ is from a discrete uniform distribution over the entire time span.

In Figure 2.2.1, we give a graphical visualization of this, where arrows denote `parent-child` relationships (provided by the Daft Python library, `http://daft-pgm.org/`).

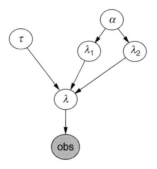

Figure 2.2.1: Graphical model of how our observations may have been generated

PyMC, and other probabilistic programming languages, have been designed to tell these data-generation *stories*. More generally, Cronin writes:[1]

Probabilistic programming will unlock narrative explanations of data, one of the holy grails of business analytics and the unsung hero of scientific persuasion. People think in terms of stories—thus the unreasonable power of the anecdote to drive decision-making, well-founded or not. But existing analytics largely fails to provide this kind of story; instead, numbers seemingly appear out of thin air, with little of the causal context that humans prefer when weighing their options.

2.2.1 Same Story, Different Ending

Interestingly, we can create *new datasets* by retelling the story. For example, if we reverse
the six steps we just discussed, we can simulate a possible realization of the dataset.

In the following, we use PyMC's internal functions for generating random variables
(but that are not `Stochastic` variables.) The function `rdiscrete_uniform`
will create random output from a discrete uniform distribution (similar to
`numpy.random.randint`).

1. Specify when the user's behavior switches by sampling from DiscreteUniform$(0, 80)$:

```
tau = pm.rdiscrete_uniform(0, 80)
print tau
```

```
[Output]:

29
```

2. Draw λ_1 and λ_2 from an $Exp(\alpha)$ distribution:

```
alpha = 1./20.
lambda_1, lambda_2 = pm.rexponential(alpha, 2)
print lambda_1, lambda_2
```

```
[Output]:

27.5189090326 6.54046888135
```

3. For days before τ, $\lambda = \lambda_1$; for days after τ, $\lambda = \lambda_2$.

```
lambda_ = np.r_[ lambda_1*np.ones(tau), lambda_2*np.ones(80-tau) ]
print lambda_
```

```
[Output]:

[ 27.519  27.519  27.519  27.519  27.519  27.519  27.519  27.519  27.519
  27.519  27.519  27.519  27.519  27.519  27.519  27.519  27.519  27.519
  27.519  27.519  27.519  27.519  27.519  27.519  27.519  27.519  27.519
  27.519  27.519   6.54    6.54    6.54    6.54    6.54    6.54    6.54
   6.54    6.54    6.54    6.54    6.54    6.54    6.54    6.54    6.54
   6.54    6.54    6.54    6.54    6.54    6.54    6.54    6.54    6.54
   6.54    6.54    6.54    6.54    6.54    6.54    6.54    6.54    6.54
   6.54    6.54    6.54    6.54    6.54    6.54    6.54    6.54    6.54
   6.54    6.54    6.54    6.54    6.54    6.54    6.54    6.54 ]
```

4. Sample from Poi(λ_1), and sample from Poi(λ_2) for days after τ. For example:

```
data = pm.rpoisson(lambda_)
print data
```

```
[Output]:

[36 22 28 23 25 18 30 27 34 26 33 31 26 26 32 26 23 32 33 33 27 26 35 20 32
 44 23 30 26  9 11  9  6  8  7  1  8  5  6  5  9  5  7  6  5 11  5  5 10  9
  4  5  7  5  9  8 10  5  7  9  5  6  3  8  7  4  6  7  7  4  5  3  5  6  8
 10  5  6  8  5]
```

5. Plot the artificial dataset:

```
plt.bar(np.arange(80), data, color="#348ABD")
plt.bar(tau-1, data[tau - 1], color="r", label="user behavior changed")
plt.xlabel("Time (days)")
plt.ylabel("Text messages received")
plt.title("Artificial dataset from simulating the model")
plt.xlim(0, 80)
plt.legend();
```

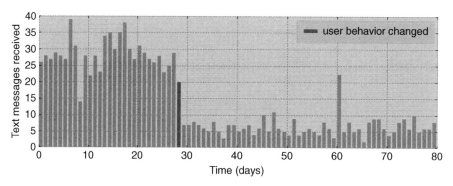

Figure 2.2.2: Artificial dataset from simulating the model

It is okay that the fictional dataset in Figure 2.2.2 does not look like our observed dataset; indeed, the probability is incredibly small that it would. PyMC's engine is designed to find good parameters—λ_i, τ—that maximize this probability.

The ability to generate an artificial dataset is an interesting side effect of our modeling, and we will see that this ability is a very important method of Bayesian inference. For example, we'll produce a few more datasets in Figure 2.2.3.

```
def plot_artificial_sms_dataset():
    tau = pm.rdiscrete_uniform(0, 80)
    alpha = 1./20.
    lambda_1, lambda_2 = pm.rexponential(alpha, 2)
```

```
    data = np.r_[pm.rpoisson(lambda_1, tau), pm.rpoisson(lambda_2,
            80 - tau)]
    plt.bar(np.arange(80), data, color="#348ABD")
    plt.bar(tau - 1, data[tau-1], color="r",
            label="user behavior changed")
    plt.xlim(0, 80)
    plt.xlabel("Time (days)")
    plt.ylabel("Text messages received")

figsize(12.5, 5)
plt.title("More examples of artificial datasets from\
        simulating our model")
for i in range(4):
    plt.subplot(4, 1, i+1)
    plt.xlabel("Time (days)")
    plt.ylabel("Text messages received")
    plot_artificial_sms_dataset()
```

Later we will see how we use this to make predictions and test the appropriateness of our models.

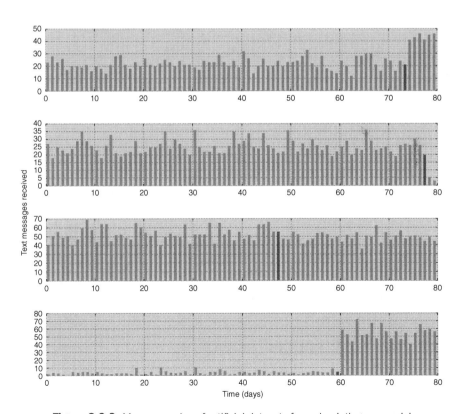

Figure 2.2.3: More examples of artificial datasets from simulating our model

2.2.2 Example: Bayesian A/B Testing

A/B testing is a statistical design pattern for determining the difference of effectiveness between two different treatments. For example, a pharmaceutical company is interested in the effectiveness of drug A versus drug B. The company will test drug A on some percentage of a patient group, and drug B on the rest (this split is often 50%/50%, but we will relax this assumption). After performing enough trials, the in-house statisticians measure the effectivenesss to determine which drug yielded better results.

Similarly, front-end Web developers are interested in which design of their Web site yields more *conversions*, where a conversion could be a visitor signing up, purchasing something, or taking some other action. They will route some fraction of visitors to site A, and the other fraction to site B (which has an alternate design), and record if the visit yielded a conversion or not. The assignments and conversions are recorded and analyzed afterward.

The key value of A/B tests is that there is only a single difference between groups. Thus, any significant change in the metrics (like drug effectiveness or conversions) can be directly attributed to the difference.

Often, the post-experiment analysis is done using something called a "hypothesis test" like a *difference of means test* or *difference of proportions test*. This involves often misunderstood quantities like a "Z-score" and even more confusing "p-values" (please don't ask). If you have taken a statistics course, you have probably been taught this technique (though not necessarily *learned* this technique). And if you were like me, you may have felt uncomfortable with their derivation. If so, good. The Bayesian approach to this problem is much more natural.

2.2.3 A Simple Case

As this is a *hacker* book, we'll continue with the Web-development example. For the moment, we will focus on the analysis of site A first. Assume that there is some probability, p_A, that users who are shown site A eventually convert. This is the true effectiveness of site A. Currently, this quantity is unknown to us.

Suppose site A was shown to N people, and n people converted. One might conclude hastily that $p_A = \frac{n}{N}$. Unfortunately, the *observed frequency* $\frac{n}{N}$ does not necessarily equal p_A; there is a difference between the *observed frequency* and the *true frequency* of an event. The true frequency can be interpreted as the probability of an event occurring, and this does not necessarily equal the observed frequency. For example, the true frequency of rolling a 1 on a six-sided die is $\frac{1}{6}$, but if we roll the dice six times we may not see a 1 show up at all (the observed frequency)! We must commonly determine the true frequency of events like:

- The fraction of users who make purchases
- The proportion of some characteristic in a population
- The percentage of Internet users with cats
- Or the probability that it will rain tomorrow

Unfortunately, noise and complexities hide the true frequency from us and we must *infer* it from observed data. We use Bayesian statistics to infer probable values of the true frequency using an appropriate prior and observed data. With respect to our conversion example, we are interested in using what we know, N (the total visitors) and n (the number of conversions), to estimate what p_A, the true frequency of conversion, might be.

To set up a Bayesian model, we need to assign prior distrbutions to our unknown quantities. *A priori*, what do we think p_A might be? For this example, we have no strong conviction about p_A, so for now, let's assume p_A is uniform over [0,1]:

```
import pymc as pm

# The parameters are the bounds of the Uniform.
p = pm.Uniform('p', lower=0, upper=1)
```

For this example, suppose $p_A = 0.05$, and $N = 1,500$ users shown site A, and we will simulate whether the user made a purchase or not. To simulate this from N trials, we will use a **Bernoulli distribution**. A Bernoulli distribution is a binary random variable (0 or 1 only), and as our observations are binary (not convert or convert), it is appropriate here. More formally, if $X \sim \text{Ber}(p)$, then X is 1 with probability p and 0 with probability $1 - p$. Of course, in practice we do not know p_A, but we will use it here to simulate artificial data.

```
# set constants
p_true = 0.05  # remember, this is unknown in real-life
N = 1500

# Sample N Bernoulli random variables from Ber(0.05).
# Each random variable has a 0.05 chance of being a 1.
# This is the data-generation step.
occurrences = pm.rbernoulli(p_true, N)

print occurrences  # Remember: Python treats True == 1, and False == 0.
print occurrences.sum()
```

```
[Output]:

[False False False False ..., False False False False]
85
```

The observed frequency is:

```
# Occurrences.mean() is equal to n/N.
print "What is the observed frequency in Group A? %.4f"\
                % occurrences.mean()
print "Does the observed frequency equal the true frequency? %s"\
                % (occurrences.mean() == p_true)
```

```
[Output]:

What is the observed frequency in Group A? 0.0567
Does the observed frequency equal the true frequency? False
```

We combine the observations into the PyMC observed variable, and run our inference algorithm:

```
# Include the observations, which are Bernoulli.
obs = pm.Bernoulli("obs", p, value=occurrences, observed=True)

# to be explained in Chapter 3
mcmc = pm.MCMC([p, obs])
mcmc.sample(20000, 1000)
```

```
[Output]:

[-----------------100%-----------------] 20000 of 20000 complete
    in 2.0 sec
```

We plot the posterior distribution of the unknown p_A in Figure 2.2.4.

```
figsize(12.5, 4)
plt.title("Posterior distribution of $p_A$, the true effectiveness\
        of site A")
plt.vlines(p_true, 0, 90, linestyle="--", label="true $p_A$ (unknown)")
plt.hist(mcmc.trace("p")[:], bins=35, histtype="stepfilled",
        normed=True)
plt.xlabel("Value of $p_A$")
plt.ylabel("Density")
plt.legend();
```

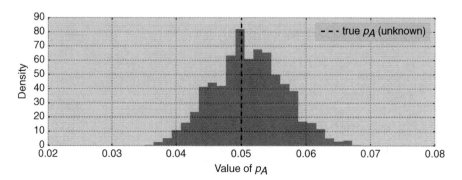

Figure 2.2.4: Posterior distribution of p_A, the true effectiveness of site A

Our posterior distribution puts weight near what our data suggests is the true value of p_A: The higher the distribution, the more likely it is there. Try changing the number of observations, N, and observe how the posterior distribution changes.

(Why is the y axis greater than 1? See the Web page in reference [2] for a great answer.)

2.2.4 *A* and *B* Together

A similar analysis can be done for site *B*'s response data to determine a posterior for p_B. What we are really interested in is the *difference* between p_A and p_B. Let's infer p_A, p_B, *and* delta $= p_A - p_B$, all at once. We can do this using PyMC's deterministic variables. We'll assume for this exercise that $p_B = 0.04$ (though we don't know this), so delta $= 0.01$, $N_B = 750$ (only half of N_A) and we will simulate site *B*'s data like we did for site *A*'s data.

```
import pymc as pm
figsize(12, 4)

# These two quantities are unknown to us.
true_p_A = 0.05
true_p_B = 0.04

# Notice the unequal sample sizes—no problem in Bayesian analysis.
N_A = 1500
N_B = 750

# Generate some observations.
observations_A = pm.rbernoulli(true_p_A, N_A)
observations_B = pm.rbernoulli(true_p_B, N_B)
print "Obs from Site A: ", observations_A[:30].astype(int), "..."
print "Obs from Site B: ", observations_B[:30].astype(int), "..."
```

```
[Output]:

Obs from Site A:  [0 0 0 0 0 0 0 0 0 0 0 0 0 0 0 0 0 0 0 0 0 0 0 1
    0 0 0 0 0 0] ...
Obs from Site B:  [0 0 0 0 0 0 0 0 0 0 0 0 0 0 0 0 0 0 0 0 0 0 0 0
    0 0 0 0 0 0] ...
```

```
print observations_A.mean()
print observations_B.mean()
```

```
[Output]:

0.0506666666667
0.0386666666667
```

(Continues)

(Continued)

```
# Set up the PyMC model. Again assume Uniform priors for p_A and p_B.
p_A = pm.Uniform("p_A", 0, 1)
p_B = pm.Uniform("p_B", 0, 1)


# Define the deterministic delta function. This is our unknown
# of interest.
@pm.deterministic
def delta(p_A=p_A, p_B=p_B):
    return p_A - p_B

# Set of observations; in this case, we have two observation datasets.
obs_A = pm.Bernoulli("obs_A", p_A, value=observations_A, observed=True)
obs_B = pm.Bernoulli("obs_B", p_B, value=observations_B, observed=True)

# to be explained in Chapter 3
mcmc = pm.MCMC([p_A, p_B, delta, obs_A, obs_B])
mcmc.sample(25000, 5000)
```

```
[Output]:

[-----------------100%-----------------] 25000 of 25000 complete
     in 3.8 sec
```

We plot the posterior distributions for the three unknowns in Figure 2.2.5.

```
p_A_samples = mcmc.trace("p_A")[:]
p_B_samples = mcmc.trace("p_B")[:]
delta_samples = mcmc.trace("delta")[:]

figsize(12.5, 10)

# histogram of posteriors

ax = plt.subplot(311)

plt.xlim(0, .1)
plt.hist(p_A_samples, histtype='stepfilled', bins=30, alpha=0.85,
         label="posterior of $p_A$", color="#A60628", normed=True)
plt.vlines(true_p_A, 0, 80, linestyle="--",
           label="true $p_A$ (unknown)")
plt.legend(loc="upper right")
plt.title("Posterior distributions of $p_A$, $p_B$,\
          and delta unknowns")
plt.ylim(0,80)

ax = plt.subplot(312)
```

```
plt.xlim(0, .1)
plt.hist(p_B_samples, histtype='stepfilled', bins=30, alpha=0.85,
        label="posterior of $p_B$", color="#467821", normed=True)
plt.vlines(true_p_B, 0, 80, linestyle="--",
        label="true $p_B$ (unknown)")
plt.legend(loc="upper right")
plt.ylim(0,80)

ax = plt.subplot(313)
plt.hist(delta_samples, histtype='stepfilled', bins=30, alpha=0.85,
        label="posterior of delta", color="#7A68A6", normed=True)
plt.vlines(true_p_A - true_p_B, 0, 60, linestyle="--",
        label="true delta (unknown)")
plt.vlines(0, 0, 60, color="black", alpha=0.2)
plt.xlabel("Value")
plt.ylabel("Density")
plt.legend(loc="upper right");
```

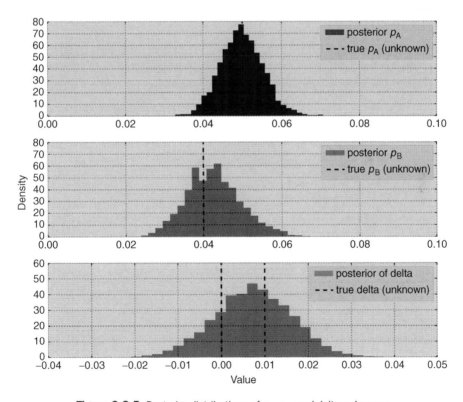

Figure 2.2.5: Posterior distributions of p_A, p_B, and delta unknowns

Notice that as a result of N_B < N_A—that is, we have less data from site *B*—our posterior distribution of p_B is fatter, implying we are less certain about the true value of p_B than we are of p_A. This is easier to see if we plot the two posteriors on the same figure:

```
figsize(12.5, 3)

# histogram of posteriors

plt.xlim(0, .1)
plt.hist(p_A_samples, histtype='stepfilled', bins=30, alpha=0.80,
        label="posterior of $p_A$", color="#A60628", normed=True)

plt.hist(p_B_samples, histtype='stepfilled', bins=30, alpha=0.80,
        label="posterior of $p_B$", color="#467821", normed=True)
plt.legend(loc="upper right")
plt.xlabel("Value")
plt.ylabel("Density")
plt.title("Posterior distributions of $p_A$ and $p_B$")
plt.ylim(0,80);
```

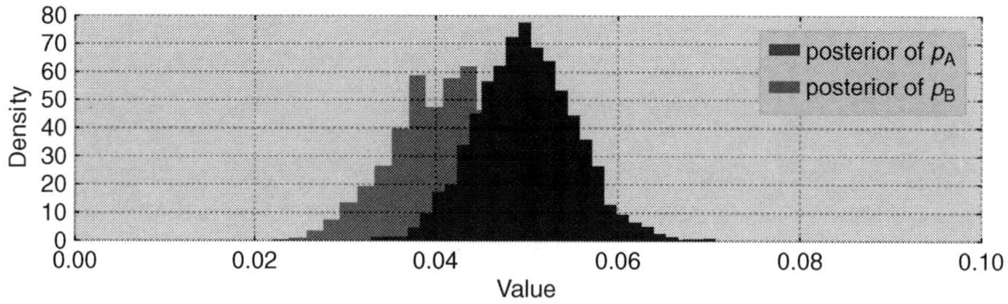

Figure 2.2.6: Posterior distributions of p_A and p_B

With respect to the posterior distribution of delta, we can see in Figure 2.2.6 that the majority of the distribution is above delta $= 0$, implying that site *A*'s response is likely better than site *B*'s response. The probability that this inference is incorrect is easily computable:

```
# Count the number of samples less than 0, i.e., the area under the curve
# before 0, representing the probability that site A is worse than site B.
print "Probability site A is WORSE than site B: %.3f" % \
    (delta_samples < 0).mean()

print "Probability site A is BETTER than site B: %.3f" % \
    (delta_samples > 0).mean()
```

```
[Output]:

Probability site A is WORSE than site B: 0.102
Probability site A is BETTER than site B: 0.897
```

If this probability is too high for comfortable decision-making, we can perform more trials on site B (as site B has less samples to begin with, each additional data point for site B contributes more inferential "power" than each additional data point for site A).

Try playing with the parameters true_p_A, true_p_B, N_A, and N_B to see what the posterior of delta looks like. Notice that in all this, the difference in sample sizes between site A and site B was never mentioned; it naturally fits into Bayesian analysis.

I hope the readers feel that this style of A/B testing is more natural than hypothesis testing, which has probably confused more than helped practitioners. In Chapter 5, we will see two extensions of this model: the first to help dynamically adjust for good sites, and the second to improve the speed of this computation by reducing the analysis to a single equation.

2.2.5 Example: An Algorithm for Human Deceit

Social data has an additional layer of interest. People are not always honest with responses, which adds further complication into inference. For example, simply asking individuals "Have you ever cheated on a test?" will surely contain some rate of dishonesty. What you can say for certain is that the true rate is less than your observed rate (assuming individuals lie *only* about *not cheating*; I cannot imagine respondents who would claim to have cheated when in fact they hadn't).

To present an elegant solution to circumventing this dishonesty problem and to demonstrate Bayesian modeling, we first need to introduce the binomial distribution.

2.2.6 The Binomial Distribution

The binomial distribution is one of the most popular distributions, mostly because of its simplicity and usefulness. Unlike the other distributions we have encountered thus far in the book, the binomial distribution has two parameters: N, a positive integer representing the number of trials or number of instances of potential events, and p, the probability of an event occurring in a single trial. Like the Poisson distribution, it is a discrete distribution, but unlike the Poisson distribution, it only assigns probabilities to integers from 0 to N (the Poisson assigns probabilities to all integers from 0 to infinity). The probability mass distribution looks like:

$$P(X = k) = \binom{N}{k} p^k (1 - p)^{N-k}$$

If X is a binomial random variable with parameters p and N, denoted $X \sim \text{Bin}(N, p)$, then X is the number of events that occurred in the N trials ($0 \le X \le N$). The larger p is (while still remaining between 0 and 1), the more events are likely to occur. The expected value of a binomial is equal to Np. In Figure 2.2.7, we plot the mass probability distribution for varying parameters.

```
figsize(12.5, 4)

import scipy.stats as stats
binomial = stats.binom
```

(Continues)

(*Continued*)

```
parameters = [(10, .4), (10, .9)]
colors = ["#348ABD", "#A60628"]

for i in range(2):
    N, p = parameters[i]
    _x = np.arange(N + 1)
    plt.bar(_x - 0.5, binomial.pmf(_x, N, p), color=colors[i],
            edgecolor=colors[i],
            alpha=0.6,
            label="$N$: %d, $p$: %.1f" % (N, p),
            linewidth=3)

plt.legend(loc="upper left")
plt.xlim(0, 10.5)
plt.xlabel("$k$")
plt.ylabel("$P(X = k)$")
plt.title("Probability mass distributions of binomial random variables");
```

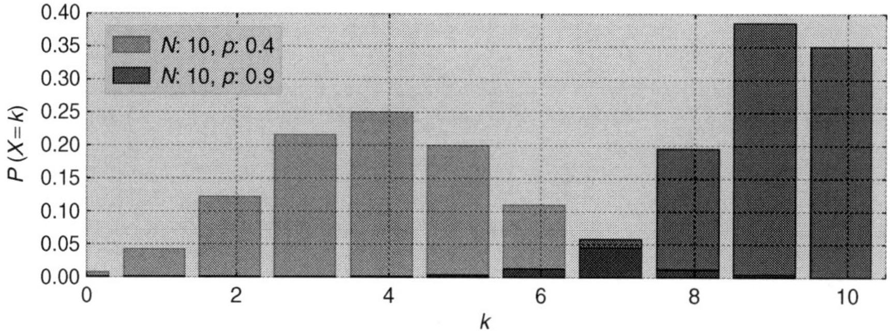

Figure 2.2.7: Probability mass distributions of binomial random variables

The special case when $N = 1$ corresponds to the Bernoulli distribution. There is another connection between Bernoulli and binomial random variables. If we have $X_1, X_2, ..., X_N$ Bernoulli random variables with equal parameter p, then $Z = X_1 + X_2 + ... + X_N \sim \text{Binomial}(N, p)$.

2.2.7 Example: Cheating Among Students

We will use the binomial distribution to determine the frequency of students cheating during an exam. If we let N be the total number of students who took the exam, and assuming each student is interviewed post-exam (answering without consequence), we will receive integer X "Yes, I did cheat" answers. We then find the posterior distribution of p, given N, some specified prior on p, and observed data X.

This is a completely absurd model. No student, even with a free pass against punishment, would admit to cheating. What we need is a better *algorithm* to ask students if they cheated. Ideally, the algorithm should encourage individuals to be honest while preserving privacy. The following proposed algorithm is a solution I greatly admire for its ingenuity and effectiveness:[3]

> In the interview process for each student, the student flips a coin, hidden from the interviewer. The student agrees to answer honestly if the coin comes up heads. Otherwise, if the coin comes up tails, the student (secretly) flips the coin again, and answers "Yes, I did cheat" if the coin flip lands heads, and "No, I did not cheat", if the coin flip lands tails. This way, the interviewer does not know if a "Yes" was the result of a guilty plea, or a Heads on a second coin toss. Thus privacy is preserved and the researchers receive honest answers.

I call this the Privacy Algorithm. One could argue that the interviewers are still receiving false data since some "Yes" answers are not confessions but instead due to randomness. An alternative way to say this is that the researchers are discarding approximately half of their original dataset since half of the responses will be due to randomness. On the other hand, they have gained a systematic data-generation process that can be modeled. Furthermore, they do not have to incorporate (perhaps somewhat naively) the possibility of deceitful answers. We can use PyMC to dig through this noisy model, and find a posterior distribution for the true frequency of liars.

Suppose 100 students are being surveyed for cheating, and we wish to find p, the proportion of cheaters. There are a few ways we can model this in PyMC. I'll demonstrate the most explicit way, and later show a simplified version. Both versions arrive at the same inference. In our data-generation model, we sample p, the true proportion of cheaters, from a prior. Since we are quite ignorant about p, we will assign it a Uniform$(0, 1)$ prior.

```
import pymc as pm

N = 100
p = pm.Uniform("freq_cheating", 0, 1)
```

Again, thinking of our data-generation model, we assign Bernoulli random variables to the 100 students: 1 implies a student cheated and 0 implies the student did not.

```
true_answers = pm.Bernoulli("truths", p, size=N)
```

If we carry out the algorithm, the next step that occurs is the first coin flip each student makes. This can be modeled again by sampling 100 Bernoulli random variables with $p = 1/2$; denote a 1 as a heads and 0 a tails.

```
first_coin_flips = pm.Bernoulli("first_flips", 0.5, size=N)
print first_coin_flips.value
```

```
[Output]:

[False False True  True  True  False True  False True  True  True  True
 False False False True  True  True  True  False True  False True  False
 True  True  False False True  True  False True  True  True  False False
 False False False True  False True  True  False False False True  True
```

(Continues)

(Continued)

```
True   False False True   False True   True   False False False False True
False  True   True  False  False False False True   False True   False False
True   True   False True   True   False True   True   False True   False False
True   True   False True   True   False True   True   False True   False True
True   True   True  True]
```

Although *not everyone* flips a second time, we can still model the possible realization of second coin flips:

```
second_coin_flips = pm.Bernoulli("second_flips", 0.5, size=N)
```

Using these variables, we can return a possible realization of the *observed proportion* of "Yes" responses. We do this using a PyMC deterministic variable:

```
@pm.deterministic
def observed_proportion(t_a=true_answers,
                        fc=first_coin_flips,
                        sc=second_coin_flips):

    observed = fc*t_a + (1-fc)*sc
    return observed.sum() / float(N)
```

The line fc*t_a + (1-fc)*sc contains the heart of the Privacy Algorithm. An element in this array is 1 *if and only if* (1) the first toss is heads and the student cheated or (2) the first toss is tails, and the second is heads, and otherwise is 0. Finally, the last line sums this vector and divides by float(N), producing a proportion.

```
observed_proportion.value
```

```
[Output]:

0.26000000000000001
```

Next we need a dataset. After performing our coin-flipped interviews, the researchers received 35 "Yes" responses. To put this into a relative perspective, if there truly were no cheaters, we should expect to see on average ¼ of all responses being a "Yes" (½ chance of having the first coin land on tails, and another ½ chance of having the second coin land on heads), so about 25 responses in a cheat-free world. On the other hand, if *all students cheated*, we should expected to see approximately ¾ of all responses be "Yes."

The researchers observe a binomial random variable, with N = 100 and p = observed_proportion with value = 35:

```
X = 35

observations = pm.Binomial("obs", N, observed_proportion, observed=True,
                           value=X)
```

Next, we add all the variables of interest to a `Model` container and run our black-box algorithm over the model.

```
model = pm.Model([p, true_answers, first_coin_flips,
                  second_coin_flips, observed_proportion, observations])

# to be explained in Chapter 3
mcmc = pm.MCMC(model)
mcmc.sample(40000, 15000)
```

```
[Output]:

[----------------100%-----------------] 40000 of 40000 complete
    in 18.7 sec
```

```
figsize(12.5, 3)
p_trace = mcmc.trace("freq_cheating")[:]
plt.hist(p_trace, histtype="stepfilled", normed=True,
         alpha=0.85, bins=30, label="posterior distribution",
         color="#348ABD")
plt.vlines([.05, .35], [0, 0], [5, 5], alpha=0.3)
plt.xlim(0, 1)
plt.xlabel("Value of $p$")
plt.ylabel("Density")
plt.title("Posterior distribution of parameter $p$")
plt.legend();
```

With regard to Figure 2.2.8, we are still pretty uncertain about what the true frequency of cheaters might be, but we have narrowed it down to a range between 0.05 to 0.35 (marked by the solid lines). This is pretty good, as *a priori* we had no idea how many students might have cheated (hence the uniform distribution for our prior). On the other hand, it is also pretty bad since there is a 0.3-length window in which the true value most likely lives. Have we even gained anything, or are we still too uncertain about the true frequency?

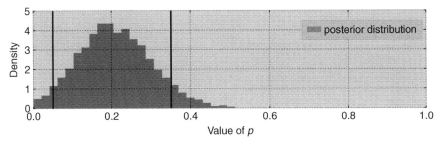

Figure 2.2.8: Posterior distribution of parameter *p*

I would argue that, yes, we have discovered something. It is implausible, according to our posterior, that there are *no cheaters*—that is, the posterior assigns low probability to $p = 0$. Since we started with an uniform prior, treating all values of p as equally plausible, but the data ruled out $p = 0$ as a possibility, we can be confident that there were cheaters.

This kind of algorithm can be used to gather private information from users and be *reasonably* confident that the data, though noisy, is truthful.

2.2.8 Alternative PyMC Model

Given a value for p (which from our godlike position we know), we can find the probability that the student will answer "Yes":

$$
\begin{aligned}
P(\text{"Yes"}) &= P(\text{heads on first coin})P(\text{cheater}) \\
&\quad + P(\text{tails on first coin})P(\text{heads on second coin}) \\
&= \frac{1}{2}p + \frac{1}{2}\frac{1}{2} \\
&= \frac{p}{2} + \frac{1}{4}
\end{aligned}
$$

Thus, knowing p, we know the probability that a student will respond "Yes." In PyMC, we can create a deterministic function to evaluate the probability of responding "Yes," given p:

```
p = pm.Uniform("freq_cheating", 0, 1)

@pm.deterministic
def p_skewed(p=p):
    return 0.5*p + 0.25
```

I could have typed p_skewed = 0.5*p + 0.25 instead for a one-liner, as the elementary operations of addition and scalar multiplication will implicitly create a deterministic variable, but I wanted to make the deterministic boilerplate explicit for clarity's sake.

If we know the probability of respondents saying "Yes," which is p_skewed, and we have $N = 100$ students, the number of "Yes" responses is a binomial random variable with parameters N and p_skewed.

This is where we include our observed 35 "Yes" responses. In the declaration of the pm.Binomial, we include value = 35 and observed = True.

```
yes_responses = pm.Binomial("number_cheaters", 100, p_skewed,
                            value=35, observed=True)
```

Next, we add all the variables of interest to a Model container and run our black-box algorithm over the model. We see the resulting posterior distribution in Figure 2.2.9.

```
model = pm.Model([yes_responses, p_skewed, p])

# to be explained in Chapter 3
mcmc = pm.MCMC(model)
mcmc.sample(25000, 2500)
```

```
[Output]:

[-----------------100%-----------------] 25000 of 25000 complete
    in 2.0 sec
```

```
figsize(12.5, 3)
p_trace = mcmc.trace("freq_cheating")[:]
plt.hist(p_trace, histtype="stepfilled", normed=True,
        alpha=0.85, bins=30, label="posterior distribution",
        color="#348ABD")
plt.vlines([.05, .35], [0, 0], [5, 5], alpha=0.2)
plt.xlim(0, 1)
plt.xlabel("Value of $p$")
plt.ylabel("Density")
plt.title("Posterior distribution of parameter $p$, from alternate model")
plt.legend();
```

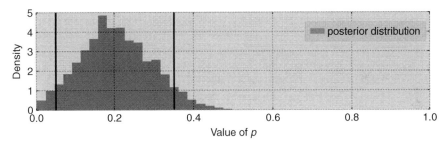

Figure 2.2.9: Posterior distribution of *p*, from alternate model

2.2.9   More PyMC Tricks

Pro Tip: *Lighter* Deterministic Variables with `Lambda` Class   Sometimes, writing
a deterministic function using the `@pm.deterministic` decorator can seem like a chore,
especially for a small function. I have already mentioned that elementary math operations
can produce deterministic variables implicitly, but what about operations like indexing or
slicing? Built-in `Lambda` functions can handle this with the elegance and simplicity
required. For example,

```
beta = pm.Normal("coefficients", 0, size=(N, 1))
x = np.random.randn((N, 1))
linear_combination = pm.Lambda(lambda x=x, beta=beta: np.dot(x.T, beta))
```

Pro Tip: Arrays of PyMC Variables   There is no reason why we cannot store multiple heterogeneous PyMC variables in a NumPy array. Just remember to set the `dtype` of the array to `object` upon initialization. For example:

```
N = 10
x = np.empty(N, dtype=object)
for i in range(0, N):
    x[i] = pm.Exponential('x_%i' % i, (i+1)**2)
```

The remainder of this chapter examines some practical examples of PyMC and PyMC modeling.

2.2.10   Example: *Challenger* Space Shuttle Disaster

On January 28, 1986, the twenty-fifth flight of the U.S. space shuttle program ended in disaster when one of the rocket boosters of the space shuttle *Challenger* exploded shortly after liftoff, killing all seven crew members. The presidential commission on the accident concluded that it was caused by the failure of an O-ring in a field joint on the rocket booster, and that this failure was due to a faulty design that made the O-ring unacceptably sensitive to a number of factors including outside temperature. Of the previous twenty-four flights, data were available on failures of O-rings on twenty-three, (one was lost at sea), and these data were discussed on the evening preceding the *Challenger* launch, but unfortunately only the data corresponding to the seven flights on which there was a damage incident were considered important, and these were thought to show no obvious trend.

The data is shown in the following code sample; the data and problem are originally from McLeish and Struthers (2012) [4] and repurposed from a problem in [5]. In Figure 2.2.10, we plot the occurrence of an incident versus the outside temperature to give you a rough idea of the relationship. (Data is available in the Github repository: `https://github.com/CamDavidsonPilon/Probabilistic-Programming-and-Bayesian-Methods-for-Hackers/blob/master/Chapter2_MorePyMC/data/challenger_data.csv`)

```
figsize(12.5, 3.5)
np.set_printoptions(precision=3, suppress=True)
challenger_data = np.genfromtxt("data/challenger_data.csv",
                                skip_header=1, usecols=[1, 2],
                                missing_values="NA",
                                delimiter=",")
# Drop the NA values.
challenger_data = challenger_data[~np.isnan(challenger_data[:, 1])]

# Plot it, as a function of temperature (the first column).
print "Temp (F), O-ring failure?"
print challenger_data

plt.scatter(challenger_data[:, 0], challenger_data[:, 1], s=75,
            color="k", alpha=0.5)
plt.yticks([0, 1])
plt.ylabel("Damage incident?")
```

```
plt.xlabel("Outside temperature (Fahrenheit)")
plt.title("Defects of the space shuttle O-rings versus temperature");
```

```
[Output]:

Temp (F), O-ring failure?
[[ 66.    0.]
 [ 70.    1.]
 [ 69.    0.]
 [ 68.    0.]
 [ 67.    0.]
 [ 72.    0.]
 [ 73.    0.]
 [ 70.    0.]
 [ 57.    1.]
 [ 63.    1.]
 [ 70.    1.]
 [ 78.    0.]
 [ 67.    0.]
 [ 53.    1.]
 [ 67.    0.]
 [ 75.    0.]
 [ 70.    0.]
 [ 81.    0.]
 [ 76.    0.]
 [ 79.    0.]
 [ 75.    1.]
 [ 76.    0.]
 [ 58.    1.]]
```

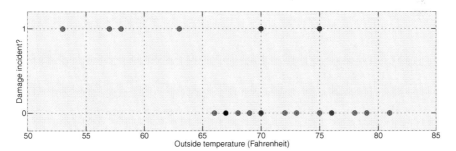

Figure 2.2.10: Defects of the space shuttle O-rings versus temperature

It looks clear that *the probability* of damage incidents occurring increases as the outside temperature decreases. We are interested in modeling the probability here because it does not look like there is a strict cutoff point between temperature and a damage incident occurring. The best we can do is ask "At temperature t, what is the probability of a damage incident?" The goal of this example is to answer that question.

We need a function of temperature—call it $p(t)$—that is bounded between 0 and 1 (so as to model a probability) and changes from 1 to 0 as we increase temperature. There are actually many such functions, but the most popular choice is the *logistic function*.

$$p(t) = \frac{1}{1 + e^{\beta t}}$$

In this model, β is the variable we are uncertain about. In Figure 2.2.11, the function plotted for $\beta = 1, 3, -5$.

```
figsize(12, 3)

def logistic(x, beta):
    return 1.0 / (1.0 + np.exp(beta * x))

x = np.linspace(-4, 4, 100)
plt.plot(x, logistic(x, 1), label=r"$\beta = 1$")
plt.plot(x, logistic(x, 3), label=r"$\beta = 3$")
plt.plot(x, logistic(x, -5), label=r"$\beta = -5$")
plt.xlabel("$x$")
plt.ylabel("Logistic function at $x$")
plt.title("Logistic function for different $\beta$ values")
plt.legend();
```

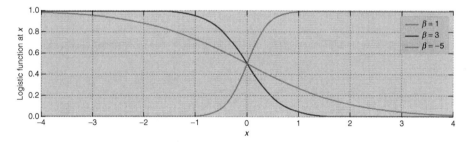

Figure 2.2.11: Logistic function for different β values

But something is missing. In the plot of the logistic function, Figure 2.2.11, the probability changes only near 0, but in our *Challenger* data, shown in Figure 2.2.10, the probability changes around 65 to 70 degrees Fahrenheit. We need to add a *bias* term to our logistic function:

$$p(t) = \frac{1}{1 + e^{\beta t + \alpha}}$$

Figure 2.2.12 demonstrates the logistic function with differing α values.

```
def logistic(x, beta, alpha=0):
    return 1.0 / (1.0 + np.exp(np.dot(beta, x) + alpha))
```

```
x = np.linspace(-4, 4, 100)

plt.plot(x, logistic(x, 1), label=r"$\beta = 1$", ls="--", lw=1)
plt.plot(x, logistic(x, 3), label=r"$\beta = 3$", ls="--", lw=1)
plt.plot(x, logistic(x, -5), label=r"$\beta = -5$", ls="--", lw=1)

plt.plot(x, logistic(x, 1, 1), label=r"$\beta = 1, \alpha = 1$",
         color="#348ABD")
plt.plot(x, logistic(x, 3, -2), label=r"$\beta = 3, \alpha = -2$",
         color="#A60628")
plt.plot(x, logistic(x, -5, 7), label=r"$\beta = -5, \alpha = 7$",
         color="#7A68A6")

plt.title("Logistic function for different $\beta$ and\
          $\alpha$ values")
plt.xlabel("$x$")
plt.ylabel("Logistic function at $x$")
plt.legend(loc="lower left");
```

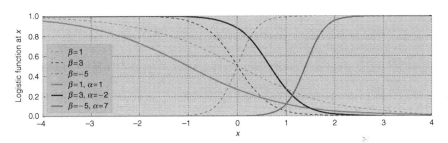

Figure 2.2.12: Logistic function for different β and α values

Adding a constant term α amounts to shifting the curve left or right (hence the name *bias*).

Let's start modeling this in PyMC. The β, α parameters have no reason to be positive, bounded, or relatively large, so they are best modeled by a *Normal random variable*, introduced next.

2.2.11 The Normal Distribution

A Normal random variable, denoted $X \sim N(\mu, 1/\tau)$, has a distribution with two parameters: the mean, μ, and the *precision*, τ. Those familiar with the Normal distribution already have probably seen σ^2 instead of τ^{-1}. They are in fact reciprocals of each other. The change was motivated by simpler mathematical analysis. Just remember: The smaller the τ, the wider the distribution (i.e., we are more uncertain); the larger the τ, the tighter the distribution (i.e., we are more certain). Regardless, τ is always positive.

The probability density function of a $N(\mu, 1/\tau)$ random variable is:

$$f(x|\mu, \tau) = \sqrt{\frac{\tau}{2\pi}} \exp\left(-\frac{\tau}{2}(x - \mu)^2\right)$$

We plot some different density functions of the Normal distribution in Figure 2.2.13.

```
import scipy.stats as stats

nor = stats.norm
x = np.linspace(-8, 7, 150)
mu = (-2, 0, 3)
tau = (.7, 1, 2.8)
colors = ["#348ABD", "#A60628", "#7A68A6"]
parameters = zip(mu, tau, colors)

for _mu, _tau, _color in parameters:
    plt.plot(x, nor.pdf(x, _mu, scale=1./_tau),
             label="$\mu = %d,\;\\tau = %.1f$" % (_mu, _tau),
             color=_color)
    plt.fill_between(x, nor.pdf(x, _mu, scale=1./_tau), color=_color,
                     alpha=.33)

plt.legend(loc="upper right")
plt.xlabel("$x$")
plt.ylabel("Density function at $x$")
plt.title("Probability distribution of three different Normal random \
          variables");
```

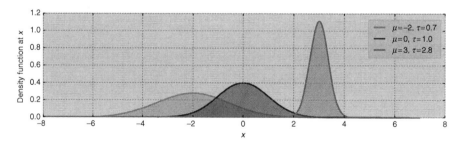

Figure 2.2.13: Probability distribution of three different Normal random variables

A Normal random variable can take on any real number, but the variable is very likely to be relatively close to μ. In fact, the expected value of a Normal is equal to its μ parameter:

$$E[X|\mu, \tau] = \mu$$

and its variance is equal to the inverse of τ:

$$Var(X|\mu, \tau) = \frac{1}{\tau}$$

Let's continue our modeling of the *Challenger* space craft.

```
import pymc as pm

temperature = challenger_data[:, 0]
D = challenger_data[:, 1]   # defect or not?

# Notice the "value" here. We will explain it later.
beta = pm.Normal("beta", 0, 0.001, value=0)
alpha = pm.Normal("alpha", 0, 0.001, value=0)


@pm.deterministic
def p(t=temperature, alpha=alpha, beta=beta):
    return 1.0 / (1. + np.exp(beta*t + alpha))
```

We have our probabilities, but how do we connect them to our observed data? We can use a *Bernoulli* random variable, introduced in Section 2.2.3. Thus, our model can look like:

$$\text{Defect Incident, } D_i \sim \text{Ber}(\, p(t_i)\,), \quad i = 1 \ldots N$$

where $p(t)$ is our logistic function (and strictly between 0 and 1) and t_i is the temperatures we have observations about. Notice that in this code we had to set the values of `beta` and `alpha` to 0. The reason for this is that if `beta` and `alpha` are very large, they make p equal to 1 or 0. Unfortunately, `pm.Bernoulli` does not like probabilities of exactly 0 or 1, though they are mathematically well-defined probabilities. So by setting the coefficient values to 0, we set the variable p to be a reasonable starting value. This has no effect on our results, nor does it mean we are including any additional information in our prior. It is simply a computational caveat in PyMC.

```
p.value
```

```
[Output]:
array([ 0.5,  0.5,  0.5,  0.5,  0.5,  0.5,  0.5,  0.5,  0.5,  0.5,  0.5,
        0.5,  0.5,  0.5,  0.5,  0.5,  0.5,  0.5,  0.5,  0.5,  0.5,
        0.5])
```

```
# Connect the probabilities in "p" with our observations through a
# Bernoulli random variable.
observed = pm.Bernoulli("bernoulli_obs", p, value=D, observed=True)

model = pm.Model([observed, beta, alpha])
```

(Continues)

(*Continued*)

```
# mysterious code to be explained in Chapter 3
map_ = pm.MAP(model)
map_.fit()
mcmc = pm.MCMC(model)
mcmc.sample(120000, 100000, 2)
```

```
[Output]:

[-----------------100%-----------------] 120000 of 120000 complete
    in 15.3 sec
```

We have trained our model on the observed data; now we can sample values from the posterior. Let's look at the posterior distributions for α and β, illustrated in Figure 2.2.14.

```
alpha_samples = mcmc.trace('alpha')[:, None]   # best to make them 1D
beta_samples = mcmc.trace('beta')[:, None]

figsize(12.5, 6)

# histogram of the samples
plt.subplot(211)
plt.title(r"Posterior distributions of the model parameters \
        $\alpha, \beta$")
plt.hist(beta_samples, histtype='stepfilled', bins=35, alpha=0.85,
        label=r"posterior of $\beta$", color="#7A68A6", normed=True)
plt.legend()

plt.subplot(212)
plt.hist(alpha_samples, histtype='stepfilled', bins=35, alpha=0.85,
        label=r"posterior of $\alpha$", color="#A60628", normed=True)
plt.xlabel("Value of parameter")
plt.xlabel("Density")
plt.legend();
```

All samples of β are greater than 0. If instead the posterior was centered around 0, we might suspect that $\beta = 0$, implying that temperature has no effect on the probability of defect. Similarly, all α posterior values are negative and far away from 0, implying that it is correct to believe that α is significantly less than 0. Regarding the spread of the data, we are very uncertain about what the true parameters might be (though considering the small sample size and the large overlap of defects and non-defects, this behavior is perhaps expected).

Next, let's look at the *expected probability* for a specific value of the temperature. That is, we average over all samples from the posterior to get a likely value for $p(t_i)$.

```
t = np.linspace(temperature.min() - 5, temperature.max()+5, 50)[:, None]
p_t = logistic(t.T, beta_samples, alpha_samples)

mean_prob_t = p_t.mean(axis=0)
```

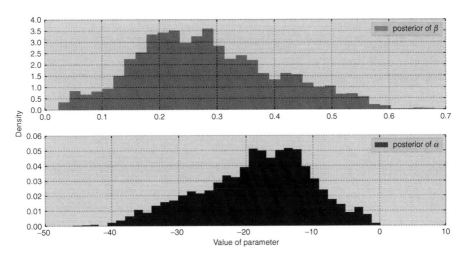

Figure 2.2.14: Posterior distributions of the model parameters α and β

```
figsize(12.5, 4)

plt.plot(t, mean_prob_t, lw=3, label="average posterior \nprobability \
            of defect")
plt.plot(t, p_t[0, :], ls="--", label="realization from posterior")
plt.plot(t, p_t[-2, :], ls="--", label="realization from posterior")
plt.scatter(temperature, D, color="k", s=50, alpha=0.5)
plt.title("Posterior expected value of the probability of defect, \
            including two realizations")
plt.legend(loc="lower left")
plt.ylim(-0.1, 1.1)
plt.xlim(t.min(), t.max())
plt.ylabel("Probability")
plt.xlabel("Temperature");
```

In Figure 2.2.15, we also plot two possible realizations of what the actual underlying system might be. Both are equally as likely as any other draw. The blue line is what occurs when we average all the 20,000 possible dotted lines together.

An interesting question to ask is, For what temperatures are we most uncertain about the defect probability? In Figure 2.2.16, we plot the expected value line *and* the associated 95% credible intervals (CI) for each temperature.

```
from scipy.stats.mstats import mquantiles

# vectorized bottom and top 2.5% quantiles for "credible interval"
qs = mquantiles(p_t, [0.025, 0.975], axis=0)
plt.fill_between(t[:, 0], *qs, alpha=0.7,
                color="#7A68A6")
```

(Continues)

(Continued)

```
plt.plot(t[:, 0], qs[0], label="95% CI", color="#7A68A6", alpha=0.7)

plt.plot(t, mean_prob_t, lw=1, ls="--", color="k",
         label="average posterior \nprobability of defect")

plt.xlim(t.min(), t.max())
plt.ylim(-0.02, 1.02)
plt.legend(loc="lower left")
plt.scatter(temperature, D, color="k", s=50, alpha=0.5)
plt.xlabel("Temperature, $t$")

plt.ylabel("Probability estimate")
plt.title("Posterior probability of estimates, given temperature $t$");
```

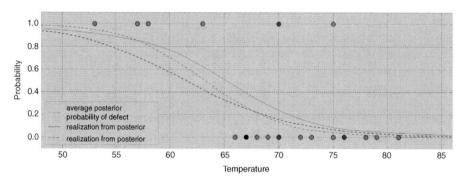

Figure 2.2.15: Posterior expected value of the probability of defect, including two realizations

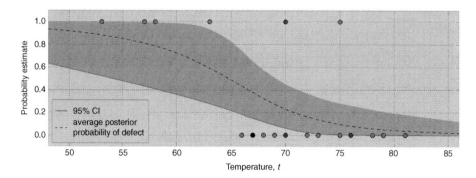

Figure 2.2.16: Posterior probability of estimates, given temperature *t*

    The **95% credible interval**, or 95% CI, painted in purple, represents the interval, for
each temperature, that contains 95% of the distribution. For example, at 65 degrees, we
can be 95% sure that the probability of defect lies between 0.25 and 0.75. This is different
from the frequentist *confidence interval*, which does not have the same interpretation.

More generally, we can see that as the temperature nears 60 degrees, the CIs spread out over [0,1] quickly. As we pass 70 degrees, the CIs tighten again. This can give us insight about how to proceed next; we should probably test more O-rings at temperatures between 60 and 65 degrees to get a better estimate of probabilities in that range. Similarly, when reporting to scientists your estimates, you should be very cautious about simply telling them the expected probability, as we can see that this does not reflect how *wide* the posterior distribution is.

2.2.12   What Happened the Day of the *Challenger* Disaster?

On the day of the *Challenger* disaster, the outside temperature was 31 degrees Fahrenheit. What is the posterior distribution of a defect occurring, given this temperature? The distribution is plotted in Figure 2.2.17. It looks almost guaranteed that the *Challenger* was going to be subject to defective O-rings.

```
figsize(12.5, 2.5)

prob_31 = logistic(31, beta_samples, alpha_samples)

plt.xlim(0.995, 1)
plt.hist(prob_31, bins=1000, normed=True, histtype='stepfilled')
plt.title("Posterior distribution of probability of defect,
          given $t = 31$")
plt.ylabel("Density")
plt.xlabel("Probability of defect occurring in O-ring");
```

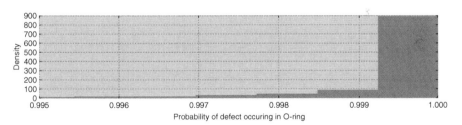

Figure 2.2.17: Posterior distribution of probability of defect, given $t = 31$

2.3   Is Our Model Appropriate?

The skeptical reader will say, "You deliberately chose the logistic function for $p(t)$ and the specific priors. Perhaps other functions or priors will give different results. How do I know I have chosen a good model?" This is absolutely true. To consider an extreme situation, what if I had chosen the function $p(t) = 1$, for all t, which would guarantee defect occurs for any t? I would have again predicted disaster on January 28. Yet this is clearly a poorly chosen model. On the other hand, if I did choose the logistic function for $p(t)$, but specified all my priors to be very tight around 0, we would likely have had very different posterior distributions. How do we know our model is an expression of the data? This encourages us to measure the model's **goodness of fit**, or the measure of how well the model fits our observations.

How can we test whether our model is a bad fit? One way is to compare observed data (which, you will recall, is a *fixed* stochastic variable) with an artificial dataset that we simulate. The rationale is that if the simulated dataset does not appear similar, statistically, to the observed dataset, then our model likely does not accurately represent the observed data.

Previously in this chapter, we simulated an artificial dataset for the text-messaging example. To do this, we sampled values from the priors (that is, we sampled values from a model that was not fitted to the data). We saw how varied the resulting datasets looked, and rarely did they mimic our observed dataset. In the current example, we should sample from the posterior distributions to create very plausible datasets. Luckily, our Bayesian framework makes this very easy. We simply create a new `Stochastic`-type variable that is exactly the same as our variable that stored the observations but minus the observations themselves. If you recall, our `Stochastic` variable that stored our observed data was

```
observed = pm.Bernoulli("bernoulli_obs", p, value=D, observed=True)
```

Hence we initialize the following variable to create plausible datasets:

```
simulated_data = pm.Bernoulli("simulation_data", p)

simulated = pm.Bernoulli("bernoulli_sim", p)
N = 10000

mcmc = pm.MCMC([simulated, alpha, beta, observed])
mcmc.sample(N)
```

```
[Output]:

[-----------------100%-----------------] 10000 of 10000 complete
     in 2.4 sec
```

```
figsize(12.5, 5)

simulations = mcmc.trace("bernoulli_sim")[:].astype(int)
print "Shape of simulations array: ", simulations.shape

plt.title("Simulated datasets using posterior parameters")
figsize(12.5, 6)
for i in range(4):
    ax = plt.subplot(4, 1, i+1)
    plt.scatter(temperature, simulations[1000*i, :], color="k",
                s=50, alpha=0.6);
```

```
[Output]:

Shape of simulations array: (10000, 23)
```

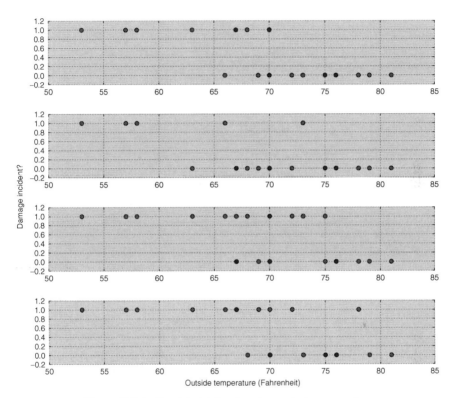

Figure 2.3.1: Simulated datasets using posterior parameters

Note that the plots in Figure 2.3.1 are different because the underlying data is different. What is true, though, is that the datasets are all derived from the same underlying model: Randomness makes them appear different, statistics binds them together. Do these datasets appear (statistically) similar to our original observed data?

We wish to assess how good our model is. "Good" is a subjective term, of course, so results must be relative to other models.

We will be doing this graphically as well, which may seem like an even less objective method. The alternative is to use **Bayesian p-values**, which are a statistical summary of our model, and analogous to frequentist p-values. Bayesian p-values are still subjective, as the proper cutoff between what is deeemed *good* and *bad* is arbitrary. Gelman emphasizes that the graphical tests are more illuminating[6] than p-value tests. We agree.

2.3.1   Separation Plots

The following graphical test is a novel data-visualization approach to logistic regression fitting. The plots are called **separation plots**. Separation plots allow the user to graphically compare a suite of models against each other. I leave most of the technical details about separation plots to the very accessible original paper,[7] but I'll summarize their use here.

For each model, we calculate the proportion of times the posterior simulation proposed a value of 1 for a particular temperature—that is, estimate $P(\text{Defect} = 1|t)$—averaging over all the returned simulations. This gives us the posterior probability of a defect at each data point in our dataset. For example, for the model we used:

```
posterior_probability = simulations.mean(axis=0)

print "Obs. | Array of Simulated Defects\
            | Posterior Probability of Defect | Realized Defect "
for i in range(len(D)):
    print "%s   | %s |   %.2f                      |   %d" %\
        (str(i).zfill(2),str(simulations[:10,i])[:-1] + "...]".ljust(12),
        posterior_probability[i], D[i])
```

```
[Output]:

Obs. | Array of Simulated Defects      | Posterior     | Realized
     |                                 | Probability   | Defect
     |                                 | of Defect
00   | [0 0 1 0 0 1 0 0 0 1...]         | 0.45          |   0
01   | [0 1 1 0 0 0 0 0 0 1...]         | 0.22          |   1
02   | [1 0 0 0 0 0 0 0 0 0...]         | 0.27          |   0
03   | [0 0 0 0 0 0 0 1 0 1...]         | 0.33          |   0
04   | [0 0 0 0 0 0 0 0 0 0...]         | 0.39          |   0
05   | [1 0 1 0 0 1 0 0 0 0...]         | 0.14          |   0
06   | [0 0 1 0 0 0 1 0 0 0...]         | 0.12          |   0
07   | [0 0 0 0 0 0 1 0 0 1...]         | 0.22          |   0
08   | [1 1 0 0 1 1 0 0 1 0...]         | 0.88          |   1
09   | [0 0 0 0 0 0 0 0 0 1...]         | 0.65          |   1
10   | [0 0 0 0 0 1 0 0 0 0...]         | 0.22          |   1
11   | [0 0 0 0 0 0 0 0 0 0...]         | 0.04          |   0
12   | [0 0 0 0 0 1 0 0 0 0...]         | 0.39          |   0
13   | [1 1 0 0 0 1 1 0 0 1...]         | 0.95          |   1
14   | [0 0 0 0 1 0 0 1 0 0...]         | 0.39          |   0
15   | [0 0 0 0 0 0 0 0 0 0...]         | 0.08          |   0
16   | [0 0 0 0 0 0 0 0 1 0...]         | 0.23          |   0
17   | [0 0 0 0 0 0 1 0 0 0...]         | 0.02          |   0
18   | [0 0 0 0 0 0 0 1 0 0...]         | 0.06          |   0
19   | [0 0 0 0 0 0 0 0 0 0...]         | 0.03          |   0
20   | [0 0 0 0 0 0 0 1 1 0...]         | 0.07          |   1
21   | [0 1 0 0 0 0 0 0 0 0...]         | 0.06          |   0
22   | [1 0 1 1 0 1 1 1 0 0...]         | 0.86          |   1
```

Next we sort each column by the posterior probabilities.

```
ix = np.argsort(posterior_probability)
print "Posterior Probability of Defect | Realized Defect"
for i in range(len(D)):
    print "%.2f                          |   %d" %
            (posterior_probability[ix[i]], D[ix[i]])
```

```
[Output]:

Posterior Probability of Defect | Realized Defect
0.02                            |   0
0.03                            |   0
0.04                            |   0
0.06                            |   0
0.06                            |   0
0.07                            |   1
0.08                            |   0
0.12                            |   0
0.14                            |   0
0.22                            |   1
0.22                            |   0
0.22                            |   1
0.23                            |   0
0.27                            |   0
0.33                            |   0
0.39                            |   0
0.39                            |   0
0.39                            |   0
0.45                            |   0
0.65                            |   1
0.86                            |   1
0.88                            |   1
0.95                            |   1
```

We can present this data better in a figure. I've wrapped this up into a separation_plot function in Figure 2.3.2.

```
from separation_plot import separation_plot

figsize(11, 1.5)
separation_plot(posterior_probability, D)
```

The snaking line is the sorted posterior probabilities, blue bars denote realized defects, and empty space (or gray bars for the optimistic readers) denote non-defects. As the probability rises, we see more and more defects occur. The plot suggests that as the posterior probability is large (line close to 1), then more defects are realized. This is good

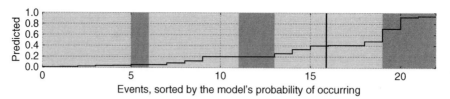

Figure 2.3.2: Temperature-dependent model

behavior. Ideally, all the blue bars *should* be close to the right-hand side, and deviations from this reflect missed predictions.

The black vertical line is located at the expected number of defects we should observe, given this model (see Appendix 2.5 for how this is calculated). This allows the user to see how the total number of events predicted by the model compares to the actual number of events in the data.

It is much more informative to compare this separation plot to the separation plots of other models. In Figures 2.3.3–2.3.6, we compare our model (top) versus three others:

1. The perfect-prediction model, which sets the posterior probability to be equal to 1 if a defect did occur and 0 if a defect did not occur

2. A completely random model, which predicts random probabilities regardless of the temperature

3. And a constant model, where $P(D = 1 \mid t) = c, \ \forall t$. The best choice for c is the observed frequency of defects—in this case, 7/23.

```
figsize(11, 1.25)

# our temperature-dependent model
separation_plot(posterior_probability, D)
plt.title("Our Bayesian temperature-dependent model")

# perfect model
# (the probability of defect is equal to if a defect occurred or not)
p = D
separation_plot(p, D)
plt.title("Perfect model")

# random predictions
p = np.random.rand(23)
separation_plot(p, D)
plt.title("Random model")

# constant model
constant_prob = 7./23*np.ones(23)
separation_plot(constant_prob, D)
plt.title("Constant-prediction model");
```

In the random model, we can see that as the probability increases, there is no clustering of defects to the right-hand side. This is similar to the constant model.

In the perfect model, Figure 2.3.4, the probability line is not well shown, as it is stuck to the bottom and top of the figure. Of course the perfect model is only for demonstration, and we cannot make any scientific inference from it.

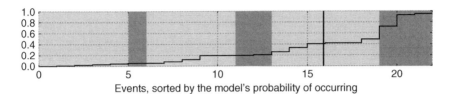

Figure 2.3.3: Our Bayesian temperature-dependent model

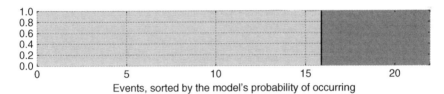

Figure 2.3.4: Perfect model

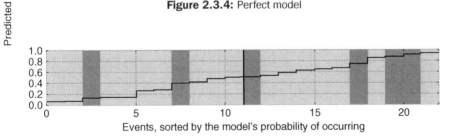

Figure 2.3.5: Random model

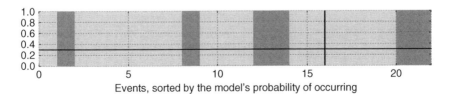

Figure 2.3.6: Constant-prediction model

2.4 Conclusion

In this chapter, we've reviewed syntax for building a PyMC model, gone through the logic of Bayesian model-building, and investigated some real-life examples: A/B testing, using the Privacy Algorithm, and the *Challenger* space shuttle crash.

The modeling in this chapter assumes a basic understanding of the distributions used, and this is important in future Bayesian modeling. As I mentioned previously, distributions are the building blocks of Bayesian modeling, so it's best to be comfortable with them. It's common to make mistakes when choosing distributions, but PyMC will be forgiving; it should scream that something is wrong. When this happens, it's best to go back and reevaluate the chosen distributions.

In Chapter 3, we'll explore what is happening under PyMC's hood, which will help with debugging improper modeling.

2.5 Appendix

How is the expected number of defects (more generally: the expected number instances of some category) computed, given a fit model? Suppose we have N observations, each with unique characteristics (temperature in our example); we can produce a probability of a category (*defect*, in our example) for each observation.

We can think of each observation, indexed by i, as a Bernoulli random variable, denoted B_i, given our model: $B_i = 1$ (i.e., we are correct) with probability p_i, and $B_i = 0$ (i.e., we are wrong) with probability $1 - p_i$, where each p_i comes from putting the observation into the fitted model and being returned a probability. The sum of all these Bernoullis is the total number of instances in that category, given our model. For example, if we are systematically biasing each p_i to be way too high, then our sum will be too high, and this may depart from what is observed in reality (where the total number of some category may in fact be low).

The *expected* number of defects is the expected value of the sum

$$S = \sum_{i=0}^{N} X_i$$

$$E[S] = \sum_{i=0}^{N} E[X_i] = \sum_{i=0}^{N} p_i$$

since the expected value of a Bernoulli is equal to the probability that it is a 1. Thus, for the separation plots, we compute this sum of probabilities, and place a vertical line at that point.

With respect to cross-validation: This step is done before any evaluating on testing data, and can be part of the training process to compare different models' goodness of fit.

2.6 Exercises

1. Try putting in extreme values for our observations in the cheating example. What happens if we observe 25 "Yes" responses? 10? 50?

2. Try plotting α samples versus β samples. Why might the resulting plot look like this?

2.6.1 Answers

1. Suppose we observe 0 affirmative responses. This would be very extreme; it would mean that those who flipped heads on the first toss all were non-cheaters, and those who flipped tails all then flipped tails again. If we were to run the model, we would see that there would be still some posterior mass at values away from 0. Why is this? The reason is that, according to our setup, a cheater might have flipped tails on his or her first toss, and we would have never heard the cheater's honest answer. Our model deals with this possibility by suggesting more probability mass on values away from 0. A similar behavior would occur if we observed 100 affirmative responses, but we would see the posterior have some weight away from 1 in this case.

2. `figsize(12.5, 4)`

```
plt.scatter(alpha_samples, beta_samples, alpha=0.1)
plt.title("Why does the plot look like this?")
plt.xlabel(r"$\alpha$")
plt.ylabel(r"$\beta$")
```

2.7 References

1. Cronin, Beau. "Why Probabilistic Programming Matters," last modified March 24, 2013, https://plus.google.com/u/0/107971134877020469960/posts/KpeRdJKR6Z1.

2. "A Probability Distribution Value Exceeding 1 Is OK?" Cross Validated, accessed December 29, 2014, http://stats.stackexchange.com/questions/4220/a-probability-distribution-value-exceeding-1-is-ok/.

3. Warner, Stanley L., "Randomized Response: A Survey Technique for Eliminating Evasive Answer Bias," *Journal of the American Statistical Association*, 60, no. 309 (Mar., 1965): 63–69.

4. McLeish, Don and Cynthia Struthers. *STATISTICS 450/850: Estimation and Hypothesis Testing, Supplementary Lecture Notes.* Ontario: University of Waterloo, Winter 2013.

5. Dalal, Siddhartha R., Edward B. Fowlkes, and Bruce Hoadley. "Risk Analysis of the Space Shuttle: Pre-Challenger Prediction of Failure," *Journal of the American Statistical Association*, 84, no. 408 (Dec., 1989): 945–957.

6. Gelman, Andrew and Cosma Rohilla Shalizi. "Philosophy and the Practice of Bayesian Statistics," *British Journal of Mathematical and Statistical Psychology* 66 (2013): 8-38.

7. Greenhill, Brian, Michael D. Ward, and Audrey Sacks. "The Separation Plot: A New Visual Method for Evaluating the Fit of Binary Models," *American Journal of Political Science* 55, no. 4 (2011): 991-1002.

Opening the Black Box
of MCMC

3.1 The Bayesian Landscape

Chapters 1 and 2 hid the inner mechanics of PyMC, and more generally Markov Chain Monte Carlo (MCMC), from the reader. The reason for including this chapter is threefold. First, is that any book on Bayesian inference must discuss MCMC. I cannot fight this. Blame the statisticians. Second, knowing the process of MCMC gives you insight into whether your algorithm has converged. (Converged to what? We'll get to that.) Third, we'll understand *why* we are returned thousands of samples from the posterior as a solution, which at first thought can be odd.

When we set up a Bayesian inference problem with N-unknowns, we are implicitly creating an N-dimensional space for the prior distributions to exist in. Associated with the space is an additional dimension, which we can describe as the *surface*, or *curve*, that sits on top of the space, that reflects the *prior probability* of a particular point. The surface on the space is defined by our prior distributions. For example, if we have two unknowns p_1 and p_2, and priors for both are Uniform$(0, 5)$, the space created is a square of length 5 and the surface is a flat plane that sits on top of the square (representing that every point is equally likely, as we chose Uniform priors). This is illustrated in Figure 3.1.1.

```
%matplotlib inline
import scipy.stats as stats
from matplotlib import pyplot as plt
from IPython.core.pylabtools import figsize
import numpy as np
figsize(12.5, 4)
plt.rcParams['savefig.dpi'] = 300
plt.rcParams['figure.dpi'] = 300

import matplotlib.pyplot as plt
from mpl_toolkits.mplot3d import Axes3D

jet = plt.cm.jet
```

(Continues)

(*Continued*)

```
fig = plt.figure()
x = y = np.linspace(0, 5, 100)
X, Y = np.meshgrid(x, y)

plt.subplot(121)
uni_x = stats.uniform.pdf(x, loc=0, scale=5)
uni_y = stats.uniform.pdf(y, loc=0, scale=5)
M = np.dot(uni_x[:, None], uni_y[None, :])
im = plt.imshow(M, interpolation='none', origin='lower',
                cmap=jet, vmax=1, vmin=-.15, extent=(0, 5, 0, 5))

plt.xlim(0, 5)
plt.ylim(0, 5)
plt.title("Overhead view of landscape formed by Uniform priors")

ax = fig.add_subplot(122, projection='3d')
ax.plot_surface(X, Y, M, cmap=plt.cm.jet, vmax=1, vmin=-.15)
ax.view_init(azim=390)
ax.set_xlabel('Value of $p_1$')
ax.set_ylabel('Value of $p_2$')
ax.set_zlabel('Density')
plt.title("Alternate view of landscape formed by Uniform priors");
```

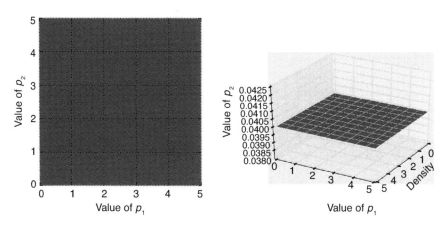

Figure 3.1.1: Left: Overhead view of landscape formed by Uniform priors. Right: Alternate view of landscape formed by Uniform priors

Alternatively, if the two priors are *Exp*(3) and *Exp*(10), then the space is all positive numbers on the 2D plane, and the surface induced by the priors looks like a waterfall that starts at the point (0,0) and flows over the positive numbers.

The plots in Figure 3.1.2 visualize this. The more the color tends toward dark red, the more prior probability is assigned to that location. Conversely, the more the area tends toward darker blue, the lower the probability our priors assign to that location.

```
figsize(12.5, 5)
fig = plt.figure()
plt.subplot(121)

exp_x = stats.expon.pdf(x, scale=3)
exp_y = stats.expon.pdf(x, scale=10)
M = np.dot(exp_x[:, None], exp_y[None, :])
CS = plt.contour(X, Y, M)
im = plt.imshow(M, interpolation='none', origin='lower',
                cmap=jet, extent=(0, 5, 0, 5))
plt.title("Overhead view of landscape formed by $Exp(3),\
          Exp(10)$ priors")

ax = fig.add_subplot(122, projection='3d')
ax.plot_surface(X, Y, M, cmap=jet)
ax.view_init(azim=390)
ax.set_xlabel('Value of $p_1$')
ax.set_ylabel('Value of $p_2$')
ax.set_zlabel('Density')
plt.title("Alternate view of landscape\nformed by $Exp(3),\
          Exp(10)$ priors");
```

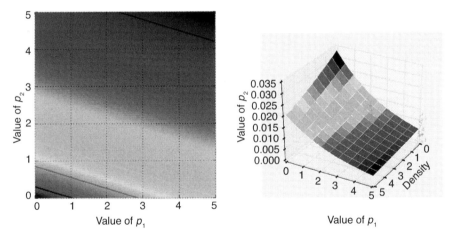

Figure 3.1.2: Left: Overhead view of landscape formed by *Exp*(3), *Exp*(10) priors. Right: Alternate view of landscape formed by *Exp*(3), *Exp*(10) priors

These are simple examples in 2D space, where our brains can understand surfaces well. In practice, spaces and surfaces generated by our priors can be much higher-dimensional.

If these surfaces describe our *prior distributions* on the unknowns, what happens to our space after we incorporate our observed data X? The data X does not change the space, but it changes the surface of the space by *pulling and stretching the fabric of the prior surface* to reflect where the true parameters likely live. More data means more pulling and stretching, and our original surface may become mangled or insignificant compared to the newly formed surface. Less data, and our original shape is more present. Regardless, the resulting surface describes the new *posterior distribution*.

Again I must stress that it is, unfortunately, impossible to visualize this in large dimensions. For two dimensions, the data essentially *pushes up* the original surface to make *tall mountains*. The tendency of the observed data to *push up* the posterior probability in certain areas is checked by the prior probability distribution, so that less prior probability means more resistance. Thus in the preceding double-exponential prior case, a mountain (or multiple mountains) that might erupt near the (0,0) corner would be much higher than mountains that erupt closer to (5,5), since there is more resistance (low prior probability) near (5,5). The mountain reflects the posterior probability of where the true parameters are likely to be found. It is important to note that if the prior has assigned a probability of 0 to a point, then no posterior probability will be assigned there.

Suppose we are interested in performing inference on two Poisson distributions, each with an unknown λ parameter. We'll compare using both a Uniform prior and an Exponential prior for the λ unknowns. Suppose we observe a data point; we visualize the "before" and "after" landscapes in Figure 3.1.3.

```
## Create the Observed Data

# sample size of data we observe, try varying this (keep it
# less than 100)
N = 1

# the true parameters, but of course we do not see
# these values...
lambda_1_true = 1
lambda_2_true = 3

# ...we see the data generated, dependent on the preceding
# two values
data = np.concatenate([
    stats.poisson.rvs(lambda_1_true, size=(N, 1)),
    stats.poisson.rvs(lambda_2_true, size=(N, 1))
], axis=1)
print "observed (2-dimensional,sample size = %d):" % N, data

# plotting details
x = y = np.linspace(.01, 5, 100)
likelihood_x = np.array([stats.poisson.pmf(data[:, 0], _x)
                        for _x in x]).prod(axis=1)
likelihood_y = np.array([stats.poisson.pmf(data[:, 1], _y)
                        for _y in y]).prod(axis=1)
L = np.dot(likelihood_x[:, None], likelihood_y[None, :])
```

```
[Output]:

observed (2-dimensional,sample size = 1): [[0 6]]
```

```
figsize(12.5, 12)
# matplotlib heavy lifting follows-beware!
plt.subplot(221)
uni_x = stats.uniform.pdf(x, loc=0, scale=5)
uni_y = stats.uniform.pdf(x, loc=0, scale=5)
M = np.dot(uni_x[:, None], uni_y[None, :])
im = plt.imshow(M, interpolation='none', origin='lower',
                cmap=jet, vmax=1, vmin=-.15, extent=(0, 5, 0, 5))
plt.scatter(lambda_2_true, lambda_1_true, c="k", s=50,
            edgecolor="none")
plt.xlim(0, 5)
plt.ylim(0, 5)
plt.title("Landscape formed by Uniform priors on $p_1, p_2$")


plt.subplot(223)
plt.contour(x, y, M * L)
im = plt.imshow(M * L, interpolation='none', origin='lower',
                cmap=jet, extent=(0, 5, 0, 5))
plt.title("Landscape warped by %d data observation;\
          \nUniform priors on $p_1, p_2$" % N)
plt.scatter(lambda_2_true, lambda_1_true, c="k", s=50,
            edgecolor="none")
plt.xlim(0, 5)
plt.ylim(0, 5)


plt.subplot(222)
exp_x = stats.expon.pdf(x, loc=0, scale=3)
exp_y = stats.expon.pdf(x, loc=0, scale=10)
M = np.dot(exp_x[:, None], exp_y[None, :])

plt.contour(x, y, M)
im = plt.imshow(M, interpolation='none', origin='lower',
                cmap=jet, extent=(0, 5, 0, 5))
plt.scatter(lambda_2_true, lambda_1_true, c="k", s=50,
            edgecolor="none")
plt.xlim(0, 5)
plt.ylim(0, 5)
plt.title("Landscape formed by Exponential priors on $p_1, p_2$")


plt.subplot(224)
# This is the likelihood times prior that results in
# the posterior.
plt.contour(x, y, M * L)
im = plt.imshow(M * L, interpolation='none', origin='lower',
                cmap=jet, extent=(0, 5, 0, 5))

plt.scatter(lambda_2_true, lambda_1_true, c="k", s=50,
            edgecolor="none")
plt.title("Landscape warped by %d data observation;\
          \nExponential priors on \ $p_1, p_2$" % N)
```

(Continues)

(Continued)

```
plt.xlim(0, 5)
plt.ylim(0, 5)
plt.xlabel('Value of $p_1$')
plt.ylabel('Value of $p_2$');
```

The black dot in each of the four figures represents the true parameters. The plot on the bottom left is the deformed landscape with the Uniform$(0, 5)$ priors, and the plot on the bottom right is the deformed landscape with the Exponential priors. Notice that the posterior landscapes look different from one another, though the data observed is identical in both cases. The reason is as follows. Notice that the posterior with the exponential-prior landscape, bottom-right figure, puts very little *posterior* weight on values in the upper-right corner of the figure; this is because *the prior does not put much weight there*. On the other hand, the Uniform-prior landscape is happy to put posterior weight in the upper-right corner, as the prior puts more weight there compared to the Exponential prior.

Notice also that the highest point, corresponding to the darkest red, is biased toward (0,0) in the Exponential prior case, which is the result of the Exponential prior putting more prior weight in the (0,0) corner. Even with 1 sample point, the mountains attempt to contain the true parameter. Of course, inference with a sample size of 1 is incredibly naive, and choosing such a small sample size was only illustrative. It's a great exercise to try changing the sample size to other values (try 2? 5? 10? 100?) and observing how our "mountain" posterior changes.

3.1.1   Exploring the Landscape Using MCMC

We should explore the deformed posterior space generated by our prior surface and observed data to find the posterior mountain. However, we cannot naively search the space. Any computer scientist will tell you that traversing N-dimensional space is exponentially difficult in N: The size of the space quickly blows up as we increase N (see the curse of dimensionality: `http://en.wikipedia.org/wiki/Curse_of_dimensionality`). What hope do we have of finding these hidden mountains? The idea behind MCMC is to perform an intelligent search of the space. To say "search" implies we are looking for a particular point, which is perhaps not an accurate description, as we are really looking for a broad mountain.

Recall that MCMC returns *samples* from the posterior distribution, not the distribution itself. Stretching our mountainous analogy to its limit, MCMC performs a task similar to repeatedly asking "How likely is this pebble I found to be from the mountain I am searching for?" and completes its task by returning thousands of accepted pebbles in hopes of reconstructing the original mountain. In MCMC and PyMC lingo, the "pebbles" returned in the sequence are the samples, cumulatively called the **traces**.

When I say that MCMC "intelligently searches," I am really saying that we *hope* that MCMC will converge toward the areas of posterior probability. MCMC does this by

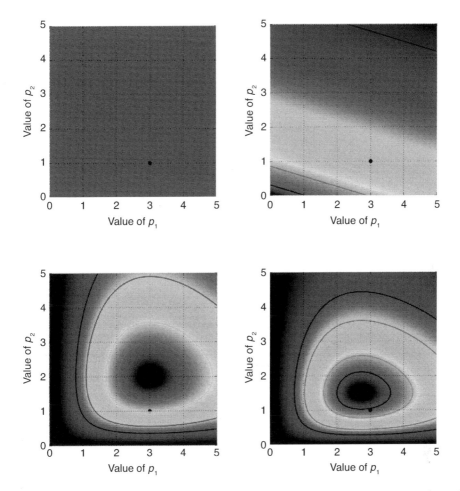

Figure 3.1.3: Top left: Landscape formed by Uniform priors on p_1, p_2. Top right: Landscape formed by Exponential priors on p_1, p_2. Bottom left: Landscape warped by 1 data observation with Uniform priors on p_1, p_2. Bottom right: Landscape warped by 1 data observation with Exponential priors on p_1, p_2

exploring nearby positions and moving into areas with higher probability. "Converging" usually implies moving toward a point in space, but MCMC moves toward a *broad area* in the space and randomly walks around in that area, picking up samples from that area.

Why Thousands of Samples? At first, returning thousands of samples to the user might sound like an inefficient way to describe the posterior distributions. I would argue that this is actually extremely efficient. Consider the alternative possibilities.

1. Returning a mathematical formula for the "mountain ranges" would involve describing an N-dimensional surface with arbitrary peaks and valleys. This is not easy.

2. Returning the "peak" of the landscape (the highest point of the mountain), while mathematically possible and a sensible thing to do (the highest point corresponds to the most probable estimate of the unknowns), ignores the shape of the landscape, which we have previously argued is very important in determining posterior confidence in unknowns.

Besides computational reasons, likely the strongest reason for returning samples is that we can easily use the *Law of Large Numbers* to solve otherwise intractable problems. I postpone this discussion to Chapter 4. With the thousands of samples, we can reconstruct the posterior surface by organizing them in a histogram.

3.1.2   Algorithms to Perform MCMC

There is a large family of algorithms that perform MCMC. Most of these algorithms can be expressed at a high level as follows.

1. Start at the current position.

2. Propose moving to a new position (investigate a pebble near you).

3. Accept/Reject the new position based on the position's adherence to the data and prior distributions (ask if the pebble likely came from the mountain).

4. (a) If you accept: Move to the new position. Return to Step 1.

   (b) Else: Do not move to the new position. Return to Step 1.

5. After a large number of iterations, return all accepted positions.

In this way, we move in the general direction toward the regions where the posterior distributions exist, and collect samples sparingly on the journey. Once we reach the posterior distribution, we can easily collect samples, as they likely all belong to the posterior distribution.

If the current position of the MCMC algorithm is in an area of extremely low probability, which is often the case when the algorithm begins (typically at a random location in the space), the algorithm will move in positions that are *likely not from the posterior* but *better than everything else nearby*. Thus the first moves of the algorithm are not very reflective of the posterior. We'll deal with this later.

In the preceding algorithm's pseudocode, notice that only the current position matters (new positions are investigated only near the current position). We can describe this property as *memorylessness*; that is, the algorithm does not care *how* it arrived at its current position, only that it is there.

3.1.3 Other Approximation Solutions to the Posterior

Besides MCMC, there are other procedures available for determining the posterior distributions. A *Laplace approximation* is an approximation of the posterior using simple functions. A more advanced method is *variational Bayes*. All three methods—Laplace approximations, variational Bayes, and classical MCMC—have their pros and cons. We will only focus on MCMC in this book. That being said, a friend of mine likes to classify MCMC algorithms as either "they suck" or "they really suck." He classifies the particular flavor of MCMC used by PyMC as just "sucks."

3.1.4 Example: Unsupervised Clustering Using a Mixture Model

Suppose we are given the following dataset:

```
figsize(12.5, 4)
data = np.loadtxt("data/mixture_data.csv", delimiter=",")

plt.hist(data, bins=20, color="k", histtype="stepfilled", alpha=0.8)
plt.title("Histogram of the dataset")
plt.ylim([0, None])
plt.xlabel('Value')
plt.ylabel('Count')
print data[:10], "..."
```

```
[Output]:

[ 115.8568 152.2615 178.8745 162.935 107.0282 105.1914 118.3829
   125.377 102.8805 206.7133] ...
```

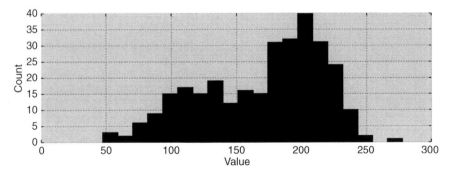

Figure 3.1.4: Histogram of the dataset

What does the data suggest? In Figure 3.1.4, it appears the data has a bimodal form; that is, it appears to have two peaks: one near 120 and the other near 200. Perhaps there are *two clusters* within this dataset.

This dataset is a good example of the data-generation modeling technique from Chapter 2. We can propose *how* the data might have been created. I suggest the following data-generation algorithm.

1. For each data point, choose cluster 1 with probability p, else choose cluster 2.
2. Draw a random variate from a Normal distribution with parameters μ_i and σ_i where i was chosen in step 1.
3. Repeat.

This algorithm would create a similar effect as the observed dataset, so we choose this as our model. Of course, we do not know p or the parameters of the Normal distributions. Hence we must infer, or *learn*, these unknowns.

Denote the Normal distributions Nor_0 and Nor_1 (having variables' index start at 0 is just Pythonic). Both currently have unknown mean and unknown standard deviation, denoted μ_i and σ_i, $i = 0, 1$ respectively. A specific data point can be from either Nor_0 or Nor_1, and we assume that the data point is assigned to Nor_0 with probability p. *A priori*, we do not know what the probability of assignment to cluster 1 is, so we create a uniform variable over 0 to 1 to model this. Call this p.

An appropriate way to assign data points to clusters is to use a PyMC Categorical stochastic variable. Its parameter is a k-length array of probabilities that must sum to 1 and its value attribute is an integer between 0 and $k - 1$ randomly chosen according to the crafted array of probabilities (in our case, $k = 2$). Thus, the probability array we enter into the Categorical variable is [p, 1-p].

```
import pymc as pm

p = pm.Uniform("p", 0., 1.)

assignment = pm.Categorical("assignment", [p, 1 - p],
                            size=data.shape[0])
print "prior assignment, with p = %.2f:" % p.value
print assignment.value[:10], "..."
```

```
[Output]:

prior assignment, with p = 0.80:
[0 0 0 0 0 0 1 1 0 0] ...
```

Looking at the preceding dataset, I would guess that the standard deviations of the two Normals are different. To maintain ignorance of what the standard deviations might be, we will initially model them as Uniform on 0 to 100. Really we are talking about τ, the *precision* of the Normal distribution, but it is easier to think in terms of standard deviation.

Our PyMC code will need to transform our standard deviation into precision by the relation

$$\tau = \frac{1}{\sigma^2}$$

In PyMC, we can do this in one step by writing

```
taus = 1.0 / pm.Uniform("stds", 0, 100, size=2) ** 2
```

Notice that we specified `size=2`: We are modeling both τs as a single PyMC variable. Note that this does not induce a necessary relationship between the two τs; it is simply for succinctness.

We also need to specify priors on the centers of the clusters. The centers are really the μ parameters in this Normal distribution. Their priors can be modeled by a Normal distribution. Looking at the data, I have an idea where the two centers might be—I would guess somewhere around 120 and 190, respectively, though I am not very confident in these eyeballed estimates. Hence I will set $\mu_0 = 120, \mu_1 = 190$, and $\sigma_{0,1} = 10$ (recall that we enter the τ parameter, so enter $1/\sigma^2 = 0.01$ in the PyMC variable).

```
taus = 1.0 / pm.Uniform("stds", 0, 33, size=2) ** 2
centers = pm.Normal("centers", [120, 190], [0.01, 0.01], size=2)

"""
The following deterministic functions map an assignment, in this
case 0 or 1, to a set of parameters, located in the (1,2) arrays
"taus" and "centers".
"""

@pm.deterministic
def center_i(assignment=assignment, centers=centers):
    return centers[assignment]

@pm.deterministic
def tau_i(assignment=assignment, taus=taus):
    return taus[assignment]

print "Random assignments: ", assignment.value[:4], "..."
print "Assigned center: ", center_i.value[:4], "..."
print "Assigned precision: ", tau_i.value[:4], "..."
```

```
[Output]:

Random assignments:  [0 0 0 0] ...
Assigned center:  [ 118.9889 118.9889 118.9889 118.9889] ...
Assigned precision:  [ 0.0041 0.0041 0.0041 0.0041] ...
```

```
# We combine it with the observations.
observations = pm.Normal("obs", center_i, tau_i, value=data,
                         observed=True)
```

(*Continues*)

(*Continued*)

```
# Now we create a model class.
model = pm.Model([p, assignment, taus, centers])
```

PyMC has an MCMC class, MCMC in the main namespace of PyMC, that implements the MCMC exploring algorithm. We initialize it by passing in a Model instance:

```
mcmc = pm.MCMC(model)
```

The method for asking the MCMC to explore the space is pm.sample(iterations), where iterations is the number of steps you wish the algorithm to perform. The following code tries 50,000 steps:

```
mcmc = pm.MCMC(model)
mcmc.sample(50000)
```

```
[Output]:

[----------------100%----------------] 50000 of 50000 complete
    in 31.5 sec
```

In Figure 3.1.5, I plot the paths—also called the *traces*—that the unknown parameters (centers, precisions, and p) have taken thus far. The traces can be retrieved using the trace method in the MCMC object created, which accepts the assigned PyMC variable name. For example, mcmc.trace("centers") will retrieve a Trace object that can be indexed (using [:] or .gettrace() to retrieve all traces, or fancy-indexing like [1000:]).

```
figsize(12.5, 9)
plt.subplot(311)
line_width = 1
center_trace = mcmc.trace("centers")[:]

# for pretty colors later in the book
colors = ["#348ABD", "#A60628"]
if center_trace[-1, 0] < center_trace[-1, 1]:
    colors = ["#A60628", "#348ABD"]

plt.plot(center_trace[:, 0], label="trace of center 0",
        c=colors[0], lw=line_width)
plt.plot(center_trace[:, 1], label="trace of center 1",
        c=colors[1], lw=line_width)
plt.title("Traces of unknown parameters")
leg = plt.legend(loc="upper right")
leg.get_frame().set_alpha(0.7)

plt.subplot(312)
std_trace = mcmc.trace("stds")[:]
```

```
plt.plot(std_trace[:, 0], label="trace of standard deviation of
         cluster 0", c=colors[0], lw=line_width)
plt.plot(std_trace[:, 1], label="trace of standard deviation of
         cluster 1", c=colors[1], lw=line_width)
plt.legend(loc="upper left")

plt.subplot(313)
p_trace = mcmc.trace("p")[:]
plt.plot(p_trace, label="$p$: frequency of assignment
         to cluster 0", color="#467821", lw=line_width)
plt.xlabel("Steps")
plt.ylim(0, 1)
plt.ylabel('Value')
plt.legend();
```

Notice the following characteristics in Figure 3.1.5.

1. The traces converge, not to a single point, but to a *distribution* of possible points. This is *convergence* in an MCMC algorithm.

2. Inference using the first few thousand points is a bad idea, as they are unrelated to the final distribution we are interested in. Thus, it is a good idea to discard those samples before using the samples for inference. We call this period before converge the *burn-in period*.

3. The traces appear as a random "walk" around the space; that is, the paths exhibit a relationship with previous positions. This is both good and bad. We will always have a relationship between current positions and the previous positions, but too much of it means we are not exploring the space well. This will be detailed in the Diagnostics section later in this chapter.

To achieve further convergence, we will perform more MCMC steps. Starting the MCMC again after it has already been called does not mean starting the entire search over. In the preceding pseudocode algorithm of MCMC, the only position that matters is the current position (new positions are investigated near the current position), implicitly stored in PyMC variables' `value` attribute. Thus it is fine to halt an MCMC algorithm and inspect its progress, with the intention of starting it up again later. The `value` attributes are not overwritten.

We will sample the MCMC 100,000 more times and visualize the progress in Figure 3.1.6.

```
mcmc.sample(100000)
```

```
[Output]:

[-----------------100%-----------------] 100000 of 100000 complete
    in 60.1 sec
```

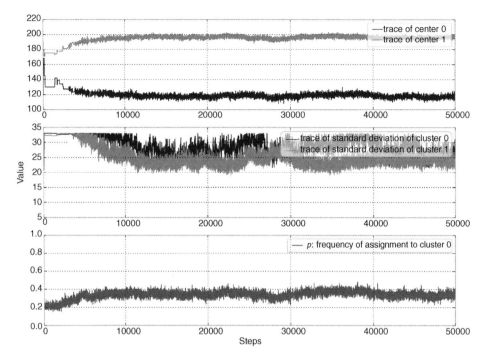

Figure 3.1.5: Traces of unknown parameters

(Continued)

```
figsize(12.5, 4)
center_trace = mcmc.trace("centers", chain=1)[:]
prev_center_trace = mcmc.trace("centers", chain=0)[:]

x = np.arange(50000)
plt.plot(x, prev_center_trace[:, 0], label="previous trace of center 0",
         lw=line_width, alpha=0.4, c=colors[1])
plt.plot(x, prev_center_trace[:, 1], label="previous trace of center 1",
         lw=line_width, alpha=0.4, c=colors[0])

x = np.arange(50000, 150000)
plt.plot(x, center_trace[:, 0], label="new trace of center 0",
         lw=line_width, c="#348ABD")
plt.plot(x, center_trace[:, 1], label="new trace of center 1",
         lw=line_width, c="#A60628")

plt.title("Traces of unknown center parameters after\
          sampling 100,000 more times")
leg = plt.legend(loc="upper right")
leg.get_frame().set_alpha(0.8)
```

```
plt.ylabel('Value')
plt.xlabel("Steps");
```

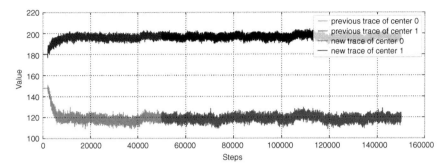

Figure 3.1.6: Traces of unknown center parameters after sampling 100,000 more times

The `trace` method in the MCMC instance has a keyword argument `chain` that indexes which call to `sample` you would like to be returned. (Often we need to call `sample` multiple times, and the ability to retrieve past samples is a useful procedure.) The default for `chain` is −1, which will return the samples from the latest call to `sample`.

Cluster Investigation   We have not forgotten our main challenge to identify the clusters. We have determined posterior distributions for our unknowns. We plot the posterior distributions of the center and standard deviation variables in Figure 3.1.7.

```
figsize(11.0, 4)
std_trace = mcmc.trace("stds")[:]

_i = [1, 2, 3, 0]
for i in range(2):
    plt.subplot(2, 2, _i[2 * i])
    plt.title("Posterior distribution of center of cluster %d" % i)
    plt.hist(center_trace[:, i], color=colors[i], bins=30,
            histtype="stepfilled")

    plt.subplot(2, 2, _i[2 * i + 1])
    plt.title("Posterior distribution of standard deviation of cluster %d" % i)
    plt.hist(std_trace[:, i], color=colors[i], bins=30,
            histtype="stepfilled")
    plt.ylabel('Density')
    plt.xlabel('Value')

plt.tight_layout();
```

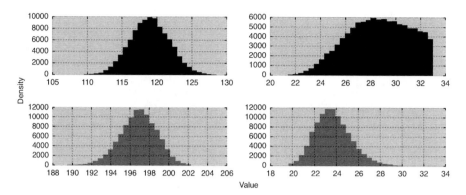

Figure 3.1.7: Top left: Posterior distribution of center of cluster 0. Top right: Posterior distribution of standard deviation of cluster 0. Bottom left: Posterior distribution of center of cluster 1. Bottom right: Posterior distribution of standard deviation of cluster 1.

The MCMC algorithm has proposed that the most likely centers of the two clusters are near 120 and 200. Similar inference can be applied to the standard deviation.

We are also given the posterior distributions for the labels of the data point, which is present in mcmc.trace("assignment"). Figure 3.1.8 is a visualization of this. The y axis represents a subsample of the posterior labels for each data point. On the x axis are the sorted values of the data points. A red square is an assignment to cluster 1, and a blue square is an assignment to cluster 0.

```
import matplotlib as mpl
figsize(12.5, 4.5)
plt.cmap = mpl.colors.ListedColormap(colors)
plt.imshow(mcmc.trace("assignment")[::400, np.argsort(data)],
        cmap=plt.cmap, aspect=.4, alpha=.9)
plt.xticks(np.arange(0, data.shape[0], 40),
        ["%.2f" % s for s in np.sort(data)[::40]])
plt.ylabel("Posterior sample")
plt.xlabel("Value of $i$th data point")
plt.title("Posterior labels of data points");
```

Looking at Figure 3.1.8, it appears that the most uncertainty is between 150 and 170. This slightly misrepresents things, as the x axis is not a true scale (it displays the value of the ith sorted data point). Figure 3.1.9 presents a more clear diagram, where we have estimated the *frequency* of each data point belonging to the clusters 0 and 1.

```
cmap = mpl.colors.LinearSegmentedColormap.from_list("BMH",
        colors)
assign_trace = mcmc.trace("assignment")[:]
plt.scatter(data, 1 - assign_trace.mean(axis=0), cmap=cmap,
        c=assign_trace.mean(axis=0), s=50)
plt.ylim(-0.05, 1.05)
```

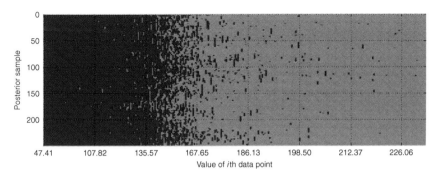

Figure 3.1.8: Posterior labels of data points

```
plt.xlim(35, 300)
plt.title("Probability of data point belonging to cluster 0")
plt.ylabel("Probability")
plt.xlabel("Value of data point");
```

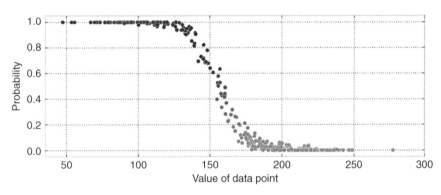

Figure 3.1.9: Probability of data point belonging to cluster 0

Even though we modeled the clusters using Normal distributions, we didn't get just a single Normal distribution that *best* fits the data (whatever our definition of best is), but a distribution of values for the Normal's parameters. How can we choose just a single pair of values for the mean and variance and determine a *sorta-best-fit* Gaussian?

One quick and dirty way (which has nice theoretical properties, as we will see in Chapter 5), is to use the *mean* of the posterior distributions. In Figure 3.1.10, we overlay the Normal density functions, using the mean of the posterior distributions as the chosen parameters, with our observed data.

```
norm = stats.norm
x = np.linspace(20, 300, 500)
posterior_center_means = center_trace.mean(axis=0)
```

(*Continues*)

(Continued)

```
posterior_std_means = std_trace.mean(axis=0)
posterior_p_mean = mcmc.trace("p")[:].mean()

plt.hist(data, bins=20, histtype="step", normed=True, color="k",
        lw=2, label="histogram of data")
y = posterior_p_mean * norm.pdf(x, loc=posterior_center_means[0],
                                scale=posterior_std_means[0])
plt.plot(x, y, label="cluster 0 (using posterior-mean
        parameters)", lw=3)
plt.fill_between(x, y, color=colors[1], alpha=0.3)

y = (1 - posterior_p_mean) * norm.pdf(x,
                    loc=posterior_center_means[1],
                    scale=posterior_std_means[1])
plt.plot(x, y, label="cluster 1 (using posterior-mean
        parameters)", lw=3)
plt.fill_between(x, y, color=colors[0], alpha=0.3)

plt.legend(loc="upper left")
plt.title("Visualizing clusters using posterior-mean\
        parameters");
```

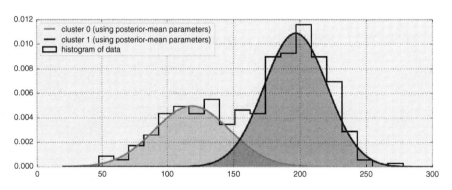

Figure 3.1.10: Visualizing clusters using posterior-mean parameters

3.1.5   Don't Mix Posterior Samples

In Figure 3.1.10, a possible (though less likely) scenario is that cluster 0 has a very large standard deviation, and cluster 1 has a small standard deviation. This would still satisfy the evidence, albeit less so than our original inference. Alternatively, it would be incredibly unlikely for *both* distributions to have a small standard deviation, as the data does not support this hypothesis at all. Thus the two standard deviations are *dependent* on each other: If one is small, the other must be large. In fact, *all* the unknowns are related in a similar manner. For example, if a standard deviation is large, the mean has a wider possible space of realizations. Conversely, a small standard deviation restricts the mean to a small area.

During MCMC, we are returned vectors representing samples from the unknown posteriors. Elements of different vectors cannot be used together, as this would break our logic. Perhaps a sample has returned that cluster 1 has a small standard deviation, hence all the other variables in that sample would incorporate that and be adjusted accordingly. It is easy to avoid this problem, though; just make sure you are indexing traces correctly.

Another small example to illustrate the point. Suppose two variables, x and y, are related by $x + y = 10$. In Figure 3.1.11, we model x as a Normal random variable with mean 4 and explore 500 samples.

```python
import pymc as pm

x = pm.Normal("x", 4, 10)
y = pm.Lambda("y", lambda x=x: 10 - x, trace=True)

ex_mcmc = pm.MCMC(pm.Model([x, y]))
ex_mcmc.sample(500)

plt.plot(ex_mcmc.trace("x")[:])
plt.plot(ex_mcmc.trace("y")[:])
plt.xlabel('Steps')
plt.ylabel('Value')
plt.title("Displaying (extreme) case of dependence between\
        unknowns");
```

```
[Output]:

[------------------100%------------------] 500 of 500 complete in 0.0 sec
```

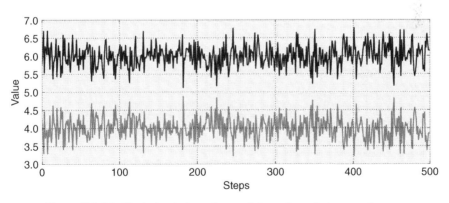

Figure 3.1.11: Displaying (extreme) case of dependence between unknowns

As you can see, the two variables are not unrelated, and it would be wrong to add the ith sample of x to the jth sample of y, unless $i = j$.

Returning to Clustering: Prediction   The preceding clustering can be generalized to k clusters. Choosing $k = 2$ allowed us to visualize the MCMC better, and examine some very interesting plots.

What about prediction? Suppose we observe a new data point, say $x = 175$, and we wish to label it to a cluster. It is foolish to simply assign it to the *closer* cluster center, as this ignores the standard deviation of the clusters, and we have seen from the preceding plots that this consideration is very important. More formally: We are interested in the *probability* (as we cannot be certain about labels) of assigning $x = 175$ to cluster 1. Denote the assignment of x as L_x, which is equal to 0 or 1, and we are interested in $P(L_x = 1 \mid x = 175)$.

A naive method to compute this is to re-run the preceding MCMC with the additional data point appended. The disadvantage with this method is that it will be slow to infer for each novel data point. Alternatively, we can try a *less precise*, but much quicker method.

We will use Bayes' Theorem for this. As you'll recall, Bayes' Theorem looks like:

$$P(A|X) = \frac{P(X|A)P(A)}{P(X)}$$

In our case, A represents $L_x = 1$ and X is the evidence we have. We observe that $x = 175$. For a particular sample set of parameters for our posterior distribution, $(\mu_0, \sigma_0, \mu_1, \sigma_1, p)$, we are interested in asking, "Is the probability that x is in cluster 1 *greater* than the probability it is in cluster 0?" where the probability is dependent on the chosen parameters.

$$P(L_x = 1|x = 175) > P(L_x = 0|x = 175)$$

$$\frac{P(x = 175|L_x = 1)P(L_x = 1)}{P(x = 175)} > \frac{P(x = 175|L_x = 0)P(L_x = 0)}{P(x = 175)}$$

As the denominators are equal, they can be ignored—and good riddance, because computing the quantity $P(x = 175)$ can be difficult.

$$P(x = 175|L_x = 1)P(L_x = 1) > P(x = 175|L_x = 0)P(L_x = 0)$$

```
norm_pdf = stats.norm.pdf
p_trace = mcmc.trace("p")[:]
x = 175

v = p_trace * norm_pdf(x, loc=center_trace[:, 0],
            scale=std_trace[:, 0]) > \
    (1 - p_trace) * norm_pdf(x, loc=center_trace[:, 1],
            scale=std_trace[:, 1])

print "Probability of belonging to cluster 1:", v.mean()
```

```
[Output]:

Probability of belonging to cluster 1: 0.025
```

Giving us a probability instead of a label is a very useful thing. Instead of the naive

```
L = 1 if prob > 0.5 else 0
```

we can optimize our guesses using a *loss function*, to which the entirety of Chapter 5 is devoted.

3.1.6 Using MAP to Improve Convergence

If you ran the preceding example yourself, you may have noticed that our results were not consistent; perhaps your cluster division was more scattered, or perhaps less scattered. The problem is that our traces are a function of the *starting values* of the MCMC algorithm.

It can be mathematically shown that if we let the MCMC run long enough, by performing many steps, then the algorithm *should forget its initial position*. In fact, this is what it means to say the MCMC converged (in practice, though, we can never achieve total convergence). Hence, if we observe different posterior analyses, it is likely because our MCMC has not fully converged yet, and we should not use samples from it yet (we should use a larger burn-in period).

In fact, poor starting values can prevent any convergence, or significantly slow it down. Ideally, we would like to have the chain start at the *peak* of our landscape, as this is exactly where the posterior distributions exist. Hence, if we started at the "peak," we could avoid a lengthy burn-in period and incorrect inference. Generally, we call this "peak" the *maximum a posterior* or, more simply, the *MAP*.

Of course, we do not know where the MAP is. PyMC provides an object that will approximate, if not find, the MAP location. In the PyMC main namespace is the MAP object that accepts a PyMC Model instance. Calling .fit() from the MAP instance sets the variables in the model to their MAP values.

```
map_ = pm.MAP(model)
map_.fit()
```

The MAP.fit() methods have the flexibility of allowing the user to choose which optimization algorithm to use (after all, this is an optimization problem; we are looking for the values that maximize our landscape), as not all optimization algorithms are created equal. The default optimization algorithm in the call to fit is SciPy's fmin algorithm (which attempts to minimize the *negative of the landscape*). An alternative algorithm that is available is Powell's method, a favorite of PyMC blogger Abraham Flaxman,[1] by calling fit(method='fmin_powell'). From my experience, I use the default, but if my convergence is slow or not guaranteed, I experiment with Powell's method.

The MAP can also be used as a solution to the inference problem, as mathematically it is the *most likely* value for the unknowns. But as mentioned earlier in this chapter, this location ignores the uncertainty and doesn't return a distribution.

Typically, it is always a good idea, and rarely a bad idea, to prepend your call to mcmc with a call to `MAP(model).fit()`. The intermediate call to `fit` is hardly computationally intensive, and will save you time later due to a shorter burn-in period.

Speaking of the Burn-in Period   It is still a good idea to provide a burn-in period, even if we are using `MAP` prior to calling `MCMC.sample`, just to be safe. We can have PyMC automatically discard the first *n* samples by specifying the `burn` parameter in the call to `sample`. As one does not know when the chain has fully converged, I like to assign the first *half* of my samples to be discarded, and sometimes up to 90% of my samples for longer runs. To continue the clustering example, my new code would look something like:

```
model = pm.Model([p, assignment, taus, centers])

map_ = pm.MAP(model)
map_.fit() # stores the fitted variables' values in foo.value

mcmc = pm.MCMC(model)
mcmc.sample(100000, 50000)
```

3.2 Diagnosing Convergence

3.2.1 Autocorrelation

Autocorrelation is a measure of how related a series of numbers is to itself. A measurement of 1 is perfect positive autocorrelation, 0 is no autocorrelation, and −1 is perfect negative correlation. If you are familiar with standard *correlation*, then autocorrelation is just how correlated a series, x_τ, at time t is with the same series at time $t - k$:

$$R(k) = Corr(x_t, x_{t-k})$$

For example, consider the two series

$$x_t \sim \text{Normal}(0, 1), \quad x_0 = 0$$

$$y_t \sim \text{Normal}(y_{t-1}, 1), \quad y_0 = 0$$

which have example paths like:

```
figsize(12.5, 4)

import pymc as pm
x_t = pm.rnormal(0, 1, 200)
x_t[0] = 0
```

```
y_t = np.zeros(200)
for i in range(1, 200):
    y_t[i] = pm.rnormal(y_t[i - 1], 1)

plt.plot(y_t, label="$y_t$", lw=3)
plt.plot(x_t, label="$x_t$", lw=3)
plt.xlabel("Time, $t$")
plt.ylabel('Value')
plt.title("Two different series of random values")
plt.legend();
```

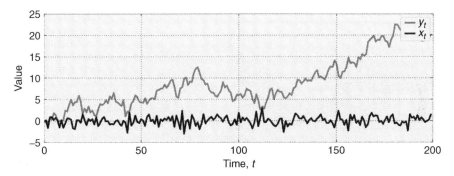

Figure 3.2.1: Two different series of random values

One way to think of autocorrelation is "If I know the position of the series at time s, can it help me know where I am at time t?" In the series x_t, the answer is no. By construction, x_t are independent random variables. If I told you that $x_2 = 0.5$, could you give me a better guess about x_3? No.

On the other hand, y_t is autocorrelated. By construction, if I knew that $y_2 = 10$, I could be very confident that y_3 would not be very far from 10. Similarly, I can even make a (less confident) guess about y_4: It will probably not be near 0 or 20, but a value of 5 is not too unlikely. I can make a similar argument about y_5, but again, I am less confident. Taking this to its logical conclusion, we must concede that as k (the lag between time points) increases, the autocorrelation decreases. We can visualize this in Figure 3.2.1. The red series is white noise (no autocorrelation), and the blue series is recursive (highly correlated).

```
def autocorr(x):
    # from http://tinyurl.com/afz57c4
    result = np.correlate(x, x, mode='full')
    result = result / np.max(result)
    return result[result.size / 2:]

colors = ["#348ABD", "#A60628", "#7A68A6"]
```

(*Continues*)

(Continued)

```
x = np.arange(1, 200)
plt.bar(x, autocorr(y_t)[1:], width=1, label="$y_t$",
        edgecolor=colors[0], color=colors[0])
plt.bar(x, autocorr(x_t)[1:], width=1, label="$x_t$",
        color=colors[1], edgecolor=colors[1])

plt.legend(title="autocorrelation")
plt.ylabel("Measured correlation \nbetween $y_t$ and $y_{t-k}$.")
plt.xlabel("$k$ (lag)")
plt.title("Autocorrelation plot of $y_t$ and $x_t$ for differing\
        $k$ lags");
```

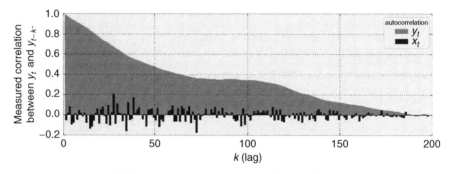

Figure 3.2.2: Autocorrelation plot of y_t and x_t for differing k lags

In Figure 3.2.2, notice that as k increases, the autocorrelation of y_t decreases from a very high point. Compare with the autocorrelation of x_t, which looks like noise (which it really is), hence we can conclude no autocorrelation exists in this series.

How Does This Relate to MCMC Convergence?   By the nature of the MCMC algorithm, we will always be returned samples that exhibit autocorrelation (this is because of the algorithm's "walk": From your current position, move to a position near you).

A chain that is exploring the space well will exhibit very high autocorrelation. Visually, if the trace seems to meander like a river, and not settle down, the chain will have high autocorrelation. For example, here's my definition of a meandering river.

Imagine you are a water molecule in the river in Figure 3.2.3. If I know where you are on the water, I can guess where you are going to be next, with decent probability. On the other hand, we say a chain is "mixing well" if it has low correlation. "Mixing well" is more than a saying. Ideally, you want your chain to behave like the river in Figure 3.2.4. In this case, I have little idea where you might end up next. This "mixes well" and has low autocorrelation. PyMC has a built-in autocorrelation plotting function in the `Matplot` module.

Figure 3.2.3: A meandering river[2]

Figure 3.2.4: A turbulent, well-mixed river[3]

3.2.2 Thinning

Another issue can arise if there is high autocorrelation between posterior samples. Many post-processing algorithms require samples to be *independent* of each other. This can be solved, or at least reduced, by only returning to the user every nth sample, thus removing some autocorrelation. In Figure 3.2.5, we perform an autocorrelation plot for y_t with differing levels of thinning:

```
max_x = 200 / 3 + 1
x = np.arange(1, max_x)

plt.bar(x, autocorr(y_t)[1:max_x], edgecolor=colors[0],
        label="no thinning", color=colors[0], width=1)
plt.bar(x, autocorr(y_t[::2])[1:max_x], edgecolor=colors[1],
        label="keeping every 2nd sample", color=colors[1],
        width=1)
plt.bar(x, autocorr(y_t[::3])[1:max_x], width=1,
        edgecolor=colors[2], label="keeping every 3rd sample",
        color=colors[2])

plt.autoscale(tight=True)
plt.legend(title="Autocorrelation plot for $y_t$",
           loc="lower left")
plt.ylabel("Measured correlation \nbetween $y_t$ and $y_{t-k}$.")
plt.xlabel("$k$ (lag)")
plt.title("Autocorrelation of $y_t$ (no thinning versus\
           thinning) at differing $k$ lags");
```

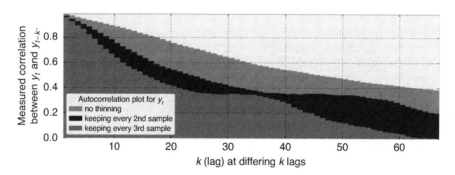

Figure 3.2.5: Autocorrelation of y_t (no thinning versus thinning) at differing k lags

With more thinning, the autocorrelation drops more quickly. There is a trade-off, though: Higher thinning requires more MCMC iterations to achieve the same number of returned samples. For example, 10,000 samples unthinned is equal to 100,000 samples with a thinning of 10 (though the latter samples have less autocorrelation).

What is a good amount of thinning? The returned samples will always exhibit some autocorrelation, regardless of how much thinning is done. So long as the autocorrelation tends to 0 quickly, you are probably okay. Typically thinning of more than 10 is not necessary.

PyMC exposes a `thinning` parameter in the call to `sample`, for example: `sample(10000, burn = 5000, thinning = 5)`.

3.2.3 `pymc.Matplot.plot()`

It seems redundant to have to manually create histograms, autocorrelation plots, and trace plots each time we perform MCMC. The authors of PyMC have included a visualization tool for just this purpose.

As the title suggests, the `pymc.Matplot` module contains a poorly named function `plot`. I prefer to import as `mcplot` so there is no conflict with other namespaces. `plot`, or `mcplot` as I suggest, accepts an MCMC object and will return posterior distributions, traces and autocorrelations for each variable (up to ten variables).

In Figure 3.2.6, we use the tool to plot the centers of the clusters, after sampling 25,000 more times and `thinning = 10`.

```
from pymc.Matplot import plot as mcplot

mcmc.sample(25000, 0, 10)
mcplot(mcmc.trace("centers", 2), common_scale=False)
```

```
[Output]:

[------------------100%------------------] 25000 of 25000 complete
     in 16.1 sec
Plotting centers_0
Plotting centers_1
```

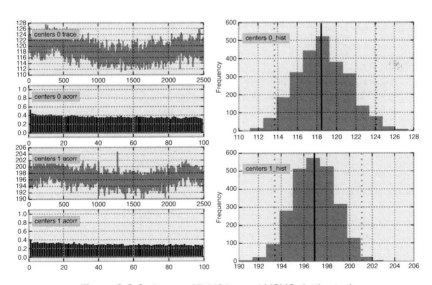

Figure 3.2.6: Output of PyMC internal MCMC plotting tool

There are really two figures here, one for each unknown in the `centers` variable. In each figure, the subfigure in the top left corner is the trace of the variable. This is useful for inspecting that possible "meandering" property that is a result of non-convergence.

The largest plot on the right-hand side is the histograms of the samples, plus a few extra features. The thickest vertical line represents the posterior mean, which is a good summary of posterior distribution. The interval between the two dashed vertical lines in each of the posterior distributions represents the *95% credible interval*, not to be confused with a *95% confidence interval*. I won't get into the latter, but the former can be interpreted as "there is a 95% chance the parameter of interest lies in this interval." (Changing default parameters in the call to `mcplot` provides alternatives to 95%.) When communicating your results to others, it is incredibly important to state this interval. One of our purposes for studying Bayesian methods is to have a clear understanding of our uncertainty in unknowns. Combined with the posterior mean, the 95% credible interval provides a reliable interval to communicate the likely location of the unknown (provided by the mean) *and* the uncertainty (represented by the width of the interval).

The plots labeled `centers_0_acorr` and `centers_1_acorr` are the generated autocorrelation plots. They look different from the ones in Figure 3.2.6, but the only difference is that 0-lag is centered in the middle of the figure, whereas I have 0 centered to the left.

3.3 Useful Tips for MCMC

Bayesian inference would be the de facto method if it weren't for MCMC's computational difficulties. In fact, MCMC is what turns most users off from practical Bayesian inference. In this section, I present some good heuristics to help convergence and speed up the MCMC engine.

3.3.1 Intelligent Starting Values

It would be great to start the MCMC algorithm off near the posterior distribution, so that it will take little time to start sampling correctly. We can aid the algorithm by telling it where we *think* the posterior distribution will be by specifying the `value` parameter in the `Stochastic` variable creation. In many cases, we can produce a reasonable guess for the parameter. For example, if we have data from a Normal distribution, and we wish to estimate the μ parameter, then a good starting value would be the *mean* of the data.

```
mu = pm.Uniform( "mu", 0, 100, value = data.mean() )
```

There are frequentist estimates for most parameters in models. These estimates are a good starting value for our MCMC algorithms. Of course, this is not always possible for some variables, but including as many appropriate initial values as possible is always a good idea. Even if your guesses are wrong, the MCMC will still converge to the proper distribution, so there is little to lose. This is what using MAP tries to do by giving good initial values to the MCMC. So why bother specifying user-defined values? Well, even giving MAP good values will help it find the maximum a posterior. Also important, *bad initial values* are a source of major bugs in PyMC and can hurt convergence.

3.3.2 Priors

If the priors are poorly chosen, the MCMC algorithm may not converge, or at least have difficulty converging. Consider what may happen if the prior chosen does not even contain the true parameter: The prior assigns 0 probability to the unknown, hence the posterior will assign 0 probability as well. This can cause pathological results.

For this reason, it is best to carefully choose the priors. Often, lack of covergence or evidence of samples crowding to boundaries implies something is wrong with the chosen priors (see the following *The Folk Theorem of Statistical Computing*).

3.3.3 The Folk Theorem of Statistical Computing

A folk theorem, if you haven't heard the term, is a truth that everyone in a certain field knows, but never really needs to write down. The folk theorem of Bayesian computations is as follows:

If you are having computational problems, your model is probably wrong.

3.4 Conclusion

PyMC provides a very strong back end to performing Bayesian inference, mostly because it has abstracted the inner mechanics of MCMC from the user. Despite this, some care must be applied to ensure your inference is not being biased by the iterative nature of MCMC.

Other MCMC libraries, like Stan, use alternative algorithms for MCMC based on modern research in the field. These algorithms suffer less often from convergence issues, and hence have abstracted MCMC even further away from the user.

In Chapter 4, we will explore what I consider the most important theorem, half because of its usefulness and half because of how often it is misused: the Law of Large Numbers.

3.5 References

1. Flaxman, Abraham. "Powell's Methods for Maximization in PyMC," Healthy Algorithms. N.p., 9 02 2012. Web. 28 Feb 2013. `http://healthyalgorithms.com/2012/02/09/powells-method-for-maximization-in-pymc/`.

2. From "Meandering river blue" by The- LizardQueen, licensed under CC BY 2.0., `https://flic.kr/p/95jKe`

3. From "close up to lower water falls..." by Tim Pearce, licensed under CC BY 2.0., `https://flic.kr/p/92V9ip`

4

The Greatest Theorem
Never Told

4.1 Introduction

This chapter focuses on an idea that is always bouncing around our minds, but is rarely made explicit outside books devoted to statistics. In fact, we've been using this simple idea in every example thus far.

4.2 The Law of Large Numbers

Let Z_i be N independent samples from some probability distribution. According to the Law of Large Numbers, so long as the expected value $E[Z]$ is not infinity, the following holds:

$$\frac{1}{N}\sum_{i=1}^{N} Z_i \to E[Z], \quad N \to \infty.$$

In words:

The average of a set of random variables from the same distribution converges to the expected value of that distribution.

This may seem like a boring result, but it will be the most useful tool you use.

4.2.1 Intuition

If the Law is somewhat surprising, it can be made clearer by examining a simple example.

Consider a random variable Z that can take only two values, c_1 and c_2. Suppose we have a large number of samples of Z, denoting a specific sample Z_i. The Law says that we can approximate the expected value of Z by averaging over all samples. Consider the average:

$$\frac{1}{N}\sum_{i=1}^{N} Z_i$$

By construction, Z_i can only take on c_1 or c_2, so we can partition the sum over these two values:

$$\frac{1}{N}\sum_{i=1}^{N} Z_i = \frac{1}{N}\Big(\sum_{Z_i=c_1} c_1 + \sum_{Z_i=c_2} c_2\Big)$$

$$= c_1 \sum_{Z_i=c_1} \frac{1}{N} + c_2 \sum_{Z_i=c_2} \frac{1}{N}$$

$$= c_1 \times \ (\text{approximate frequency of } c_1)$$
$$+ c_2 \times \ (\text{approximate frequency of } c_2)$$

$$\approx c_1 \times P(Z = c_1) + c_2 \times P(Z = c_2)$$

$$= E[Z]$$

Equality holds in the limit, but we can get closer and closer by using more and more samples in the average. This Law holds for almost *any distribution*, minus a few important cases.

4.2.2　Example: Convergence of Poisson Random Variables

In Figure 4.2.1 is a diagram of the Law of Large Numbers in action for three different sequences of Poisson random variables.

We sample `sample_size = 100000` Poisson random variables with parameter $\lambda = 4.5$. (Recall that the expected value of a Poisson random variable is equal to its parameter.) We calculate the average for the first n samples, for $n = 1$ to `sample_size`.

```
%matplotlib inline
import numpy as np
from IPython.core.pylabtools import figsize
import matplotlib.pyplot as plt
plt.rcParams['savefig.dpi'] = 300
plt.rcParams['figure.dpi'] = 300

figsize(12.5, 5)
import pymc as pm

sample_size = 100000
expected_value = lambda_ = 4.5
poi = pm.rpoisson
N_samples = range(1,sample_size,100)

for k in range(3):

    samples = poi(lambda_, size = sample_size)
```

```
    partial_average = [samples[:i].mean() for i in N_samples]

    plt.plot(N_samples, partial_average, lw=1.5,label="average \
            of $n$ samples; seq. %d"%k)


plt.plot(N_samples, expected_value*np.ones_like(partial_average),
        ls="--", label="true expected value", c="k")

plt.ylim(4.35, 4.65)
plt.title("Convergence of the average of \n random variables to their \
        expected value")
plt.ylabel("Average of $n$ samples")
plt.xlabel("Number of samples, $n$")
plt.legend();
```

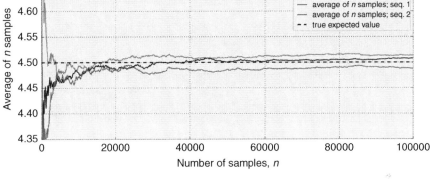

Figure 4.2.1: Convergence of the average of random variables to their expected value

Looking at Figure 4.2.1, it is clear that when the sample size is small, there is greater variation in the average (compare how jagged and jumpy the average is initially to when it smooths out). All three paths approach the value 4.5, but just flirt with it as n gets large. Mathematicians and statisticians have another name for this "flirting": *convergence*.

Another very relevant question we can ask is, How quickly am I converging to the expected value? Let's plot something new. For a specific n, let's do these trials thousands of times and compute how far away we are from the true expected value on average. But wait—compute on average? This is simply the Law of Large Numbers again! For example, we are interested in, for a specific n, the quantity

$$D(n) = \sqrt{E\left[\left(\frac{1}{n}\sum_{i=1}^{n} Z_i - 4.5\right)^2\right]}$$

This formula is interpretable as a distance away from the true value (on average) for some n. (We take the square root so the dimensions of this quantity and our random variables are the same.) Because this is an expected value, it can be approximated using the Law of Large Numbers: Instead of averaging Z_i, we calculate the following multiple times and average them:

$$Y_{n,k} = \left(\frac{1}{n} \sum_{i=1}^{n} Z_i - 4.5 \right)^2$$

By computing $Y_{n,k}$ many times, each time with new Z_is, and averaging them:

$$\frac{1}{N} \sum_{k=1}^{N} Y_{n,k} \rightarrow E[Y_n] = E \left[\left(\frac{1}{n} \sum_{i=1}^{n} Z_i - 4.5 \right)^2 \right]$$

Finally, taking the square root:

$$\sqrt{ \frac{1}{N} \sum_{k=1}^{N} Y_{n,k} } \approx D(n)$$

```
figsize(12.5, 4)

N_Y = 250 # Use this many to approximate D(N).
# Use this many samples in the approximation to the variance.
N_array = np.arange(1000, 50000, 2500)
D_N_results = np.zeros(len(N_array))

lambda_ = 4.5
expected_value = lambda_ # for X ~ Poi(lambda), E[X] = lambda

def D_N(n):
    """
    This function approximates D_n, the average variance of using
    n samples.
    """
    Z = poi(lambda_, size = (n, N_Y))
    average_Z = Z.mean(axis=0)
    return np.sqrt(((average_Z - expected_value)**2).mean())


for i,n in enumerate(N_array):
    D_N_results[i] =  D_N(n)
```

```
plt.xlabel("$N$")
plt.ylabel("Expected squared-distance from true value")
plt.plot(N_array, D_N_results, lw=3,
        label="expected distance between\n\
expected value and \naverage of $N$ random variables")
plt.plot(N_array, np.sqrt(expected_value)/np.sqrt(N_array), lw=2,
        ls="--", label=r"$\frac{\sqrt{\lambda}}{\sqrt{N}}$")
plt.legend()
plt.title("How "quickly" is the sample average converging?");
```

As expected, the expected distance between our sample average and the actual expected value shrinks as N grows large. But also notice that the *rate* of convergence decreases; that is, we need only 10,000 additional samples to move from 0.020 to 0.015, a difference of 0.005, but *20,000* more samples to again decrease from 0.015 to 0.010, again a difference of only 0.005.

It turns out we can measure this rate of convergence. In Figure 4.2.2, I have plotted a second line, the function $\sqrt{\lambda}/\sqrt{N}$. This was not chosen arbitrarily. In most cases, given a sequence of random variables distributed like Z, the rate of converge to $E[Z]$ of the Law of Large Numbers is

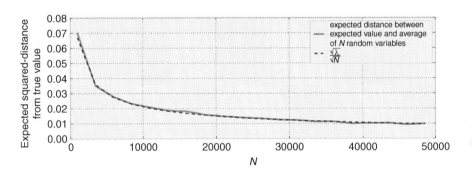

Figure 4.2.2: How "quickly" is the sample average converging?

$$\frac{\sqrt{Var(Z)}}{\sqrt{N}}$$

This is useful to know: For a given large N, we know (on average) how far away we are from the estimate. On the other hand, in a Bayesian setting, this can seem like a useless result: Bayesian analysis is okay with uncertainty, so what's the statistical point of adding extra precise digits? Drawing samples can be so computationally cheap that having a larger N is fine, too.

4.2.3   How Do We Compute *Var(Z)*?

The variance is simply another expected value that can be approximated! Consider the following: Once we have the expected value (by using the Law of Large Numbers to estimate it, denoting it μ), we can estimate the variance.

$$\frac{1}{N}\sum_{i=1}^{N}(Z_i - \mu)^2 \rightarrow E[\,(Z-\mu)^2\,] = Var(Z)$$

4.2.4   Expected Values and Probabilities

There is an even less explicit relationship between expected value and estimating probabilities. Define the *indicator function*

$$\mathbb{1}_A(x) = \begin{cases} 1 & x \in A \\ 0 & else \end{cases}$$

Then, by the Law of Large Numbers, if we have many samples X_i, we can estimate the probability of an event A, denoted $P(A)$, by

$$\frac{1}{N}\sum_{i=1}^{N}\mathbb{1}_A(X_i) \rightarrow E[\mathbb{1}_A(X)] = P(A)$$

Again, this is fairly obvious after a moment's thought: The indicator function is only 1 if the event occurs, so we are summing only the times the event occurs and dividing by the total number of trials (consider how we usually approximate probabilities using frequencies). For example, suppose we wish to estimate the probability that a $Z \sim Exp(0.5)$ is greater than 10, and we have many samples from a $Exp(0.5)$ distribution.

$$P(Z > 10) = \sum_{i=1}^{N}\mathbb{1}_{z>10}(Z_i)$$

```
import pymc as pm
N = 10000
print np.mean([pm.rexponential(0.5)>10 for i in range(N)])
```

```
[Output]:

0.0069
```

4.2.5   What Does All This Have to Do with Bayesian Statistics?

Point estimates, to be introduced in Chapter 5, in Bayesian inference are computed using expected values. In more analytical Bayesian inference, we would have been required to evaluate complicated expected values represented as multidimensional integrals. No longer. If we can sample from the posterior distribution directly, we simply need to evaluate averages—much easier. If accuracy is a priority, plots like the ones in Figure 4.2.2 show how quickly you are converging. And if further accuracy is desired, just take more samples from the posterior.

When is enough enough? When can you stop drawing samples from the posterior? That is the practitioner's decision, and also dependent on the variance of the samples (recall that a high variance means the average will converge more slowly).

We also should understand when the Law of Large Numbers fails. As the name implies, and comparing our graphs for small N, the Law is only true for large sample sizes. Without this, the asymptotic result is not reliable. Knowing in what situations the Law fails can give us confidence in how *unconfident* we should be. Section 4.3 deals with this issue.

4.3   The Disorder of Small Numbers

The Law of Large Numbers is only valid as N gets infinitely large, which is never truly attainable. While the Law is a powerful tool, it is foolhardy to apply it liberally. Our next example illustrates this.

4.3.1   Example: Aggregated Geographic Data

Data often comes in aggregated form. For instance, data may be grouped by state, county, or city. Of course, the population numbers vary per geographic area. If the data is an average of some characteristic of each of the geographic areas, we must be conscious of the Law of Large Numbers and how it can *fail* for areas with small populations.

We will observe this on a toy dataset. Suppose there are 5,000 counties in our dataset. Furthermore, population numbers in each state are uniformly distributed between 100 and 1,500 (the way the population numbers are generated is irrelevant to the discussion). We are interested in measuring the average height of individuals per county. Unbeknownst to us, height does *not* vary across county, and each individual has the same height distribution, which is independent of the county in which he or she lives.

$$\text{height} \sim \text{Normal}(150, 15)$$

We aggregate the individuals at the county level, so we only have data for the average in the county. What might our dataset look like?

```
figsize(12.5, 4)
std_height = 15
mean_height = 150
```

(Continues)

(*Continued*)

```
n_counties = 5000
pop_generator = pm.rdiscrete_uniform
norm = pm.rnormal

# generate some artificial population numbers
population = pop_generator(100, 1500, size = n_counties)

average_across_county = np.zeros(n_counties)
for i in range(n_counties):
    # generate some individuals and take the mean
    average_across_county[i] = norm(mean_height, 1./std_height**2,
                                    size=population[i]).mean()

# locate the counties with the apparently most extreme average heights
i_min = np.argmin(average_across_county)
i_max = np.argmax(average_across_county)

# plot population size versus recorded average
plt.scatter(population, average_across_county, alpha=0.5, c="#7A68A6")
plt.scatter([population[i_min], population[i_max]],
            [average_across_county[i_min], average_across_county[i_max]],
            s=60, marker="o", facecolors="none",
            edgecolors="#A60628", linewidths=1.5,
             label="extreme heights")

plt.xlim(100, 1500)
plt.title("Average height versus county population")
plt.xlabel("County population")
plt.ylabel("Average height in county")
plt.plot([100, 1500], [150, 150], color="k", label="true expected \
height", ls="--")
plt.legend(scatterpoints = 1);
```

What do we observe? Without accounting for population sizes, we run the risk of making an enormous inference error: If we ignore population size, we would say that the counties with the shortest and tallest individuals have been correctly circled in Figure 4.3.1. But this inference is wrong for the following reason. These two counties do *not* necessarily have the most extreme heights. The error results from the calculated average of smaller populations not being a good reflection of the true expected value of the population (which in truth should be $\mu = 150$). The sample size/population size/N—whatever you wish to call it—is simply too small to invoke the Law of Large Numbers effectively.

We provide more damning evidence against this inference. Recall that the population numbers were uniformly distributed over 100 to 1,500. Our intuition should tell us that the counties with the most extreme population heights should also be uniformly spread over 100 to 4,000, and certainly independent of the county's population. Not so. Following are the population sizes of the counties with the most extreme heights.

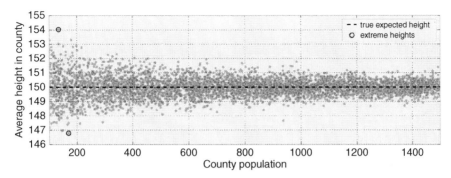

Figure 4.3.1: Average height versus county population

```
print "Population sizes of 10 'shortest' counties: "
print population[np.argsort(average_across_county)[:10]]
print
print "Population sizes of 10 'tallest' counties: "
print population[np.argsort(-average_across_county)[:10]]
```

```
[Output]:

Population sizes of 10 'shortest' counties:
[111 103 102 109 110 257 164 144 169 260]

Population sizes of 10 'tallest' counties:
[252 107 162 141 141 256 144 112 210 342]
```

The populations are not at all uniform over 100 to 1,500. This is an absolute failure of the Law of Large Numbers.

4.3.2   Example: Kaggle's *U.S. Census Return Rate Challenge*

Following is data from the 2010 U.S. census, which partitions populations beyond counties to the level of block groups (which are aggregates of city blocks or equivalents). The dataset is from a Kaggle machine-learning competition in which some colleagues and I participated. The objective was to predict the census letter mail-back rate of a block group, measured between 0 and 100, using census variables (median income, number of females in the block group, number of trailer parks, average number of children, etc.). In Figure 4.3.2, we plot the census mail-back rate versus block-group population:

```
figsize(12.5, 6.5)
data = np.genfromtxt("data/census_data.csv", skip_header=1,
                     delimiter=",")
plt.scatter(data[:,1], data[:,0], alpha=0.5, c="#7A68A6")
plt.title("Census mail-back rate versus population")
plt.ylabel("Mail-back rate")
```

(Continues)

(*Continued*)

```
plt.xlabel("Population of block group")
plt.xlim(-100, 15e3)
plt.ylim(-5, 105)

i_min = np.argmin(data[:,0])
i_max = np.argmax(data[:,0])

plt.scatter([data[i_min,1], data[i_max, 1]],
            [data[i_min,0],  data[i_max,0]],
            s=60, marker="o", facecolors="none",
            edgecolors="#A60628", linewidths=1.5,
            label="most extreme points")

plt.legend(scatterpoints = 1);
```

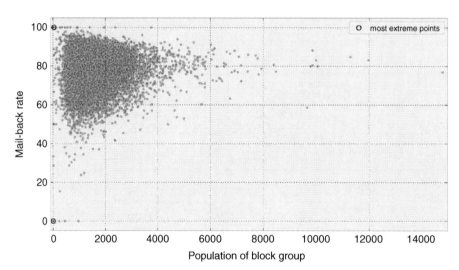

Figure 4.3.2: Census mail-back rate versus population

This is a classic phenomenon in statistics. I say *classic* referring to the "shape" of the scatter plot in Figure 4.3.2. It follows a classic triangular form that tightens as we increase the sample size (as the Law of Large Numbers becomes more exact).

I am perhaps overstressing the point, and maybe I should have titled the book *You Don't Have Big Data Problems!* but here again is an example of the trouble with *small datasets*, not big ones. Simply, small datasets cannot be processed using the Law of Large Numbers, while you can apply the Law without hassle to big datasets (actual "big data"). I mentioned earlier that, paradoxically, big-data prediction problems are solved by relatively simple algorithms. The paradox is partially resolved by understanding that the Law of

Large Numbers creates solutions that are *stable*—that is, adding or subtracting a few data points will not affect the solution much. On the other hand, adding data points to or removing data points from a small dataset can create very different results.

For further reading on the hidden dangers of the Law of Large Numbers, I would highly recommend the excellent manuscript *The Most Dangerous Equation* (`http://faculty.cord.edu/andersod/MostDangerousEquation.pdf`).

4.3.3 Example: How to Sort Reddit Comments

You may have disagreed with the original statement that the Law of Large Numbers is known to everyone, but only implicitly in our subconscious decision-making. Consider ratings on online products: How often do you trust an average 5-star rating if there is only one reviewer? Two reviewers? Three reviewers? We implicitly understand that with so few reviewers, the average rating is *not* a good reflection of the true value of the product.

This has created flaws in how we sort items, and more generally, how we compare items. Many people have realized that sorting online search results by their rating, whether the objects be books, videos, or online comments, returns poor results. Often, the seemingly "top" videos or comments have perfect ratings only from a few enthusiastic fans, and videos or comments of truly higher quality are hidden in later pages with *falsely substandard* ratings of around 4.8. How can we correct this?

Consider the popular site Reddit (I purposefully am not linking to Reddit here, as Reddit is notoriously addictive, and you might never return to this text). The site hosts links to stories or images, and a very popular part of the site is the comments associated with each link. "Redditors" (that's what the site's users are called) can vote up or down on each comment (called *upvotes* and *downvotes*). Reddit, by default, will sort comments by Top—that is, the best comments. How would you determine which comments are the best? There are a number of ways to achieve this.

1. *Popularity*: A comment is considered good if it has many upvotes. A problem with this model is when a comment has hundreds of upvotes, but thousands of downvotes. While being very *popular*, the comment is likely more controversial than "best."

2. *Difference*: Using the *difference* of upvotes and downvotes. This solves the problem in using the Popularity metric, but fails when we consider the temporal nature of comments. Comments can be posted many hours after the original link submission. The difference method will bias the *Top* comments to be the oldest comments, which have accumulated more upvotes than newer comments, but are not necessarily the best.

3. *Time adjusted*: Consider using Difference divided by the age of the comment. This creates a *rate*, something like *difference per second*, or *per minute*. An immediate counterexample is, if we use per second, a 1-second-old comment with 1 upvote would be "better" than a 100-second-old comment with 99 upvotes. One can avoid this by only considering at least t-second-old comments. But what is a good t value?

Does this mean no comment younger than t is good? We end up comparing unstable quantities with stable quantities (young versus old comments).

4. *Ratio*: Rank comments by the ratio of upvotes to total number of votes (upvotes plus downvotes). This solves the temporal issue, such that new comments that score well can be considered Top just as likely as older comments, provided they have many upvotes to total votes. The problem here is that a comment with a single upvote (ratio = 1.0) will beat a comment with 999 upvotes and 1 downvote (ratio = 0.999), but clearly the latter comment is *more likely* to be "better."

I used the phrase *more likely* for good reason. It is possible that the former comment, with a single upvote, is in fact a better comment than the later with 999 upvotes. We should hesitate to agree with this because we have not seen the other 999 potential votes the former comment might get. Perhaps it will achieve an additional 999 upvotes and 0 downvotes and be considered better than the latter, though this scenario is not likely.

What we really want is an estimate of the *true upvote ratio*. Note that the true upvote ratio is not the same as the observed upvote ratio; the true upvote ratio is hidden, and we only observe upvotes versus downvotes (one can think of the true upvote ratio as "What is the underlying probability someone gives this comment an upvote versus a downvote?"). So the 999 upvote/1 downvote comment probably has a true upvote ratio close to 1, which we can assert with confidence thanks to the Law of Large Numbers. On the other hand, we are much less certain about the true upvote ratio of the comment with only a single upvote. Sounds like a Bayesian problem to me.

One way to determine a prior on the upvote ratio is to look at the historical distribution of upvote ratios. This can be accomplished by scraping Reddit's comments and determining a distribution. There are a couple problems with this technique, though.

1. *Skewed data*: The vast majority of comments have very few votes, hence there will be many comments with ratios near the extremes (see the "triangular plot" in the Kaggle dataset in Figure 4.3.2), effectively skewing our distribution to the extremes. One could try to only use comments with votes greater than some threshold. Again, problems are encountered. There is a trade-off between number of comments available to use and a higher threshold with associated ratio precision.

2. *Biased data*: Reddit is composed of different subpages, called *subreddits*. Two examples are *r/aww*, which posts pics of cute animals, and *r/politics*. It is very likely that the user behavior toward comments of these two subreddits are very different: Visitors are likely friendly and affectionate in the former, and would therefore upvote comments more, compared to the latter, where comments are likely to be controversial and disagreed upon. Therefore, not all comments are the same.

In light of these, I think it is better to use a `Uniform` prior.

With our prior in place, we can find the posterior of the true upvote ratio. The Python script `comments_for_top_reddit_pic.py` will scrape the comments from the current top picture on Reddit. In the following, we've scraped comments from Reddit that were attached to an image submission[3]: `http://i.imgur.com/OYsHKlH.jpg`.

```
from IPython.core.display import Image
# Adding a number to the end of the %run call will get the ith top photo.
%run top_pic_comments.py 2
```

```
[Output]:

Title of submission:
Frozen mining truck
http://i.imgur.com/OYsHKlH.jpg
```

```
"""
Contents: an array of the text from all comments on the pic
Votes: a 2D NumPy array of upvotes, downvotes for each comment
"""
n_comments = len(contents)
comments = np.random.randint(n_comments, size=4)
print "Some Comments (out of %d total) \n-----------"%n_comments
for i in comments:
    print '"' + contents[i] + '"'
    print "upvotes/downvotes: ",votes[i,:]
    print
```

```
[Output]:

Some Comments (out of 77 total)
-----------
"Do these trucks remind anyone else of Sly Cooper?"
upvotes/downvotes:  [2 0]

"Dammit Elsa I told you not to drink and drive."
upvotes/downvotes:  [7 0]

"I've seen this picture before in a Duratray (the dump box supplier)
    brochure..."
upvotes/downvotes:  [2 0]

"Actually it does not look frozen just covered in a layer of wind
    packed snow."
upvotes/downvotes:  [120  18]
```

For a given true upvote ratio p and N votes, the number of upvotes will look like a binomial random variable with parameters p and N. (This is because of the equivalence between upvote ratio and probability of upvoting versus downvoting, out of *N* possible votes/trials). We create a function that performs Bayesian inference on *p*, for a particular comment's upvote/downvote pair.

```
import pymc as pm

def posterior_upvote_ratio(upvotes, downvotes, samples=20000):
    """
    This function accepts the number of upvotes and downvotes a
    particular comment received, and the number of posterior samples
    to return to the user. Assumes a uniform prior.
    """
    N = upvotes + downvotes
    upvote_ratio = pm.Uniform("upvote_ratio", 0, 1)
    observations = pm.Binomial("obs",  N, upvote_ratio,
                                    value=upvotes, observed=True)
    # Do the fitting; first do a MAP, as it is cheap and useful.
    map_ = pm.MAP([upvote_ratio, observations]).fit()
    mcmc = pm.MCMC([upvote_ratio, observations])
    mcmc.sample(samples, samples/4)
    return mcmc.trace("upvote_ratio")[:]
```

Following are the resulting posterior distributions.

```
figsize(11., 8)
posteriors = []
colors = ["#348ABD", "#A60628", "#7A68A6", "#467821", "#CF4457"]
for i in range(len(comments)):
    j = comments[i]
    label = '(%d up:%d down)\n%s...'%(votes[j, 0], votes[j,1],
                                        contents[j][:50])
    posteriors.append(posterior_upvote_ratio(votes[j, 0], votes[j,1]))
    plt.hist(posteriors[i], bins=18, normed=True, alpha=.9,
                histtype="step", color=colors[i%5], lw=3,
                label=label)
    plt.hist(posteriors[i], bins=18, normed=True, alpha=.2,
                histtype="stepfilled", color=colors[i], lw=3)

plt.legend(loc="upper left")
plt.xlim(0, 1)
plt.ylabel("Density")
plt.xlabel("Probability of upvote")
plt.title("Posterior distributions of upvote ratios on different\
            comments");
```

```
[Output]:

[*****************100%*****************] 20000 of 20000 complete
```

As you can see in Figure 4.3.3, some distributions are very tight; others have very long tails (relatively speaking), expressing our uncertainty about what the true upvote ratio might be.

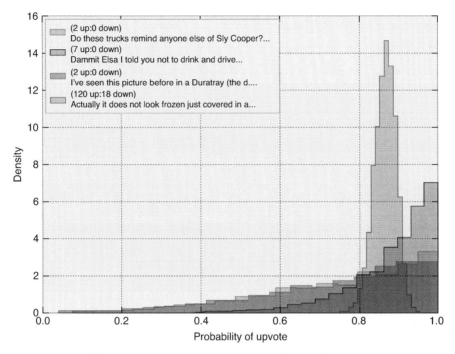

Figure 4.3.3: Posterior distributions of upvote ratios on different comments

4.3.4 Sorting!

We have been ignoring the goal of this exercise: How do we *sort* the comments from best to worst? Of course, we cannot sort distributions; we must sort scalar numbers. There are many ways to distill a distribution down to a scalar; expressing the distribution through its expected value, or mean, is one way. Choosing the mean is a bad choice, though. This is because the mean does not take into account the uncertainty of distributions.

I suggest using the **95% least plausible value**, defined as the value such that there is only a 5% chance the true parameter is lower (think of the lower bound on the 95% credible region). Following are the posterior distributions with the 95% least plausible value plotted.

```
N = posteriors[0].shape[0]
lower_limits = []
```

(Continues)

(*Continued*)

```
for i in range(len(comments)):
    j = comments[i]
    label = '(%d up:%d down)\n%s...'%(votes[j, 0], votes[j,1],
                                      contents[j][:50])
    plt.hist(posteriors[i], bins=20, normed=True, alpha=.9,
             histtype="step", color=colors[i], lw=3,
             label=label)
    plt.hist(posteriors[i], bins=20, normed=True, alpha=.2,
             histtype="stepfilled", color=colors[i], lw=3)
    v = np.sort(posteriors[i])[int(0.05*N)]
    plt.vlines(v, 0, 10 , color=colors[i], linestyles="--",
               linewidths=3)
    lower_limits.append(v)

plt.legend(loc="upper left")
plt.xlabel("Probability of upvote")
plt.ylabel("Density")
plt.title("Posterior distributions of upvote ratios on different\
          comments");

order = np.argsort(-np.array(lower_limits))
print order, lower_limits
```

```
[Output]:

[3 1 2 0] [0.36980613417267094, 0.68407203257290061,
    0.37551825562169117, 0.8177566237850703]
```

The "best" comments, according to our procedure, are the comments that are *most likely* to score a high percentage of upvotes. Visually, those are the comments with the 95% least plausible value closest to 1. In Figure 4.3.4, the vertical lines depict the 95% least plausible value.

Why is sorting based on this quantity a good idea? By ordering by the 95% least plausible value, we are being the most conservative with what we think is best. That is, even in the worst-case scenario, when we have severely overestimated the upvote ratio, we can be sure the best comments are still on top. Under this ordering, we impose the following very natural properties.

1. Given two comments with the same observed upvote ratio, we will evaluate the comment with more votes as better (since we are more confident it has a higher ratio).

2. Given two comments with the same number of votes, we still evaluate the comment with more upvotes as better.

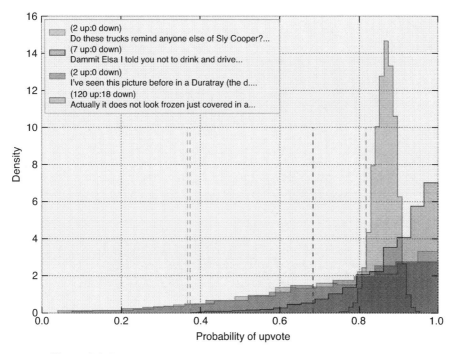

Figure 4.3.4: Posterior distributions of upvote ratios on different comments

4.3.5   But This Is Too Slow for Real-Time!

I agree; computing the posterior of every comment takes a long time, and by the time you have computed it, the data has likely changed. I postpone explaining the mathematics to the appendix, but I suggest using the following formula to compute the lower bound very quickly.

$$\frac{a}{a+b} - 1.65\sqrt{\frac{ab}{(a+b)^2(a+b+1)}}$$

where

$$a = 1 + u$$
$$b = 1 + d$$

u is the number of upvotes, and d is the number of downvotes. The formula is a shortcut in Bayesian inference, which will be further explained in Chapter 6 when we discuss priors in more detail.

```
def intervals(u,d):
    a = 1. + u
    b = 1. + d
    mu = a/(a+b)
    std_err = 1.65*np.sqrt((a*b)/((a+b)**2*(a+b+1.)))
    return (mu, std_err)

print "Approximate lower bounds:"
posterior_mean, std_err  = intervals(votes[:,0],votes[:,1])
lb = posterior_mean - std_err
print lb
print
print "Top 40 sorted according to approximate lower bounds:"
print
order = np.argsort(-lb)
ordered_contents = []
for i in order[:40]:
    ordered_contents.append(contents[i])
    print  votes[i,0], votes[i,1], contents[i]
    print "-------------"
```

```
[Output]:

Approximate lower bounds:
[ 0.83167764  0.8041293   0.8166957   0.77375237  0.72491057 0.71705212
  0.72440529  0.73158407  0.67107394  0.6931046   0.66235556 0.6530083
  0.70806405  0.60091591  0.60091591  0.66278557  0.60091591 0.60091591
  0.53055613  0.53055613  0.53055613  0.53055613  0.53055613 0.43047887
  0.43047887  0.43047887  0.43047887  0.43047887  0.43047887 0.43047887
  0.43047887  0.43047887  0.43047887  0.43047887  0.43047887 0.43047887
  0.43047887  0.43047887  0.43047887  0.47201974  0.45074913 0.35873239
  0.3726793   0.42069919  0.33529412  0.27775794  0.27775794 0.27775794
  0.27775794  0.27775794  0.27775794  0.13104878  0.13104878 0.27775794
  0.27775794  0.27775794  0.27775794  0.27775794  0.27775794 0.27775794
  0.27775794  0.27775794  0.27775794  0.27775794  0.27775794 0.27775794
  0.27775794  0.27775794  0.27775794  0.27775794  0.27775794 0.27775794
  0.27775794  0.27775794  0.27775794  0.27775794  0.27775794]

Top 40 sorted according to approximate lower bounds:

327 52 Can you imagine having to start that? I've fired up much smaller
    equipment when its around 0° out and its still a pain. It would
    probably take a crew of guys hours to get that going. Do they have
    built in heaters to make it easier? You'd think they would just let
    them idle overnight if they planned on running it the next day
    though.
-------------
120 18 Actually it does not look frozen just covered in a layer of wind
    packed snow.
-------------
```

```
70 10 That's actually just the skin of a mining truck. They shed it
    periodically like snakes do.
-------------
76 14 The model just hasn't been textured yet!
-------------
21 3 No worries, [this](http://imgur.com/KeSYJud) will help.
-------------
7 0 Dammit Elsa I told you not to drink and drive.
-------------
88 23 Speaking of mining...[BAGGER 288!](http://www.youtube.com/
    watch?v=azEvfD4C6ow)
-------------
112 32 Wonder why OP has 31,944 link karma but so few submissions?
    /u/zkool may have the worst case of karma addiction I'm aware of.

title | points | age | /r/ | comnts
:--|:--|:--|:--|:--
[Frozen mining truck](http://www.reddit.com/r/pics/comments/1mrqvh/
    frozen_mining_truck/) | 2507 | 4^mos | pics | 164
[Frozen mining truck](http://www.reddit.com/r/pics/comments/1cutbw/
    frozen_mining_truck/) | 16 | 9^mos | pics | 4
[Frozen mining truck](http://www.reddit.com/r/pics/comments/vvcrv/
    frozen_mining_truck/) | 439 | 1^yr | pics | 21
[Meanwhile, in New Zealand...](http://www.reddit.com/r/pics/comments/
    ir1pl/meanwhile_in_new_zealand/) | 39 | 2^yrs | pics | 12
[Blizzardy day](http://www.reddit.com/r/pics/comments/1uiu3y/
    blizzardy_day/) | 7 | 19^dys | pics | 3

*[Source: karmadecay](http://karmadecay.com/r/pics/comments/1w454i/
    frozen_mining_truck/)*
-------------
11 1 This is what it's typically like, living in Alberta.
-------------
6 0 That'd be a haul truck. Looks like a CAT 793. We run em at the site
    I work at, 240ton carrying capacity.
-------------
22 5 Taken in Fort Mcmurray Ab!
-------------
9 1 "EXCLUSIVE: First look at "Hoth" from the upcoming 'Star Wars:
    Episode VII'"
-------------
32 9 This is the most fun thing to drive in GTA V.
-------------
5 0 it reminds me of the movie "moon" with sam rockwell.
-------------
4 0 Also frozen drill rig.
-------------
```

(Continues)

(Continued)

```
4 0 There's just something awesome about a land vehicle so huge that
    it warrants a set of stairs on the front of it. I find myself
    wishing I were licensed to drive it.
-------------
4 0 Heaters all over the components needing heat:
    http://www.arctic-fox.com/fuel-fluid-warming-products/
    diesel-fired-coolant-pre-heaters
-------------
4 0 Or it is just an amazing snow sculpture!
-------------
3 0 I have to tell people about these awful conditions... Too bad I'm
    Snowden.
-------------
3 0 Someone let it go
-------------
3 0 Elsa, you can't do that to people's trucks.
-------------
3 0 woo Alberta represent
-------------
3 0 Just thaw it with love
-------------
6 2 Looks like the drill next to it is an IR DM30 or DM45. Good rigs.
-------------
4 1 That's the best snow sculpture I've ever seen.
-------------
2 0 [These](http://i.imgur.com/xYuwk5I.jpg) are used for removing
    the ice.
-------------
2 0 Please someone post frozen Bagger 288
-------------
2 0 It's kind of cool there are trucks so big they need both a
    ladder and a staircase...
-------------
2 0 Eight miners are just out of frame hiding inside a tauntaun.
-------------
2 0 http://imgur.com/gallery/Fxv3Oh7
-------------
2 0 It would take a god damn week just to warm that thing up.
-------------
2 0 Maybe /r/Bitcoin can use some of their mining equipment to heat
    this guy up!
-------------
2 0 Checkmate Jackie Chan
-------------
2 0 I've seen this picture before in a Duratray (the dump box supplier)
    brochure...
-------------
```

```
2 0 The Texas snow has really hit hard!
-------------
2 0 I'm going to take a wild guess and say the diesel is gelled.
-------------
2 0 Do these trucks remind anyone else of Sly Cooper?
-------------
2 0 cool
-------------
```

We can view the ordering visually by plotting the posterior mean and bounds, and
sorting by the lower bound. In Figure 4.3.5, notice that the left error bar is sorted (as we
suggested, this is the best way to determine an ordering), so the means, indicated by dots,
do not follow any particular pattern.

```
r_order = order[::-1][-40:]
plt.errorbar(posterior_mean[r_order], np.arange(len(r_order)),
             xerr=std_err[r_order],xuplims=True, capsize=0, fmt="o",
             color="#7A68A6")
plt.xlim(0.3, 1)
plt.yticks(np.arange(len(r_order)-1,-1,-1),
           map(lambda x: x[:30].replace("\n",""), ordered_contents));
```

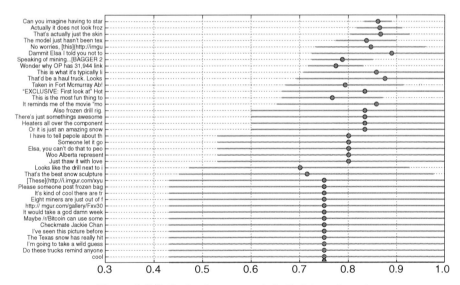

Figure 4.3.5: Sorting top comments by their lower bound

In Figure 4.3.5, you can see why sorting by mean would be suboptimal.

4.3.6   Extension to Starred Rating Systems

This procedure works well for upvote/downvote schemes, but what about systems that use star ratings, such as 5-star rating systems? Similar problems apply with simply taking the average: An item with two perfect ratings would beat an item with thousands of perfect ratings, but a single sub-perfect rating.

We can consider the upvote/downvote problem as binary: 0 is a downvote, 1 is an upvote. An N-star rating system can be seen as a more continuous version of the preceding, and we can set n stars rewarded as equivalent to rewarding $\frac{n}{N}$. For example, in a 5-star system, a 2-star rating corresponds to 0.4. A perfect rating is a 1. We can use the same formula as before, but with a, b defined differently.

$$\frac{a}{a+b} - 1.65\sqrt{\frac{ab}{(a+b)^2(a+b+1)}}$$

where

$$a = 1 + S$$
$$b = 1 + N - S$$

where N is the number of users who rated, and S is the sum of all the ratings, under the aforementioned equivalence scheme.

4.4   Conclusion

While the Law of Large Numbers is cool, it is only true to the extent its name implies: with large sample sizes only. We have seen how our inference can be affected by not considering *how the data is shaped*.

1. By (cheaply) drawing many samples from the posterior distributions, we can ensure that the Law of Large Numbers applies as we approximate expected values (which we will do in Chapter 5).

2. Bayesian inference understands that with small sample sizes, we can observe wild randomness. Our posterior distribution will reflect this by being more spread out rather than tightly concentrated. Thus, our inference should be correctable.

3. There are major implications of not considering the sample size, and trying to sort objects that are unstable leads to pathological orderings. The method provided in section 4.3.3 solves this problem.

4.5   Appendix

4.5.1   Derivation of Sorting Comments Formula

Basically, what we are doing is using a Beta prior (with parameters $a = 1, b = 1$, which is a uniform distribution), and using a binomial likelihood with observations $u, N = u + d$.

This means that our posterior is a Beta distribution with parameters $d' = 1 + u$, $b' = 1 + (N - u) = 1 + d$. We then need to find the value, x, such that 0.05 probability is less than x. This is usually done by inverting the cumulative distribution function (CDF), but the CDF of the Beta, for integer parameters, is known but is a large sum.[1]

We instead use a Normal approximation. The mean of the Beta is $\mu = d'/(d' + b')$, and the variance is

$$\sigma^2 = \frac{d'b'}{(d' + b')^2(d' + b' + 1)}$$

Hence we solve the following equation for x and have an approximate lower bound

$$0.05 = \Phi\left(\frac{(x - \mu)}{\sigma}\right)$$

with Φ being the cumulative distribution for the Normal distribution.

4.6 Exercises

1. How would you estimate the quantity $E[\cos X]$, where $X \sim Exp(4)$? What about $E[\cos X | X < 1]$ (that is, the expected value *given* we know X is less than 1)?

2. The following table was located in the paper "Going for Three: Predicting the Likelihood of Field Goal Success with Logistic Regression."[2] The table ranks football field-goal kickers by their percent of non-misses. What mistake have the researchers made?

Rank	Kicker	Make %	Number of Kicks
1	Garrett Hartley	87.7	57
2	Matt Stover	86.8	335
3	Robbie Gould	86.2	224
4	Rob Bironas	86.1	223
5	Shayne Graham	85.4	254
...	...	...	
51	Dave Rayner	72.2	90
52	Nick Novak	71.9	64
53	Tim Seder	71.0	62
54	Jose Cortez	70.7	75
55	Wade Richey	66.1	56

In August 2013, a popular post (http://bpodgursky.wordpress.com/2013/08/21/average-income-per-programming-language/)[4], on the average income per programmer of different languages was trending. Here's the summary chart. What do you notice about the extremes?

Language	Average Household Income ($)	Data Points
Puppet	87,589.29	112
Haskell	89,973.82	191
PHP	94,031.19	978
CoffeeScript	94,890.80	435
VimL	94,967.11	532
Shell	96,930.54	979
...	...	...
Scala	101,460.91	243
ColdFusion	101,536.70	109
Objective-C	101,801.60	562
Groovy	102,650.86	116
Java	103,179.39	1402
XSLT	106,199.19	123
ActionScript	108,119.47	113

4.6.1 Answers

1.
```
import scipy.stats as stats
exp = stats.expon(scale=4)
N = 1e5
X = exp.rvs(N)

# E[cos(X)]
print (cos(X)).mean()
# E[cos(X) | X<1]
print (cos(X[X<1])).mean()
```

2. Both charts are naively sorting computed statistics (conversion in the first, and average in the second) without considering the sample sizes used to determine the statistics. This leads to problems; in the table of career kicks, Garrett Hartley is clearly not the best kicker. That honor goes to Matt Stover. In the table of salaries, the extreme salaries are both populated with languages with smaller numbers of data points. A naive (and wrong) interpretation after looking at this chart might be that companies clearly have to pay more to attract developers in the rarer languages, as there is a lower supply of developers for these languages.

4.7 References

1. "Beta function," Wikipedia, The Free Encyclopedia, last modified May 26, 2015,
11:19 PM EST, accessed June 4, 2015, `http://en.wikipedia.org/wiki`
`/Beta function#Incomplete beta function`.

2. Clark, Torin K., Aaron W. Johnson, and Alexander J. Stimpson. "Going for Three:
Predicting the Likelihood of Field Goal Success with Logistic Regression." Presented at
the 7th Annual MIT Sloan Sports Analytics Conference, Cambridge, MA, March 1-2,
2013. Cambridge, MA: MIT Sloan Sports Analytics Conference,
`http://www.sloansportsconference.com/wp-content/uploads/2013/`
`Going%20for%20Three%20Predicting%20the%20Likelihood%20of%`
`20Field%20Goal%20Success%20with%20Logistic%20Regression.pdf`.

3. Commentary surrounding Imgur image posted by user Zcool. "Frozen Mining Truck."
Reddit. Web Accessed on Jan 25, 2014. Link: `http:www.reddit.com/r/pics/`
`comments/1w454i/frozen_mining_truck/`

4. Podgursky, Ben. "Average Income per Programming Language," bpodgursky.com, last
modified August 21, 2013, accessed June 4, 2015, `http://bpodgursky.com/2013/`
`08/21/average-income-per-programming-language/`.

5

Would You Rather Lose an Arm or a Leg?

5.1 Introduction

Statisticians can be a sour bunch. Instead of considering their winnings, they only measure how much they have lost. In fact, they consider their wins to be *negative losses*. But what's interesting is how they measure their losses.

For example, consider the following:

> A meteorologist is predicting the probability of a hurricane striking his city. He estimates, with 95% confidence, that the probability of it *not* striking is between 99% and 100%. He is very happy with his precision and advises the city that a major evacuation is unnecessary. Unfortunately, the hurricane does strike and the city is flooded.

This stylized example shows the flaw in using a pure accuracy metric to measure outcomes. Using a measure that emphasizes estimation accuracy, while an appealing and objective thing to do, misses the point of why you are even performing the statistical inference in the first place: results of inference. Furthermore, we'd like a method that stresses the importance of payoffs of decisions, not the accuracy of the estimation alone. Read puts this succinctly: "It is better to be roughly right than precisely wrong."[1]

5.2 Loss Functions

We introduce what statisticians and decision theorists call **loss functions**. A loss function is a function of the true parameter, and an estimate of that parameter

$$L(\theta, \hat{\theta}) = f(\theta, \hat{\theta})$$

The important point of loss functions is that they measure how *bad* our current estimate is: The larger the loss, the worse the estimate is according to the loss function. A simple, and very common, example of a loss function is the **squared-error loss**, a type of loss function that increases quadratically with the difference, used in estimators like linear regression, calculation of unbiased statistics, and many areas of machine learning

$$L(\theta, \hat{\theta}) = (\theta - \hat{\theta})^2$$

The squared-error loss function is used in estimators like linear regression, calculation of unbiased statistics, and many areas of machine learning. We can also consider an asymmetric squared-error loss function, something like:

$$L(\theta,\hat{\theta}) = \begin{cases} (\theta - \hat{\theta})^2 & \hat{\theta} < \theta \\ \\ c(\theta - \hat{\theta})^2 & \hat{\theta} \geq \theta, \ \ 0 < c < 1 \end{cases}$$

which represents that estimating a value larger than the true estimate is preferable to estimating a value that is smaller. A situation where this might be useful is in estimating Web traffic for the next month, where an overestimated outlook is preferred so as to avoid an underallocation of server resources.

A negative property about the squared-error loss is that it puts a disproportionate emphasis on large outliers. This is because the loss increases quadratically, and not linearly, as the estimate moves away. That is, the penalty of being 3 units away is much less than being 5 units away, but the penalty is not much greater than being 1 unit away, though in both cases the magnitude of difference is the same:

$$\frac{1^2}{3^2} < \frac{3^2}{5^2}, \ \ \text{although} \ \ 3 - 1 = 5 - 3$$

This loss function implies that large errors are very bad. A more robust loss function that increases linearly with the difference is the **absolute-loss**, a type of loss function that increases linearly with the difference, often used in machine learning and robust statistics.

$$L(\theta,\hat{\theta}) = |\theta - \hat{\theta}|$$

Other popular loss functions include the following.

- $L(\theta,\hat{\theta}) = \mathbf{1}_{\hat{\theta} \neq \theta}$ is the *zero-one loss* often used in machine-learning classification algorithms.
- $L(\theta,\hat{\theta}) = -\hat{\theta}\log(\theta) - (1 - \hat{\theta})\log(1 - \theta)$, $\hat{\theta} \in 0, 1$, $\theta \in [0, 1]$, called the *log-loss*, is also used in machine learning.

Historically, loss functions have been motivated from (1) mathematical ease and (2) their robustness to application (that is, they are objective measures of loss). The first motivation has really held back the full breadth of loss functions. With computers being agnostic to mathematical convenience, we are free to design our own loss functions, which we take full advantage of later in this chapter.

With respect to the second motivation, the above loss functions are indeed objective in that they are most often a function of the difference between estimate and true parameter, independent of positivity or negativity, or payoff of choosing that estimate. This last point—its independence of payoff—causes quite pathological results, though. Consider our hurricane example: The statistician equivalently predicted that the probability of the hurricane striking was between 0% and 1%. But if he had ignored being precise and instead focused on outcomes (99% chance of no flood, 1% chance of flood), he might have advised differently.

By shifting our focus from trying to be incredibly precise about parameter estimation to focusing on the outcomes of our parameter estimation, we can customize our estimates to be optimized for our application. This requires us to design new loss functions that reflect our goals and outcomes. Some examples of more interesting loss functions include the following.

- $L(\theta, \hat{\theta}) = \frac{|\theta - \hat{\theta}|}{\theta(1-\theta)}$, $\hat{\theta}, \theta \in [0, 1]$ emphasizes an estimate closer to 0 or 1, since if the true value θ is near 0 or 1, the loss will be very large unless $\hat{\theta}$ is similarly close to 0 or 1. This loss function might be used by a political pundit who's job requires him or her to give confident "Yes/No" answers. This loss reflects that if the true parameter is close to 1 (for example, if a political outcome is very likely to occur), he or she would want to strongly agree so as to not look like a skeptic.

- $L(\theta, \hat{\theta}) = 1 - e^{-(\theta - \hat{\theta})^2}$ is bounded between 0 and 1 and reflects that the user is indifferent to sufficiently-far-away estimates. It is similar to the zero-one loss, but not quite as penalizing to estimates that are close to the true parameter.

- Complicated non-linear loss functions can programmed:

```
def loss(true_value, estimate):
    if estimate*true_value > 0:
        return abs(estimate - true_value)
    else:
        return abs(estimate)*(estimate - true_value)**2
```

- Another example in everyday life is the loss function that weather forecasters use. Weather forecasters have an incentive to report accurately on the probability of rain, but also to err on the side of suggesting rain. Why is this? People much prefer to prepare for rain, even when it may not occur, than to be rained on when they are unprepared. For this reason, forecasters tend to artificially bump up the probability of rain and report this inflated estimate, as this provides a better payoff than the uninflated estimate.

5.2.1 Loss Functions in the Real World

So far, we have been acting under the unrealistic assumption that we know the true parameter. Of course, if we know the true parameter, bothering to guess an estimate is pointless. Hence a loss function is really only practical when the true parameter is unknown.

In Bayesian inference, we have a mindset that the unknown parameters are really random variables with prior and posterior distributions. Concerning the posterior distribution, a value drawn from it is a possible realization of what the true parameter could be. Given that realization, we can compute a loss associated with an estimate. As we have a whole distribution of what the unknown parameter could be (the posterior), we should be more interested in computing the *expected loss* given an estimate. This expected loss is a better estimate of the true loss than comparing the given loss from only a single sample from the posterior.

First, it will be useful to explain a **Bayesian point estimate**. The systems and machinery present in the modern world are not built to accept posterior distributions as input. It is also rude to hand someone over a distribution when all they asked for was an estimate. In the course of our day, when faced with uncertainty, we still act by distilling our uncertainty down to a single action. Similarly, we need to distill our posterior distribution down to a single value (or vector, in the multivariate case). If the value is chosen intelligently, we can avoid the flaw of frequentist methodologies that mask the uncertainty and provide a more informative result. The value chosen, if from a Bayesian posterior, is a Bayesian point estimate.

If $P(\theta|X)$ is the posterior distribution of θ after observing data X, then the following function is understandable as the *expected loss of choosing estimate $\hat{\theta}$ to estimate θ*:

$$ l(\hat{\theta}) = E_\theta \left[L(\theta, \hat{\theta}) \right] $$

This is also known as the *risk* of estimate $\hat{\theta}$. The subscript θ under the expectation symbol is used to denote that θ is the unknown (random) variable in the expectation, something that at first can be difficult to consider.

We spent all of Chapter 4 discussing how to approximate expected values. Given N samples θ_i, $i = 1, ..., N$ from the posterior distribution, and a loss function L, we can approximate the expected loss of using estimate $\hat{\theta}$ by the Law of Large Numbers:

$$ \frac{1}{N} \sum_{i=1}^{N} L(\theta_i, \hat{\theta}) \approx E_\theta \left[L(\theta, \hat{\theta}) \right] = l(\hat{\theta}) $$

Notice that measuring your loss via an expected value uses more information from the distribution than the MAP estimate—which, if you recall, will only find the maximum value of the distribution and ignore the shape of the distribution. Ignoring information can overexpose yourself to tail risks, like the unlikely hurricane, and leaves your estimate ignorant of how ignorant you really are about the parameter.

Similarly, compare this with frequentist methods, that traditionally only aim to minimize the error, and do not consider the loss associated with the result of that error. Compound this with the fact that frequentist methods are almost guaranteed to never be absolutely accurate. Bayesian point estimates fix this by planning ahead: If your estimate is going to be wrong, you might as well err on the right side of wrong.

5.2.2 Example: Optimizing for the Showcase on *The Price Is Right*

Bless you if you are ever chosen as a contestant on *The Price Is Right*, for here we will show you how to optimize your final price on the Showcase. For those who don't know the rules:

1. Two contestants compete in the Showcase.
2. Each contestant is shown a unique suite of prizes.
3. After the viewing, the contestants are asked to bid on the price for their unique suite of prizes.
4. If a bid price is over the actual price, the bid's owner is disqualified from winning.
5. If a bid price is under the true price by less than $250, the winner is awarded both prizes.

The difficulty in the game is balancing your uncertainty in the prices, keeping your bid low enough so as to not bid over, and to bid close to the price.

Suppose we have recorded the Showcases from previous *The Price Is Right* episodes and have prior beliefs about what distribution the true price follows. For simplicity, suppose it follows a Normal:

$$\text{True Price} \sim \text{Normal}(\mu_p, \sigma_p)$$

For now, we will assume $\mu_p = 35,000$ and $\sigma_p = 7,500$.

We need a model of how we should be playing the Showcase. For each prize in the prize suite, we have an idea of what it might cost, but this guess could differ significantly from the true price. (Couple this with increased pressure from being onstage, and you can see why some bids are so wildly off.) Let's suppose your beliefs about the prices of prizes also follow Normal distributions:

$$\text{Prize}_i \sim \text{Normal}(\mu_i, \sigma_i), \quad i = 1, 2$$

This is really why Bayesian analysis is great: We can specify what we think a fair price is through the μ_i parameter, and express uncertainty of our guess in the σ_i parameter. We'll assume two prizes per suite for brevity, but this can be extended to any number. The true price of the prize suite is then given by $\text{Prize}_1 + \text{Prize}_2 + \epsilon$, where ϵ is some error term. We are interested in the updated true price given we have observed both prizes and have belief distributions about them. We can perform this using PyMC.

Let's make some values concrete. Suppose there are two prizes in the observed prize suite:

1. A trip to wonderful Toronto, Canada!
2. A lovely new snowblower!

We have some guesses about the true prices of these objects, but we are also pretty uncertain about them. We can express this uncertainty through the parameters of the Normals:

$$\text{Snowblower} \sim \text{Normal}(3000, 500)$$
$$\text{Toronto} \sim \text{Normal}(12000, 3000)$$

For example, I believe that the true price of the trip to Toronto is 12,000 dollars, and that there is a 68.2% chance the price falls 1 standard deviation away from this; that is, my confidence is that there is a 68.2% chance the trip is in [9000, 15000]. These priors are graphically represented in Figure 5.2.1.

We can create some PyMC code to perform inference on the true price of the suite, as shown in Figure 5.2.2.

```
%matplotlib inline
import scipy.stats as stats
from IPython.core.pylabtools import figsize
import numpy as np
import matplotlib.pyplot as plt
plt.rcParams['savefig.dpi'] = 300
plt.rcParams['figure.dpi'] = 300

figsize(12.5, 9)

norm_pdf = stats.norm.pdf

plt.subplot(311)
x = np.linspace(0, 60000, 200)
sp1 = plt.fill_between(x, 0, norm_pdf(x, 35000, 7500),
                color="#348ABD", lw=3, alpha=0.6,
                label="historical total prices")
p1 = plt.Rectangle((0, 0), 1, 1, fc=sp1.get_facecolor()[0])
plt.legend([p1], [sp1.get_label()])

plt.subplot(312)
x = np.linspace(0, 10000, 200)
sp2 = plt.fill_between(x, 0, norm_pdf(x, 3000, 500),
                color="#A60628", lw=3, alpha=0.6,
                label="snowblower price guess")

p2 = plt.Rectangle((0, 0), 1, 1, fc=sp2.get_facecolor()[0])
plt.legend([p2], [sp2.get_label()])

plt.subplot(313)
x = np.linspace(0, 25000, 200)
sp3 = plt.fill_between(x , 0, norm_pdf( x, 12000, 3000),
```

```
                color="#7A68A6", lw=3, alpha=0.6,
                    label="trip price guess")
plt.autoscale(tight=True)
p3 = plt.Rectangle((0, 0), 1, 1, fc=sp3.get_facecolor()[0])
plt.title("Prior distributions for unknowns: the total price,\
            the snowblower's price, and the trip's price")
plt.legend([p3], [sp3.get_label()]);
plt.xlabel("Price");
plt.ylabel("Density")
```

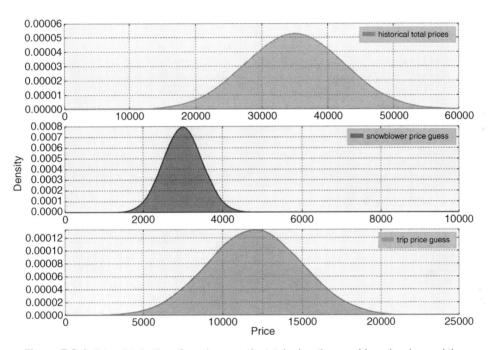

Figure 5.2.1: Prior distributions for unknowns: the total price, the snowblower's price, and the trip's price

```
import pymc as pm

data_mu = [3e3, 12e3]

data_std = [5e2, 3e3]

mu_prior = 35e3
std_prior =  75e2
```

(Continues)

(Continued)

```
true_price = pm.Normal("true_price", mu_prior, 1.0 / std_prior ** 2)


prize_1 = pm.Normal("first_prize", data_mu[0], 1.0 / data_std[0] ** 2)
prize_2 = pm.Normal("second_prize", data_mu[1], 1.0 / data_std[1] ** 2)
price_estimate = prize_1 + prize_2

@pm.potential
def error(true_price=true_price, price_estimate=price_estimate):
    return pm.normal_like(true_price,  price_estimate, 1 / (3e3) ** 2)


mcmc = pm.MCMC([true_price, prize_1, prize_2, price_estimate, error])
mcmc.sample(50000, 10000)

price_trace = mcmc.trace("true_price")[:]
```

```
[Output]:

[------------------100%------------------] 50000 of 50000 complete in
    10.9 sec
```

```
figsize(12.5, 4)

import scipy.stats as stats

# Plot the prior distribution.
x = np.linspace(5000, 40000)
plt.plot(x, stats.norm.pdf(x, 35000, 7500), c="k", lw=2,
         label="prior distribution\n of suite price")

# Plot the posterior distribution, represented by samples from the MCMC.
_hist = plt.hist(price_trace, bins=35, normed=True, histtype="stepfilled")
plt.title("Posterior of the true price estimate")
plt.vlines(mu_prior, 0, 1.1*np.max(_hist[0]), label="prior's mean",
           linestyles="--")
plt.vlines(price_trace.mean(), 0, 1.1*np.max(_hist[0]), \
    label="posterior's mean", linestyles="-.")
plt.legend(loc="upper left");
```

Notice that because of the snowblower prize and trip prize and subsequent guesses (including uncertainty about those guesses), we shifted our mean price estimate down about \$15,000 from the previous mean price.

A frequentist, seeing the two prizes and having the same beliefs about their prices, would bid $\mu_1 + \mu_2 = \$35,000$, regardless of any uncertainty. Meanwhile, the *naive Bayesian* would simply pick the mean of the posterior distribution. But we have more information about our eventual outcomes; we should incorporate this into our bid. We will use the loss function to find the *best* bid (*best* according to our loss).

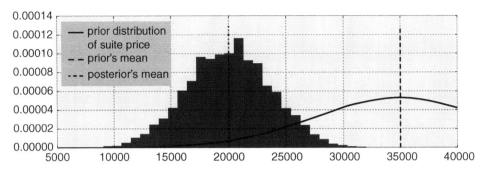

Figure 5.2.2: Posterior of the true price estimate

What might a contestant's loss function look like? I would think it would look something like:

```
def showcase_loss(guess, true_price, risk=80000):
    if true_price < guess:
        return risk
    elif abs(true_price - guess) <= 250:
        return -2 * np.abs(true_price)
    else:
        return np.abs(true_price - guess - 250)
```

where `risk` is a parameter that defines how bad it is if your guess is over the true price. I've arbitrarily picked 80,000. A lower `risk` means that you are more comfortable with the idea of going over. If we do bid under and the difference is less than $250, we receive both prizes (modeled here as receiving twice the original prize). Otherwise, when we bid under the `true_price`, we want to be as close as possible, hence the `else` loss is a increasing function of the distance between the guess and true price.

For every possible bid, we calculate the *expected loss* associated with that bid. We vary the `risk` parameter to see how it affects our loss. The results are shown in Figure 5.2.3.

```
figsize(12.5, 7)
# NumPy-friendly showdown_loss
def showdown_loss(guess, true_price, risk=80000):
        loss = np.zeros_like(true_price)
        ix = true_price < guess
        loss[~ix] = np.abs(guess - true_price[~ix])
        close_mask = [abs(true_price - guess) <= 250]
        loss[close_mask] = -2 * true_price[close_mask]
        loss[ix] = risk
        return loss
```

(Continues)

(Continued)

```
guesses = np.linspace(5000, 50000, 70)
risks = np.linspace(30000, 150000, 6)
expected_loss = lambda guess, risk: showdown_loss(guess, price_trace,
                                                   risk).mean()

for _p in risks:
    results = [expected_loss (_g, _p) for _g in guesses]
    plt.plot(guesses, results, label="%d"%_p)

plt.title("Expected loss of different guesses, \nvarious risk levels of \
        overestimating")
plt.legend(loc="upper left", title="risk parameter")
plt.xlabel("Price bid")
plt.ylabel("Expected loss")
plt.xlim(5000, 30000);
```

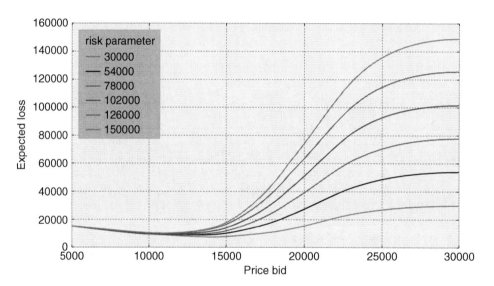

Figure 5.2.3: Expected loss of different guesses, various risk levels of overestimating

Minimizing Our Losses   It would be wise to choose the estimate that minimizes our expected loss. This corresponds to the minimum point on each of the curves on the previous figure. More formally, we would like to minimize our expected loss by finding the solution to

$$\underset{\hat{\theta}}{\arg\min} \quad E_\theta \left[L(\theta, \hat{\theta}) \right]$$

The minimum of the expected loss is called the *Bayes action*. We can solve for the Bayes action using SciPy's optimization routines. The function in `fmin` in the scipy.optimize module uses an intelligent search to find a minimum (not necessarily a *global* minimum) of any univariate or multivariate function. For most purposes, fmin will provide you with a good answer.

We'll compute the minimum loss for the Showcase example in Figure 5.2.4.

```
import scipy.optimize as sop

ax = plt.subplot(111)


for _p in risks:
    _color = ax._get_lines.color_cycle.next()
    _min_results = sop.fmin(expected_loss, 15000, args=(_p,),disp=False)
    _results = [expected_loss(_g, _p) for _g in guesses]
    plt.plot(guesses, _results , color=_color)
    plt.scatter(_min_results, 0, s=60,
                color=_color, label="%d"%_p)
    plt.vlines(_min_results, 0, 120000, color=_color, linestyles="--")
    print "minimum at risk %d: %.2f"%(_p, _min_results)

plt.title("Expected loss and Bayes actions of different guesses, \n \
          various risk levels of overestimating")
plt.legend(loc="upper left", scatterpoints=1,
           title="Bayes action at risk:")
plt.xlabel("Price guess")
plt.ylabel("Expected loss")
plt.xlim(7000, 30000)
plt.ylim(-1000, 80000);
```

```
[Output]:

minimum at risk 30000: 14189.08
minimum at risk 54000: 13236.61
minimum at risk 78000: 12771.73
minimum at risk 102000: 11540.84
minimum at risk 126000: 11534.79
minimum at risk 150000: 11265.78
```

```
[Output]:

(-1000, 80000)
```

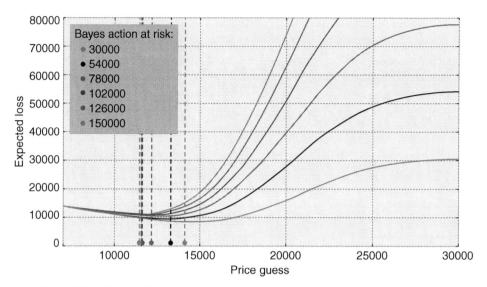

Figure 5.2.4: Expected loss and Bayes actions of different guesses, various risk levels of overestimating

As we decrease the risk threshold (care about overbidding less), we increase our bid, willing to edge closer to the true price. It is interesting how far away our optimized loss is from the posterior mean, which was about 20,000.

Suffice it to say, in higher dimensions, being able to eyeball the minimum expected loss is impossible. That is why we require use of SciPy's `fmin` function.

Shortcuts   For some loss functions, the Bayes action is known in closed form. We list some of them here.

- If using the mean-squared loss, the Bayes action is the mean of the posterior distribution; that is, the value

$$E_\theta [\theta]$$

  minimizes $E_\theta[(\theta - \hat{\theta})^2]$. Computationally, this requires us to calculate the average of the posterior samples (see Chapter 4 on the Law of Large Numbers).

- Whereas the median of the posterior distribution minimizes the expected absolute loss, the sample median of the posterior samples is an appropriate and very accurate approximation to the true median.

- In fact, it is possible to show that the MAP estimate is the solution to using a loss function that shrinks to the zero-one loss.

Maybe it is clear now why the first-introduced loss functions are used most often in the mathematics of Bayesian inference: No complicated optimizations are necessary. Luckily, we have machines to do the complications for us.

5.3 Machine Learning via Bayesian Methods

Whereas frequentist methods strive to achieve the best precision about all possible parameters, machine learning cares to achieve the best *prediction* among all possible parameters. Often, your prediction measure and what frequentist methods are optimizing for are very different.

For example, least-squares linear regression is the simplest active machine-learning algorithm. I say *active*, as it engages in some learning, whereas predicting the sample mean is technically simpler, but is learning very little (if anything). The loss that determines the coefficients of the regressors is a squared-error loss. On the other hand, if your prediction loss function (or score function, which is the negative loss) is not a squared-error, your least-squares line will not be optimal for the prediction loss function. This can lead to prediction results that are suboptimal.

Finding Bayes actions is equivalent to finding parameters that optimize not *parameter accuracy* but an *arbitrary performance measure*; however, we wish to define "performance" (loss functions, AUC, ROC, precision/recall, etc.).

The next two examples demonstrate these ideas. The first example is a linear model where we can choose to predict using the least-squares loss or a novel, outcome-sensitive loss. The second example is adapted from a Kaggle data science project. The loss function associated with our predictions is incredibly complicated.

5.3.1 Example: Financial Prediction

Suppose the future return of a stock price is very small, say 0.01 (or 1%). We have a model that predicts the stock's future price, and our profit and loss is directly tied to our acting on the prediction. How should we measure the loss associated with the model's predictions, and subsequent future predictions? A squared-error loss is agnostic to the signage and would penalize a prediction of -0.01 equally as badly as a prediction of 0.03:

$$(0.01 - (-0.01))^2 = (0.01 - 0.03)^2 = 0.004$$

If you had made a bet based on your model's prediction, you would have earned money with a prediction of 0.03, and lost money with a prediction of -0.01, yet our loss did not capture this. We need a better loss that takes into account the *sign* of the prediction and true value. We design a new loss that is better for financial applications, shown in Figure 5.3.1.

```
figsize(12.5, 4)
def stock_loss(true_return, yhat, alpha=100.):
    if true_return*yhat < 0:
        # opposite signs, not good
        return alpha*yhat**2 - np.sign(true_return)*yhat \
                        + abs(true_return)
    else:
        return abs(true_return - yhat)
```

(*Continues*)

(*Continued*)

```
true_value = .05
pred = np.linspace(-.04, .12, 75)

plt.plot(pred, [stock_loss(true_value, _p) for _p in pred], \
    label = "loss associated with\n prediction if true value = 0.05", lw=3)
plt.vlines(0, 0, .25, linestyles="--")

plt.xlabel("Prediction")
plt.ylabel("Loss" )
plt.xlim(-0.04, .12)
plt.ylim(0, 0.25)

true_value = -.02
plt.plot(pred, [stock_loss(true_value, _p) for _p in pred], alpha=0.6, \
    label="loss associated with\n prediction if true value = -0.02", lw=3)
plt.legend()
plt.title("Stock returns loss if true value = 0.05, -0.02" );
```

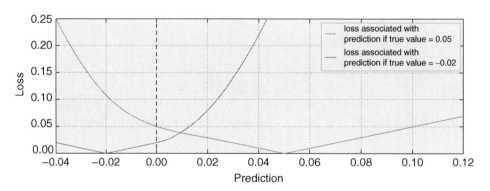

Figure 5.3.1: Stock returns loss if true value = 0.05, −0.02

Note the change in the shape of the loss as the prediction crosses 0. This loss reflects that the user really does *not* want to guess the wrong sign, and especially doesn't want to be wrong *and* with a large magnitude.

Why would the user care about the magnitude? Why is the loss not 0 for predicting the correct sign? Surely, if the return is 0.01 and we bet millions, we will still be (very) happy.

Financial institutions treat *downside risk* (as in predicting a lot on the wrong side) and *upside risk* (as in predicting a lot on the right side) similarly. Both are seen as risky behavior and are discouraged. Therefore, we have an increasing loss as we move further away from the true price, with less extreme loss in the direction of the correct sign.

We will perform a regression on a trading signal that we believe predicts future returns well. Our dataset is artificial, as most financial data is not even close to linear. In Figure 5.3.2, we plot the data along with the least-squares line.

```
# code to create artificial data
N = 100
X = 0.025 * np.random.randn(N)
Y = 0.5 * X + 0.01 * np.random.randn(N)

ls_coef_ = np.cov(X, Y)[0,1]/np.var(X)
ls_intercept = Y.mean() - ls_coef_*X.mean()

plt.scatter(X, Y, c="k")
plt.xlabel("Trading signal")
plt.ylabel("Returns")
plt.title("Empirical returns versus trading signal")
plt.plot(X, ls_coef_ * X + ls_intercept, label="least-squares line")
plt.xlim(X.min(), X.max())
plt.ylim(Y.min(), Y.max())
plt.legend(loc="upper left");
```

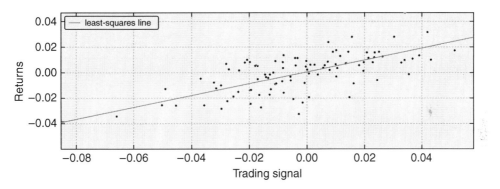

Figure 5.3.2: Empirical returns versus trading signal

We perform a simple Bayesian linear regression on this dataset. We look for a model like

$$R = \alpha + \beta x + \epsilon$$

where α, β are our unknown parameters and $\epsilon \sim \text{Normal}(0, 1/\tau)$. The most common priors on β and α are Normal priors. We will also assign a prior on τ, so that $\sigma = 1/\sqrt{\tau}$ is uniform over 0 to 100 (equivalently, then, $\tau = 1/\text{Uniform}(0, 100)^2$).

```
import pymc as pm
from pymc.Matplot import plot as mcplot

std = pm.Uniform("std", 0, 100, trace=False)

@pm.deterministic
def prec(U=std):
    return 1.0 / U **2

beta = pm.Normal("beta", 0, 0.0001)
alpha = pm.Normal("alpha", 0, 0.0001)

@pm.deterministic
def mean(X=X, alpha=alpha, beta=beta):
    return alpha + beta * X

obs = pm.Normal("obs", mean, prec, value=Y, observed=True)
mcmc = pm.MCMC([obs, beta, alpha, std, prec])

mcmc.sample(100000, 80000);
```

```
[Output]:

[------------------100%------------------] 100000 of 100000 complete in
    23.2 sec
```

For a specific trading signal, call it x, the distribution of possible returns has the form

$$R_i(x) = \alpha_i + \beta_i x + \epsilon$$

where $\epsilon \sim \text{Normal}(0, 1/\tau_i)$ and i indexes our posterior samples. We wish to find the solution to

$$\arg\min_r \quad E_{R(x)}[\, L(R(x), r)\,]$$

according to the loss given. This r is our Bayes action for trading signal x. In Figure 5.3.3, we plot the Bayes action over different trading signals. What do you notice?

```
figsize(12.5, 6)
from scipy.optimize import fmin

def stock_loss(price, pred, coef=500):
    sol = np.zeros_like(price)
    ix = price*pred < 0
    sol[ix] = coef * pred **2 - np.sign(price[ix]) * pred + abs(price[ix])
    sol[~ix] = abs(price[~ix] - pred)
    return sol

tau_samples = mcmc.trace("prec")[:]
alpha_samples = mcmc.trace("alpha")[:]
beta_samples = mcmc.trace("beta")[:]
```

```
N = tau_samples.shape[0]

noise = 1. / np.sqrt(tau_samples) * np.random.randn(N)

possible_outcomes = lambda signal: alpha_samples + beta_samples * signal \
                                    +u noise


opt_predictions = np.zeros(50)
trading_signals = np.linspace(X.min(), X.max(), 50)
for i, _signal in enumerate(trading_signals):
        _possible_outcomes = possible_outcomes(_signal)
        tomin = lambda pred: stock_loss(_possible_outcomes, pred).mean()
        opt_predictions[i] = fmin(tomin, 0, disp=False)


plt.xlabel("Trading signal")
plt.ylabel("Prediction")
plt.title("Least-squares prediction versus Bayes action prediction" )
plt.plot(X, ls_coef_ * X + ls_intercept,
        label="least-squares prediction")
plt.xlim(X.min(), X.max())
plt.plot(trading_signals, opt_predictions,
        label="Bayes action prediction")
plt.legend(loc="upper left");
```

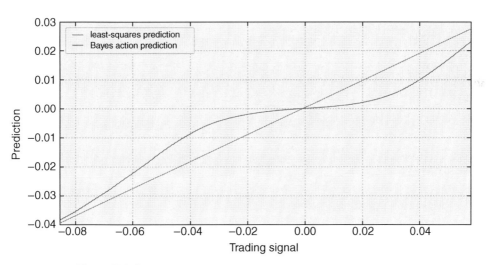

Figure 5.3.3: Least-squares prediction versus Bayes action prediction

What is interesting about Figure 5.3.3 is that when the signal is near 0, and many of the possible returns are possibly both positive and negative, our best (with respect to our loss)

move is to predict close to 0; that is, take on no position. Only when we are very confident do we enter into a position. I call this style of model a **sparse prediction**, where we feel uncomfortable with our uncertainty so choose not to act. (Compare this with the least-squares prediction, which will rarely, if ever, predict 0.)

A good sanity check that our model is still reasonable is that as the signal becomes more and more extreme, and we feel more and more confident about the positiveness/negativeness of returns, our position converges with that of the least-squares line.

The sparse-prediction model is not trying to fit the data the best according to a squared-error loss definition of fit. That honor would go to the least-squares model. The sparse-prediction model is trying to find the best prediction *with respect to our* `stock_loss`-*defined loss*. We can turn this reasoning around: The least-squares model is not trying to predict the best (according to a `stock-loss` definition of "predict"). That honor would go the sparse-prediction model. The least-squares model is trying to find the best fit of the data *with respect to the squared-error loss*.

5.3.2   Example: Kaggle Contest on Observing Dark Worlds

A personal motivation for learning Bayesian methods was trying to piece together the winning solution to Kaggle's Observing Dark Worlds contest. From the contest's website:[2]

> There is more to the Universe than meets the eye. Out in the cosmos exists a form of matter that outnumbers the stuff we can see by almost 7 to 1, and we don't know what it is. What we do know is that it does not emit or absorb light, so we call it **Dark Matter**.

> Such a vast amount of aggregated matter does not go unnoticed. In fact we observe that this stuff aggregates and forms massive structures called **Dark Matter Halos**.

> Although dark, it warps and bends spacetime such that any light from a background galaxy which passes close to the *Dark Matter* will have its path altered and changed. This bending causes the galaxy to appear as an ellipse in the sky.

The contest required predictions about where dark matter was likely to be. The winner, Tim Salimans, used Bayesian inference to find the best locations for the halos (interestingly, the second-place winner also used Bayesian inference). With Tim's permission, we provide his solution[3] here.

1. Construct a prior distribution for the halo positions $p(x)$, i.e. formulate our expectations about the halo positions before looking at the data.

2. Construct a probabilistic model for the data (observed ellipticities of the galaxies) given the positions of the dark matter halos: $p(e|x)$.

3. Use Bayes' rule to get the posterior distribution of the halo positions, i.e. use to [*sic*] the data to guess where the dark matter halos might be.

4. Minimize the expected loss with respect to the posterior distribution over the predictions for the halo positions: $\hat{x} = \arg\min_{\text{prediction}} E_{p(x|e)}[L(\text{prediction}, x)]$, i.e. tune our predictions to be as good as possible for the given error metric.

The loss function in this problem is very complicated. For the very determined, the loss function is contained in the file DarkWorldsMetric.py. Though I suggest not reading it all, suffice it to say the loss function is about 160 lines of code—not something that can be written down in a single mathematical line. The loss function attempts to measure the accuracy of prediction, in a Euclidean distance sense, such that no shift bias is present. More details can be found on the contest's homepage.

We will attempt to implement Tim's winning solution using PyMC and our knowledge of loss functions.

5.3.3 The Data

The dataset is actually 300 separate files, each representing a sky. In each file, or sky, are between 300 and 720 galaxies. Each galaxy has an x and y position associated with it, ranging from 0 to 4,200, and measures of ellipticity: e_1 and e_2. Information about what these measures mean can be found at https://www.kaggle.com/c/DarkWorlds/details/an-introduction-to-ellipticity, but we only care about that for visualization purposes. Thus, a typical sky might look like Figure 5.3.4.

```
from draw_sky2 import draw_sky

n_sky = 3 # choose a file/sky to examine
data = np.genfromtxt("data/Train_Skies/Train_Skies/\
Training_Sky%d.csv"%(n_sky),
                        dtype=None,
                        skip_header=1,
                        delimiter=",",
                        usecols=[1,2,3,4])
print "Data on galaxies in sky %d."%n_sky
print "position_x, position_y, e_1, e_2 "
print data[:3]

fig = draw_sky(data)
plt.title("Galaxy positions and ellipticities of sky %d."%n_sky)
plt.xlabel("$x$ position")
plt.ylabel("$y$ position");
```

```
[Output]:

Data on galaxies in sky 3.
position_x, position_y, e_1, e_2
[[ 1.62690000e+02 1.60006000e+03 1.14664000e-01 -1.90326000e-01]
 [ 2.27228000e+03 5.40040000e+02 6.23555000e-01  2.14979000e-01]
 [ 3.55364000e+03 2.69771000e+03 2.83527000e-01 -3.01870000e-01]]
```

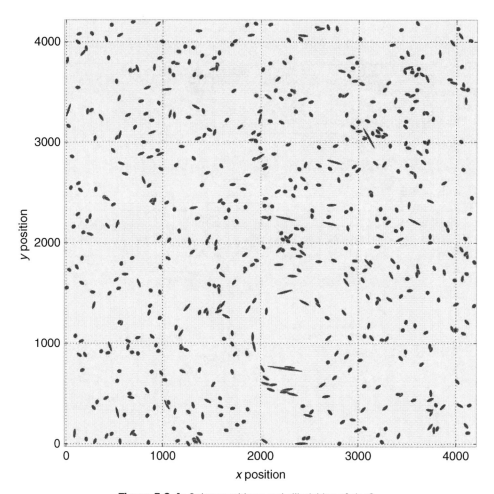

Figure 5.3.4: Galaxy positions and ellipticities of sky 3

5.3.4 Priors

Each sky has one, two, or three dark matter halos in it. Tim's solution details that his prior distribution of halo positions was uniform; that is,

$$x_i \sim \text{Uniform}(0, 4200)$$
$$y_i \sim \text{Uniform}(0, 4200), \quad i = 1, 2, 3$$

Tim and other competitors noted that most skies had one large halo, and other halos, if present, were much smaller. Larger halos, having more mass, will influence the surrounding galaxies more. He decided that the large halos would have a mass distributed as a *log*-uniform random variable between 40 and 180; that is,

$$m_{\text{large}} = \log \text{Uniform}(40, 180)$$

and in PyMC,

```
exp_mass_large = pm.Uniform("exp_mass_large", 40, 180)
@pm.deterministic
def mass_large(u = exp_mass_large):
    return np.log(u)
```

(This is what we mean when we say "*log*-uniform.") For smaller galaxies, Tim set the mass to be the logarithm of 20. Why did Tim not create a prior for the smaller mass, or treat it as a unknown? I believe this decision was made to speed up convergence of the algorithm. This is not too restrictive, as by construction, the smaller halos have less influence on the galaxies.

Tim logically assumed that the ellipticity of each galaxy is dependent on the position of the halos, the distance between the galaxy and halo, and the mass of the halos. Thus, the vector of ellipticity of each galaxy, $\mathbf{e}_i$, are *children* variables of the vector of halo positions $(\mathbf{x}, \mathbf{y})$, distance (which we will formalize), and halo masses.

Tim conceived a relationship to connect positions and ellipticity by reading literature and forum posts. He supposed the following was a reasonable relationship:

$$e_i|(\mathbf{x}, \mathbf{y}) \sim \text{Normal}\left(\sum_{j=\text{halo positions}} d_{i,j} m_j f(r_{i,j}), \sigma^2 \right)$$

where $d_{i,j}$ is the *tangential direction* (the direction in which halo j bends the light of galaxy i), m_j is the mass of halo j, and $f(r_{i,j})$ is a *decreasing function* of the Euclidean distance between halo j and galaxy i.

Tim's function f was defined:

$$f(r_{i,j}) = \frac{1}{\min(r_{i,j}, 240)}$$

for large halos, and for small halos

$$f(r_{i,j}) = \frac{1}{\min(r_{i,j}, 70)}$$

This fully bridges our observations and unknown. This model is incredibly simple, and Tim mentions that this simplicity was purposely designed; it prevents the model from overfitting.

5.3.5 Training and PyMC Implementation

For each sky, we run our Bayesian model to find the posteriors for the halo positions—we ignore the (known) halo position. This is slightly different from perhaps more traditional approaches to Kaggle competitions, where this model uses no data from other skies or from the known halo location. That does not mean other data are not necessary; in fact, the model was created by comparing different skies.

```
def euclidean_distance(x, y):
    return np.sqrt(((x - y) **2).sum(axis=1))

def f_distance(gxy_pos, halo_pos, c):
    # foo_position should be a 2D numpy array.
    return np.maximum(euclidean_distance(gxy_pos, halo_pos), c)[:,None]

def tangential_distance(glxy_position, halo_position):
    # foo_position should be a 2D numpy array.
    delta = glxy_position - halo_position
    t = (2*np.arctan(delta[:,1]/delta[:,0]))[:,None]
    return np.concatenate([-np.cos(t), -np.sin(t)], axis=1)

import pymc as pm

# Set the size of the halo's mass.
mass_large = pm.Uniform("mass_large", 40, 180, trace=False)

# Set the initial prior position of the halos; it's a 2D Uniform
# distribution.
halo_position = pm.Uniform("halo_position", 0, 4200, size=(1,2))


@pm.deterministic
def mean(mass=mass_large, h_pos=halo_position, glx_pos=data[:,:2]):
    return mass/f_distance(glx_pos, h_pos, 240)*\
            tangential_distance(glx_pos, h_pos)

ellpty = pm.Normal("ellipticity", mean, 1./0.05, observed=True,
                    value=data[:,2:] )
mcmc = pm.MCMC([ellpty, mean, halo_position, mass_large])
map_ = pm.MAP([ellpty, mean, halo_position, mass_large])
map_.fit()
mcmc.sample(200000, 140000, 3)
```

```
[Output]:

[****************100%******************] 200000 of 200000 complete
```

In Figure 5.3.5, we plot a heatmap of the posterior distribution (this is just a scatter plot of the posterior, but we can visualize it as a heatmap). As you can see in the figure, the red spot denotes our posterior distribution over where the halo is.

```
t = mcmc.trace("halo_position")[:].reshape( 20000,2)

fig = draw_sky(data)
plt.title("Galaxy positions and ellipticities of sky %d."%n_sky)
plt.xlabel("$x$ position")
plt.ylabel("$y$ position")
scatter(t[:,0], t[:,1], alpha=0.015, c="r")
plt.xlim(0, 4200)
plt.ylim(0, 4200);
```

The most probable position reveals itself like a lethal wound.

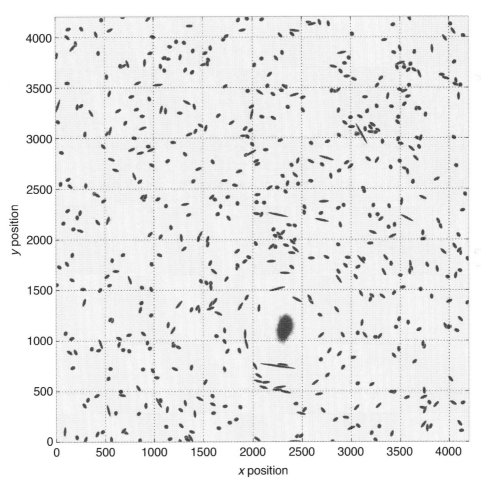

Figure 5.3.5: Galaxy positions and ellipticities of sky 3

Associated with each sky is another data point, located in `Training_halos.csv`, that holds the locations of up to three dark matter halos contained in the sky. For example, the night sky we trained on has halo locations

```
halo_data = np.genfromtxt("data/Training_halos.csv",
                          delimiter=",",
                          usecols=[1,2,3,4,5,6,7,8,9],
                          skip_header=1)
print halo_data[n_sky]
```

```
[Output]:

[ 3.00000000e+00 2.78145000e+03 1.40691000e+03 3.08163000e+03
  1.15611000e+03 2.28474000e+03 3.19597000e+03 1.80916000e+03
  8.45180000e+02]
```

The third and fourth column represent the true x and y position of the halo. It appears that the Bayesian method has located the halo within a tight vicinity, as denoted by the black dot in Figure 5.3.6.

```
fig = draw_sky(data)
plt.title("Galaxy positions and ellipticities of sky %d."%n_sky)
plt.xlabel("$x$ position")
plt.ylabel("$y$ position" )
plt.scatter(t[:,0], t[:,1], alpha=0.015, c="r")
plt.scatter(halo_data[n_sky-1][3], halo_data[n_sky-1][4],
            label="true halo position",
            c="k", s=70)
plt.legend(scatterpoints=1, loc="lower left")
plt.xlim(0, 4200)
plt.ylim(0, 4200);

print "True halo location:", halo_data[n_sky][3], halo_data[n_sky][4]
```

```
[Output]:

True halo location: 1408.61 1685.86
```

Perfect. Our next step is to use the loss function to optimize our location. A naive strategy would be to simply choose the mean:

```
mean_posterior = t.mean(axis=0).reshape(1,2)
print mean_posterior
```

```
[Output]:

[[ 2324.07677813 1122.47097816]]
```

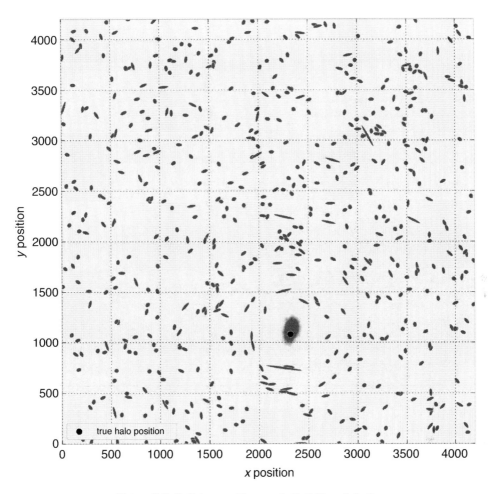

Figure 5.3.6: Galaxy positions and ellipticities of sky 3

```
from DarkWorldsMetric import main_score

_halo_data = halo_data[n_sky-1]

nhalo_all = _halo_data[0].reshape(1,1)
x_true_all = _halo_data[3].reshape(1,1)
y_true_all = _halo_data[4].reshape(1,1)
x_ref_all = _halo_data[1].reshape(1,1)
y_ref_all = _halo_data[2].reshape(1,1)
sky_prediction = mean_posterior

print "Using the mean:"
```

(*Continues*)

(Continued)

```
main_score(nhalo_all, x_true_all, y_true_all, \
           x_ref_all, y_ref_all, sky_prediction)

# What's a bad score?
print
random_guess = np.random.randint(0, 4200, size=(1,2))
print "Using a random location:", random_guess
main_score(nhalo_all, x_true_all, y_true_all, \
           x_ref_all, y_ref_all, random_guess)
print
```

```
[Output]:

Using the mean:
Your average distance in pixels away from the true halo is
    31.1499201664
Your average angular vector is 1.0
Your score for the training data is 1.03114992017

Using a random location: [[2755 53]]
Your average distance in pixels away from the true halo is
    1773.42717812
Your average angular vector is 1.0
Your score for the training data is 2.77342717812
```

This is a good guess; it is not very far from the true location, but it ignores the loss function that was provided to us. We also need to extend our code to allow for up to two additional, *smaller* halos. Let's create a function for automatizing our PyMC.

```
from pymc.Matplot import plot as mcplot

def halo_posteriors(n_halos_in_sky, galaxy_data,
                    samples = 5e5, burn_in = 34e4, thin = 4):

    # Set the size of the halo's mass.

    mass_large = pm.Uniform("mass_large", 40, 180)

    mass_small_1 = 20
    mass_small_2 = 20

    masses = np.array([mass_large,mass_small_1, mass_small_2],
                      dtype=object)

    # Set the initial prior positions of the halos; it's a 2D Uniform
    # distribution.
    halo_positions = pm.Uniform("halo_positions", 0, 4200,
                      size=(n_halos_in_sky,2))
```

```
    fdist_constants = np.array([240, 70, 70])

    @pm.deterministic
    def mean(mass=masses, h_pos=halo_positions, glx_pos=data[:,:2],
             n_halos_in_sky = n_halos_in_sky):

        _sum = 0
        for i in range(n_halos_in_sky):
            _sum += mass[i] / f_distance( glx_pos,h_pos[i, :],
                fdist_constants[i])*\
                    tangential_distance( glx_pos, h_pos[i, :])


        return _sum


    ellpty = pm.Normal("ellipticity", mean, 1. / 0.05, observed=True,
                       value = data[:,2:])

    map_ = pm.MAP([ellpty, mean, halo_positions, mass_large])
    map_.fit(method="fmin_powell")

    mcmc = pm.MCMC([ellpty, mean, halo_positions, mass_large])
    mcmc.sample(samples, burn_in, thin)
    return mcmc.trace("halo_positions")[:]

n_sky =215
data = np.genfromtxt("data/Train_Skies/Train_Skies/\
Training_Sky%d.csv"%(n_sky),
                     dtype=None,
                     skip_header=1,
                     delimiter=",",
                     usecols=[1,2,3,4])

# There are 3 halos in this file.
samples = 10.5e5
traces = halo_posteriors(3, data, samples=samples,
                             burn_in=9.5e5,
                             thin=10)
```

```
[Output]:

[*****************100%*****************] 1050000 of 1050000 complete
```

```
fig = draw_sky(data)
plt.title("Galaxy positions, ellipticities, and halos of sky %d."%n_sky)
plt.xlabel("$x$ position")
plt.ylabel("$y$ position")
```

(Continues)

(Continued)

```
colors = ["#467821", "#A60628", "#7A68A6"]

for i in range(traces.shape[1]):
    plt.scatter(traces[:, i, 0], traces[:, i, 1], c=colors[i],
                alpha=0.02)


for i in range(traces.shape[1]):
    plt.scatter(halo_data[n_sky-1][3 + 2 * i],
        halo_data[n_sky-1][4 + 2 * i],
            label="true halo position", c="k", s=90)

plt.xlim(0, 4200)
plt.ylim(0, 4200);
```

```
[Output]:

(0, 4200)
```

As you can see in Figure 5.3.7, this looks pretty good, though it took a long time for the system to (sort of) converge. Our optimization step would look something like this.

```
_halo_data = halo_data[n_sky-1]
print traces.shape

mean_posterior = traces.mean(axis=0).reshape(1,4)
print mean_posterior


nhalo_all = _halo_data[0].reshape(1,1)
x_true_all = _halo_data[3].reshape(1,1)
y_true_all = _halo_data[4].reshape(1,1)
x_ref_all = _halo_data[1].reshape(1,1)
y_ref_all = _halo_data[2].reshape(1,1)
sky_prediction = mean_posterior


print "Using the mean:"
main_score([1], x_true_all, y_true_all, \
            x_ref_all, y_ref_all, sky_prediction)

# What's a bad score?
print
random_guess = np.random.randint(0, 4200, size=(1,2))
print "Using a random location:", random_guess
main_score([1], x_true_all, y_true_all, \
            x_ref_all, y_ref_all, random_guess)
print
```

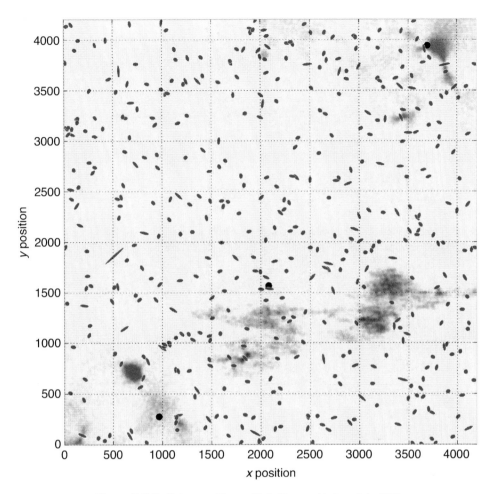

Figure 5.3.7: Galaxy positions, ellipticities, and halos of sky 215

```
[Output]:

(10000L, 2L, 2L)
[[ 48.55499317 1675.79569424 1876.46951857 3265.85341193]]
Using the mean:
Your average distance in pixels away from the true halo is
    37.3993004245
Your average angular vector is 1.0
Your score for the training data is 1.03739930042
```

(*Continues*)

(*Continued*)

```
Using a random location: [[2930 4138]]
Your average distance in pixels away from the true halo is
    3756.54446887
Your average angular vector is 1.0
Your score for the training data is 4.75654446887
```

5.4   Conclusion

Loss functions are one of the most interesting parts of statistics. They directly connect inference and the domain the problem is in. One thing *not* mentioned is that the loss function is another degree of freedom in your overall model. This is a good thing, as we saw in this chapter; loss functions can be used very effectively, but can be a bad thing, too. An extreme case is that a practitioner can change his or her loss function if the results do not fit the desired result. For this reason, it's best to set the loss function as soon as possible in the analysis, and have its derivation open and logical.

5.5   References

1. Read, Carveth. *Logic: Deductive and Inductive*. London: Simkin, Marshall, 1920, p. vi.

2. "Observing Dark Worlds," Kaggle, accessed November 30, 2014, `https://www.kaggle.com/c/DarkWorlds`.

3. Salimans, Tim. "Observing Dark Worlds," Tim Salimans on Data Analysis, accessed May 19, 2015, `http://timsalimans.com/observing-dark-worlds/`.

6

Getting Our Priorities Straight

6.1 Introduction

This chapter focuses on the most debated and discussed part of Bayesian methodologies: how to choose an appropriate prior distribution. We also present how the prior's influence changes as our dataset grows larger, and an interesting relationship between priors and penalties on linear regression.

Throughout this book, we have mostly ignored our choice of priors. This is unfortunate, as we can be very expressive with our priors, but we also must be careful about choosing them. This is especially true if we want to be objective, that is, not to express any personal beliefs in the priors.

6.2 Subjective versus Objective Priors

Bayesian priors can be classified into two classes. The first are **objective priors**, which aim to allow the data to influence the posterior the most. The second class are **subjective priors**, which allow the practitioner to express his or her views in the prior.

6.2.1 Objective Priors

What is an example of an objective prior? We have seen some already, including the **flat prior**, which is a uniform distribution over the entire range of the unknown. Using a flat prior implies that we give each possible value an equal weighting. Choosing this type of prior is invoking what is called the **Principle of Indifference**: We have no prior reason to favor one value over another. Calling a flat prior over a restricted space an objective prior is not correct, though it seems similar. If we know p in a binomial model is greater than 0.5, then Uniform(0.5, 1) is not an objective prior (since we have used external knowledge) even though that distribution is indeed "flat" over [0.5, 1]. The flat prior must be flat over the entire range of possibilities, including 0 to 0.5.

Aside from the flat prior, other examples of objective priors are less obvious, but they contain important characteristics that reflect objectivity. For now, it should be said that rarely is an objective prior *truly* objective. We will see this later.

6.2.2 Subjective Priors

On the other hand, if we add more probability mass to certain areas of the prior, and less elsewhere, we are biasing our inference toward the parameters existing in the areas with more probability mass. This is known as a subjective, or *informative*, prior.

In Figure 6.2.1, the subjective prior describes a belief that the unknown likely lives around 0.5, and not around the extremes. The objective prior is insensitive to this.

```
%matplotlib inline
import numpy as np
from IPython.core.pylabtools import figsize
import matplotlib.pyplot as plt
import scipy.stats as stats
plt.rcParams['savefig.dpi'] = 300
plt.rcParams['figure.dpi'] = 300


figsize(12.5,3)
colors = ["#348ABD", "#A60628", "#7A68A6", "#467821"]

x = np.linspace(0,1)
y1, y2 = stats.beta.pdf(x, 1, 1), stats.beta.pdf(x, 10, 10)

p = plt.plot(x, y1,
    label='An objective prior \n(uninformative, \n"Principle of\
    Indifference")')
plt.fill_between(x, 0, y1, color=p[0].get_color(), alpha=0.3)

p = plt.plot(x, y2,
    label='A subjective prior \n(informative)')
plt.fill_between(x, 0, y2, color=p[0].get_color(), alpha=0.3)

p = plt.plot(x[25:], 2*np.ones(25), label="Another subjective prior")
plt.fill_between(x[25:], 0, 2, color=p[0].get_color(), alpha=0.3)

plt.ylim(0, 4)

plt.ylim(0, 4)
leg = plt.legend(loc="upper left")
leg.get_frame().set_alpha(0.4)
plt.xlabel('Value')
plt.ylabel('Density')
plt.title("Comparing objective versus subjective priors for an unknown\
        probability");
```

The choice of a subjective prior does not always imply that we are using the practitioner's subjective opinion; more often, the subjective prior was once a posterior to a previous problem, and now the practitioner is updating this posterior with new data. A subjective prior can also be used to inject domain knowledge of the problem into the model. We will see examples of these two situations later.

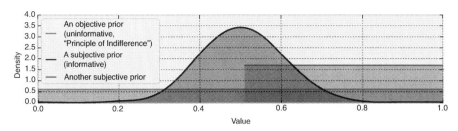

Figure 6.2.1: Comparing objective versus subjective priors for an unknown probability

6.2.3   Decisions, Decisions . . .

The choice of an objective or subjective prior mostly depends on the problem being solved, but there are a few cases where one is preferred over the other. In instances of scientific research, the choice of an objective prior is obvious, as this eliminates any biases in the results. It should be the case that two researchers with differing beliefs about the topic of research still feel that an objective prior is "fair."

Consider a more extreme situation: Suppose a tobacco company publishes a report with a Bayesian methodology that challenges sixty years of medical research on tobacco use. Would you believe the results? Unlikely. The researchers probably chose a subjective prior that too strongly biased results in their favor.

Unfortunately, choosing an objective prior is not as simple as selecting a flat prior, and even today, the problem is still not completely solved. The problem with naively choosing the uniform prior is that pathological issues can arise. Some of these issues are pedantic, but we will later see an example of when this can be an issue.

We must remember that choosing a prior, whether subjective or objective, is still part of the modeling process. To quote Gelman:[1]

> [A]fter the model has been fit, one should look at the posterior distribution and see if it makes sense. If the posterior distribution does not make sense, this implies that additional prior knowledge is available that has not been included in the model, and that contradicts the assumptions of the prior distribution that has been used. It is then appropriate to go back and alter the prior distribution to be more consistent with this external knowledge.

If the posterior does not make sense to you, then clearly you had an idea of what the posterior *should* look like (not to be confused with what one *hopes* it will look like), implying that the current prior does not contain all the prior information and should be updated. At this point, we can discard the current prior and choose one more reflective of *all* our prior information.

Gelman[2] suggests that using a uniform distribution with large bounds is often a good choice for objective priors. However, one should be wary about using uniform objective priors with large bounds, as they can assign too large of a prior probability to points that are extremely unintuitive. Ask yourself: Do you really think the unknown *could* be incredibly large? Often, quantities are naturally biased toward 0. A Normal random variable with large variance (small precision) might be a better choice, or an exponential variable with a fat tail in the strictly positive (or negative) case.

6.2.4 Empirical Bayes

Empirical Bayes is a trick that combines frequentist and Bayesian inference. As mentioned previously, for (almost) every inference problem, there is a Bayesian method and a frequentist method. The significant difference between the two is that Bayesian methods have a prior distribution, with hyperparameters α and τ, while empirical methods do not have any notion of a prior. Empirical Bayes combines the two methods by using frequentist methods to select α and τ, and then proceeds with Bayesian methods on the original problem.

A very simple example follows. Suppose we wish to estimate the parameter μ of a Normal distribution, with $\sigma = 5$. Since μ could range over the all real numbers, we can use a Normal distribution as a prior for μ. Next we must select the prior's hyperparameters, denoted (μ_p, σ_p^2). The σ_p^2 parameter can be chosen to reflect the uncertainty we have. For μ_p, we have two options.

1. Empirical Bayes suggests using the empirical sample mean, which will center the prior around the observed empirical mean:

$$\mu_p = \frac{1}{N} \sum_{i=0}^{N} X_i$$

2. Traditional Bayesian inference suggests using prior knowledge, or a more objective prior (0 mean and fat standard deviation).

In contrast to objective Bayesian inference, empirical Bayes can be argued as being semi-objective, since while the choice of prior model is ours (hence subjective), the parameters are solely determined by the data (hence objective).

Personally, I feel that the empirical Bayes approach is double-counting the data. That is, we are using the data once in the prior, which will influence our results toward the observed data, and again in the inferential engine of MCMC. This double-counting can understate our true uncertainty. To minimize this double-counting, I would only suggest using empirical Bayes when you have lots of observations, else the prior will have too strong of an influence. I would also recommend, if possible, to maintain high uncertainty (by setting a large σ_p^2 or equivalent).

Empirical Bayes also violates a philosophical point in Bayesian inference. The textbook Bayesian algorithm of

prior $\Rightarrow$ observed data $\Rightarrow$ posterior

is violated by Empirical Bayes, which instead uses

observed data $\Rightarrow$ prior $\Rightarrow$ observed data $\Rightarrow$ posterior

Ideally, all priors should be specified before we observe the data, so that the data does not influence our prior opinions (see the volumes of research by Daniel Kahneman and others about anchoring).

6.3   Useful Priors to Know About

In the following, we'll go over some distributions that are common in Bayesian analysis and methods.

6.3.1   The Gamma Distribution

A Gamma random variable, denoted $X \sim \text{Gamma}(\alpha, \beta)$, is a random variable over the positive real numbers. It is in fact a generalization of the Exponential random variable, that is,

$$Exp(\beta) \sim \text{Gamma}(1, \beta)$$

This additional parameter allows the probability density function to have more flexibility, hence allowing the practitioner to express his or her subjective priors more accurately. The density function for a $\text{Gamma}(\alpha, \beta)$ random variable is

$$f(x \mid \alpha, \beta) = \frac{\beta^{\alpha} x^{\alpha-1} e^{-\beta x}}{\Gamma(\alpha)}$$

where $\Gamma(\alpha)$ is the gamma function. In Figure 6.3.1, we plot the Gamma distribution for differing values of (α, β):

```
figsize(12.5, 5)
gamma = stats.gamma

parameters = [(1, 0.5), (9, 2), (3, 0.5), (7, 0.5)]
x = np.linspace(0.001, 20, 150)
for alpha, beta in parameters:
    y = gamma.pdf(x, alpha, scale=1./beta)
    lines = plt.plot(x, y, label="(%.1f,%.1f)"%(alpha,beta), lw=3)
    plt.fill_between(x, 0, y, alpha=0.2, color=lines[0].get_color())
    plt.autoscale(tight=True)

plt.legend(title=r"$\alpha, \beta$ - parameters")
plt.xlabel('Value')
plt.ylabel('Density')
plt.title(r "The Gamma distribution for different values of $\alpha$ and\
          $\beta$");
```

6.3.2   The Wishart Distribution

Until now, we have only seen random variables that are scalars. Of course, we can also have random matrices! Specifically, the **Wishart distribution** is a distribution over all

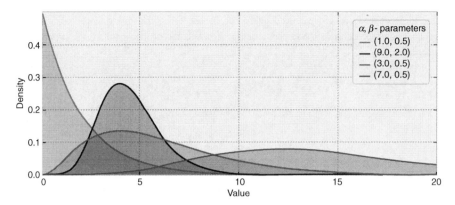

Figure 6.3.1: The Gamma distribution for different values of α and β

positive semi-definite matrices. Why is this useful to have in our arsenal? Proper covariance matrices are positive-definite, hence the Wishart is an appropriate prior for covariance matrices. We can't really visualize a distribution of matrices well, so in Figure 6.3.2, we'll plot some realizations from the 4×4 (top row) and 15×15 (bottom row) Wishart distribution.

```
import pymc as pm

n = 4
hyperparameter = np.eye(n)
for i in range(5):
    ax = plt.subplot(2, 5, i+1)
    plt.imshow(pm.rwishart(n+1, hyperparameter), interpolation="none",
               cmap=plt.cm.hot)
    ax.axis("off")

n = 15
hyperparameter = 10*np.eye(n)
for i in range(5, 10):
    ax = plt.subplot(2, 5, i+1)
    plt.imshow(pm.rwishart(n+1, hyperparameter), interpolation="none",
               cmap=plt.cm.hot)
    ax.axis("off")

plt.suptitle("Random matrices from a Wishart distribution");
```

One thing to notice is the symmetry of these matrices, which reflect that covariance matrices are symmetric, too. The Wishart distribution can be a little troubling to deal with, but we will use it in an example later.

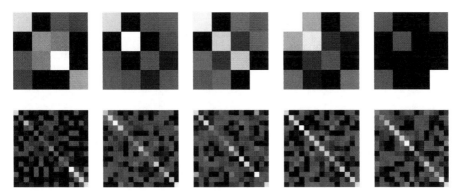

Figure 6.3.2: Random matrices of 4 × 4 (top row) and 15 × 15 (bottom row) from a Wishart distribution

6.3.3   The Beta Distribution

You may have seen the term `beta` in previous code in this book. Often, I was implementing a **Beta distribution**. The Beta distribution is very useful in Bayesian statistics. A random variable X has a Beta distribution, with parameters (α, β), if its density function is

$$f_X(x|\,\alpha, \beta) = \frac{x^{(\alpha-1)}(1-x)^{(\beta-1)}}{B(\alpha, \beta)}$$

In the previous question, B is the beta function (hence the name). The Beta distribution defines random variables between 0 and 1, making it a popular choice for modeling probabilities and proportions. The values of α and β, both positive values, provide great flexibility in the shape of the distribution. In Figure 6.3.3 we plot some distributions, varying over α and β.:

```
figsize(12.5, 5)

params = [(2,5), (1,1), (0.5, 0.5), (5, 5), (20, 4), (5, 1)]

x = np.linspace(0.01, .99, 100)
beta = stats.beta
for a, b in params:
  y = beta.pdf(x, a, b)
  lines = plt.plot(x, y, label="(%.1f,%.1f)"%(a,b), lw = 3)
  plt.fill_between(x, 0, y, alpha=0.2, color=lines[0].get_color())
  plt.autoscale(tight=True)

plt.ylim(0)
plt.legend(loc='upper left', title="(a,b)-parameters")
plt.xlabel('Value')
plt.ylabel('Density')
plt.title(r "The Beta distribution for different values of $\alpha$ and\
          $\beta$");
```

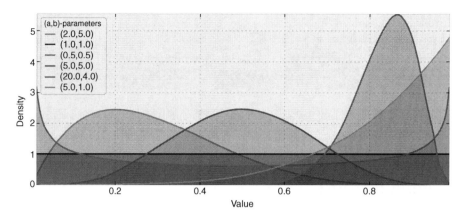

Figure 6.3.3: The Beta distribution for different values of α and β

One thing I'd like the reader to notice is the presence of the flat distribution in the previous figure, specified by parameters $(1, 1)$. This is the uniform distribution. Hence, the Beta distribution is a generalization of the uniform distribution, something we will revisit many times.

There is an interesting connection between the Beta distribution and the binomial distribution. Suppose we are interested in some unknown proportion or probability p. We assign a $\text{Beta}(\alpha, \beta)$ prior to p. We observe some data generated by a binomial process, say $X \sim \text{Binomial}(N, p)$, with p still unknown. Then our posterior *is again a Beta distribution*; that is, $p|X \sim \text{Beta}(\alpha + X, \beta + N - X)$. Succinctly, one can relate the two: a Beta prior with binomial observations creates a Beta posterior. This is a very useful property, both computationally and heuristically.

To make this concrete, if we start with a $\text{Beta}(1, 1)$ prior on p (which is a Uniform), observe data $X \sim \text{Binomial}(N, p)$, then our posterior is $\text{Beta}(1 + X, 1 + N - X)$. For example, if we observe $X = 10$ successes out of $N = 25$ trials, then our posterior for p is a $\text{Beta}(1 + 10, 1 + 25 - 10) = \text{Beta}(11, 16)$ distribution.

6.4   Example: Bayesian Multi-Armed Bandits

Suppose you are faced with ten slot machines (colorfully called *multi-armed bandits*). Each bandit has an unknown probability of distributing a prize (assume for now that the prizes are the same for each bandit; only the probabilities differ). Some bandits are very generous, others not so much. Of course, you don't know what these probabilities are. By only choosing one bandit per round, our task is devise a strategy to maximize our winnings.

Of course, if we knew the bandit with the largest probability, then always picking this bandit would yield the maximum winnings. So our task can be phrased as "Find the best bandit as quickly as possible."

The task is complicated by the stochastic nature of the bandits. A suboptimal bandit can return many winnings, purely by chance, which would make us believe that it is a very profitable bandit. Similarly, the best bandit can return many duds, by chance. Should we keep trying losers, then, or give up?

A more troublesome problem is, if we have found a bandit that returns *pretty good* results, do we keep drawing from it to maintain our *pretty good* score, or do we try other bandits in hopes of finding an even better bandit? This is the *exploration versus exploitation* dilemma.

6.4.1 Applications

The multi-armed bandit problem at first seems very artificial, something only a mathematician would love, but that is only before we address some applications.

- Internet display advertising: Companies have a suite of potential ads they can display to visitors, but the company is not sure which ad strategy to follow to maximize sales. This is similar to A/B testing, but has the added advantage of naturally minimizing groups that are not sucessful.
- Ecology: Animals have a finite amount of energy to expend, and certain behaviors have uncertain rewards. How does the animal maximize its fitness?
- Finance: Which stock option gives the highest return, under time-varying return profiles?
- Clinical trials: A researcher would like to find the best treatment, out of many possible treatments, while minimizing losses.

It turns out that the optimal solution is incredibly difficult, and it took decades for an overall solution to develop. There are also many approximately optimal solutions that are quite good. The one I wish to discuss is one of the few solutions that can scale well and is easily modified. The solution is known as *Bayesian Bandits*.[3]

6.4.2 A Proposed Solution

The algorithm starts in an ignorant state, where it knows nothing, and begins to acquire data by testing the system. As it acquires data and results, it learns what the best and worst behaviors are (in this case, it learns which bandit is the best). With this in mind, perhaps we can add an additional application of the multi-armed bandit problem:

- Psychology: How do punishment and reward affect our behavior? How do humans learn?

The Bayesian solution begins by assuming priors on the probability of winning for each bandit. In our vignette, we assumed complete ignorance of these probabilities. So a very natural prior is the flat prior over 0 to 1. The algorithm proceeds as follows:

1. Sample a random sample X_b from the prior of bandit b, for all b.
2. Select the bandit with highest sample; that is, select $B = \text{argmax } X_b$.
3. Observe the result of pulling bandit B, and update your prior on bandit B.
4. Return to 1.

That's it. Computationally, the algorithm involves sampling from N distributions. Since the initial priors are Beta($\alpha = 1, \beta = 1$), a uniform distribution, and the observed result X (a win or loss, encoded 1 and 0, respectively) is binomial, the posterior is a Beta($\alpha = 1 + X, \beta = 1 + 1 - X$).

To answer our question from before, this algorithm suggests that we should not discard losers, but rather should pick them at a decreasing rate as we gather confidence that there exist better bandits. This follows because there is always a non-zero chance that a loser will become B, the bandit with the largest sample, but the probability of this event decreases as we play more rounds (see Figure 6.4.1).

Next, we implement Bayesian Bandits using two classes: `Bandits`, which defines the slot machines, and `BayesianStrategy`, which implements the previous learning strategy.

```python
from pymc import rbeta

class Bandits(object):
    """
    This class represents N bandits.

    parameters:
        p_array: an (N,) NumPy array of probabilities >0, <1.

    methods:
        pull(i): return the results, 0 or 1, of pulling
            the ith bandit.
    """
    def __init__(self, p_array):
        self.p = p_array
        self.optimal = np.argmax(p_array)

    def pull(self, i):
        # i is which arm to pull. Returns True if a reward is earned, False else.
        return np.random.rand() < self.p[i]

    def __len__(self):
        return len(self.p)


class BayesianStrategy(object):
    """
    Implements an online learning strategy to solve
    the multi-armed bandit problem.

    parameters:
        bandits: a Bandit class with .pull method

    methods:
        sample_bandits(n): sample and train on n pulls.
```

```
attributes:
  N: the cumulative number of samples
  choices: the historical choices as an (N,) array
  bb_score: the historical score as an (N,) array
"""

def __init__(self, bandits):

    self.bandits = bandits
    n_bandits = len(self.bandits)
    self.wins = np.zeros(n_bandits)
    self.trials = np.zeros(n_bandits)
    self.N = 0
    self.choices = []
    self.bb_score = []


def sample_bandits(self, n=1):

    bb_score = np.zeros(n)
    choices = np.zeros(n)

    for k in range(n):
        # sample from the bandit's priors, and select the largest sample
        choice = np.argmax(rbeta(1 + self.wins, 1 + self.trials - self.wins))

        # sample the chosen bandit
        result = self.bandits.pull(choice)

        # update priors and score
        self.wins[choice] += result
        self.trials[choice] += 1
        bb_score[k] = result
        self.N += 1
        choices[k] = choice

    self.bb_score = np.r_[self.bb_score, bb_score]
    self.choices = np.r_[self.choices, choices]
    return
```

In Figure 6.4.1, we visualize the progression of the Bayesian Bandits algorithm.

```
figsize(11.0, 10)

beta = stats.beta
x = np.linspace(0.001, .999, 200)

def plot_priors(bayesian_strategy, prob, lw=3, alpha=0.2, plt_vlines=True):
    # plotting function
    wins = bayesian_strategy.wins
    trials = bayesian_strategy.trials
```

(Continues)

(Continued)

```
for i in range(prob.shape[0]):
  y = beta(1 + wins[i], 1 + trials[i] - wins[i])
  p = plt.plot(x, y.pdf(x), lw=lw)
  c = p[0].get_markeredgecolor()
  plt.fill_between(x,y.pdf(x),0 ,color=c, alpha=alpha,
          label="underlying probability: %.2f"%prob[i])
  if plt_vlines:
    plt.vlines(prob[i], 0, y.pdf(prob[i]),
          colors=c, linestyles="--", lw=2)
  plt.autoscale(tight="True")
  plt.title("Posteriors after %d pull"%bayesian_strategy.N +\
        "s"*(bayesian_strategy.N>1))
  plt.autoscale(tight=True)
return

hidden_prob = np.array([0.85, 0.60, 0.75])
bandits = Bandits(hidden_prob)
bayesian_strat = BayesianStrategy(bandits)

draw_samples = [1, 1, 3, 10, 10, 25, 50, 100, 200, 600]

for j,i in enumerate(draw_samples):
  plt.subplot(5, 2, j+1)
  bayesian_strat.sample_bandits(i)
  plot_priors(bayesian_strat, hidden_prob)
  plt.autoscale(tight=True)
plt.xlabel('Value')
plt.ylabel('Density')
plt.title("Posterior distributions of our inference about each bandit\
        after different numbers of pulls")
plt.tight_layout()
```

Note that we don't really care how accurate we become about the inference of the hidden probabilities—for this problem, we are more interested in choosing the best bandit (or, more accurately, becoming more confident in choosing the best bandit). For this reason, the distribution of the red bandit is very wide (representing ignorance about what that hidden probability might be), but we are reasonably confident that it is not the best, so the algorithm chooses to ignore it.

From Figure 6.4.1, we can see that after 1,000 pulls, the majority of the "blue" function leads the pack, hence we will almost always choose this arm. This is good, as this arm is indeed the best.

Deviations of the observed ratio from the highest probability is a measure of performance. For example, in the long run, optimally we can attain the reward/pull ratio of the maximum bandit probability. Long-term realized ratios less than the maximum represent inefficiencies. (Realized ratios larger than the maximum probability are due to randomness, and will eventually fall below.)

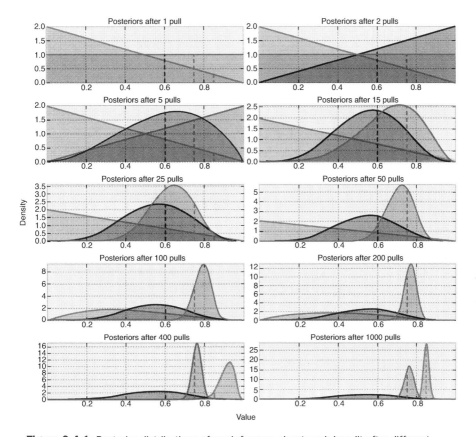

Figure 6.4.1: Posterior distributions of our inference about each bandit after different numbers of pulls

6.4.3 A Measure of Good

We need a metric to calculate how well we are doing. Recall that the absolute *best* we can do is to always pick the bandit with the largest probability of winning. Denote this best bandit's probability of winning as w_{opt}. Our score should be relative to how well we would have done had we chosen the best bandit from the beginning. This motivates the definition of the **total regret** of a strategy, defined as the difference between the payoff after T rounds of choosing the optimal strategy (always picking the bandit with the highest probability of success) and the payoff after T rounds of choosing another strategy, and mathematically defined as

$$R_T = \sum_{i=1}^{T} \left(w_{opt} - w_{B(i)} \right)$$

$$= Tw^* - \sum_{i=1}^{T} w_{B(i)}$$

In this equation, $w_{B(i)}$ is the probability of a prize of the chosen bandit in the ith round. A total regret of 0 means that the strategy is attaining the best possible score. This is likely not possible, as initially our algorithm will often make the wrong choice. Ideally, a strategy's total regret should flatten as it learns the best bandit. (Mathematically, we start to achieve $w_{B(i)} = w_{opt}$ often.)

In Figure 6.4.2, we plot the total regret of this simulation, including the scores of some other strategies.

1. Random: Randomly choose a bandit to pull. If you can't beat this, just stop.
2. Largest Bayesian credible bound: Pick the bandit with the largest upper bound in its 95% credible region of the underlying probability.
3. Bayes–UCB algorithm: Pick the bandit with the largest *score*, where score is a dynamic quantile of the posterior (see[2]).
4. Mean of posterior: Choose the bandit with the largest posterior mean. This is what a human player (sans computer) would likely do.
5. Largest proportion: Pick the bandit with the current largest observed proportion of winning.

The code for these is in the other_strats.py, where you can implement your own strategy very easily.

```
figsize(12.5, 5)
from other_strats import upper_credible_choice, bayesian_bandit_choice,
        ucb_bayesmax_mean, random_choice

# define a harder problem
hidden_prob = np.array([0.15, 0.2, 0.1, 0.05])
bandits = Bandits(hidden_prob)

# define regret
def regret(probabilities, choices):
  w_opt = probabilities.max()
  return(w_opt - probabilities[choices.astype(int)]).cumsum()

# create new strategies
strategies= [upper_credible_choice,
      bayesian_bandit_choice,
      ucb_bayes,
      max_mean,
      random_choice]
algos = []
for strat in strategies:
  algos.append(GeneralBanditStrat(bandits, strat))

# train 10,000 times
for strat in algos:
  strat.sample_bandits(10000)

# test and plot
for i,strat in enumerate(algos):
```

```
    _regret = regret(hidden_prob, strat.choices)
    plt.plot(_regret, label=strategies[i].__name__, lw = 3)

plt.title("Total regret of the Bayesian Bandits strategy versus random
          guessing")
plt.xlabel("Number of pulls")
plt.ylabel("Regret after $n$ pulls")
plt.legend(loc="upper left");
```

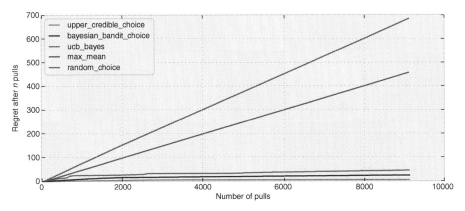

Figure 6.4.2: Total regret of the Bayesian Bandits strategy versus random guessing

Like we wanted, the Bayesian Bandits strategy and other strategies have decreasing rates of regret, representing that we are achieving optimal choices. To be more scientific so as to remove any possible luck in the previous simulation, we should instead look at the **expected total regret**, defined as the expected value of the total regret over all possible scenarios, and mathematically defined as

$$\bar{R}_T = E[R_T]$$

It can be shown that any suboptimal strategy's expected total regret is bounded below logarithmically. Formally:

$$E[R_T] = \Omega\left(\log(T)\right)$$

Thus, any strategy that matches logarithmic-growing regret is said to solve the multi-armed bandit problem.[4]

Using the Law of Large Numbers, we can approximate the Bayesian Bandits strategy's expected total regret by performing the same experiment many times (200 times, to be fair). The results are illustrated in Figure 6.4.3. To perhaps get a better idea of the differences in strategies, we also plot the same figure on a log-scale, illustrated in Figure 6.4.4.

```
# This can be slow, so I recommend NOT running it.

trials = 200
expected_total_regret = np.zeros((1000, 3))

for i_strat, strat in enumerate(strategies[:-2]):
  for i in range(trials):
    general_strat = GeneralBanditStrat(bandits, strat)
    general_strat.sample_bandits(1000)
    _regret = regret(hidden_prob, general_strat.choices)
    expected_total_regret[:,i_strat] += _regret

  plt.plot(expected_total_regret[:,i_strat]/trials, lw =3,
         label = strat.__name__)

plt.title("Expected total regret of different multi-armed bandit strategies")
plt.xlabel("Number of pulls")
plt.ylabel("Expected total regret \n after $n$ pulls")
plt.legend(loc="upper left");
```

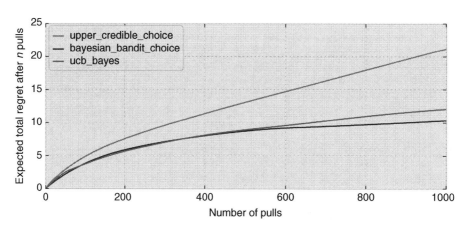

Figure 6.4.3: Expected total regret of different multi-armed bandit strategies

```
plt.figure()
[pl1, pl2, pl3] = plt.plot(expected_total_regret[:, [0,1,2]], lw = 3)
plt.xscale("log")
plt.legend([pl1, pl2, pl3],
       ["Upper credible bound", "Bayesian Bandits", "UCB-Bayes"],
       loc="upper left")
plt.ylabel(r "Expected total regret \n after $\log{n}$ pulls")
plt.xlabel("Number of pulls", $n$)
plt.title("Log-scale of the expected total regret of different multi-armed
         bandit strategies");
```

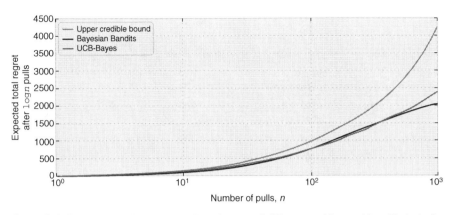

Figure 6.4.4: Log-scale of the expected total regret of different multi-armed bandit strategies

6.4.4 Extending the Algorithm

Because of the Bayesian Bandits algorithm's simplicity, it is easy to extend. Some possibilities are:

- If interested in the *minimum* probability (e.g., where prizes are a bad thing), simply choose $B = \operatorname{argmin} X_b$ and proceed.
- Adding learning rates: Suppose the underlying environment may change over time. Technically, the standard Bayesian Bandits algorithm would self-update (awesome!) by noting that what it thought was the best is starting to fail more often. We can motivate the algorithm to learn changing environments more quickly by simply adding a *rate* term upon updating.

```
self.wins[ choice ] = rate*self.wins[ choice ] + result
self.trials[ choice ] = rate*self.trials[ choice ] + 1
```

If `rate` < 1, the algorithm will forget its previous wins more quickly and there will be a downward pressure toward ignorance. Conversely, setting `rate` > 1 implies your algorithm will act in a riskier manner, and bet on earlier winners more often and be more resistant to changing environments.

- Hierarchical algorithms: We can set up a Bayesian Bandits algorithm on top of smaller bandit algorithms. Suppose we have N Bayesian Bandits models, each varying in some behavior (for example, different `rate` parameters, representing varying sensitivity to changing environments). On top of these N models is another Bayesian Bandits learner that will select a sub-Bayesian Bandits. This chosen Bayesian Bandits will then make an internal choice as to which machine to pull. The super-Bayesian Bandits updates itself depending on whether the sub-Bayesian Bandits was correct or not.
- Extending the rewards, denoted γ_a for bandit A, to random variables from a distribution $f_{\gamma_a}(\gamma)$ is straightforward. More generally, this problem can be rephrased as "Find the bandit with the largest expected value," as playing the bandit with the largest

expected value is optimal. In the preceding case, f_{y_a} was a Bernoulli random variable with probability p_a, hence the expected value for a bandit is equal to p_a, which is why it looks like we are aiming to maximize the probability of winning. If the prize is not Bernoulli, and it is non-negative, which can be accomplished by shifting the distribution (we assume we know f), then the algorithm behaves as before:

For each round,

1. Sample a random variable X_b from the prior of bandit b, for all b.
2. Select the bandit with largest sample; that is, select bandit $B = \text{argmax } X_b$.
3. Observe the result, $R \sim f_{y_b}$, of pulling bandit B, and update your prior on bandit B.
4. Return to 1.

The issue is in the sampling of the X_b drawing phase. With Beta priors and Bernoulli observations, we have a Beta posterior; this is easy to sample from. But now, with arbitrary distributions f, we have a non-trivial posterior. Sampling from these can be difficult.

There has been some interest in extending the Bayesian Bandits algorithm to commenting systems. Recall that in Chapter 4, we developed a ranking algorithm based on the Bayesian lower bound of the proportion of upvotes to the total number of votes. One problem with this approach is that it will bias the top rankings toward older comments, since older comments naturally have more votes (and hence the lower bound is tighter to the true proportion). This creates a positive feedback cycle where older comments gain more votes, hence are displayed more often, hence gain more votes, and so on. This pushes any new, potentially better comments toward the bottom. J. Neufeld proposes a system to remedy this that uses a Bayesian Bandits solution.

His proposal is to consider each comment as a bandit, with the number of pulls equal to the number of votes cast, and number of rewards as the number of upvotes, hence creating a Beta$(1 + U, 1 + D)$ posterior. As visitors visit the page, samples are drawn from each bandit/comment, but instead of displaying the comment with the max sample, the comments are ranked according to the ranking of their respective samples. From J. Neufeld's blog:[5]

> [The] resulting ranking algorithm is quite straightforward, each new time the comments page is loaded, the score for each comment is sampled from a Beta$(1 + U, 1 + D)$, comments are then ranked by this score in descending order... This randomization has a unique benefit in that even untouched comments ... have some chance of being seen even in threads with 5000+ comments (something that is not [happening] now), but, at the same time, the user will [sic] is not likely to be inundated with rating these new comments.

Just for fun, we watch the Bayesian Bandits algorithm learn 35 different options in Figure 6.4.5.

```
figsize(12.0, 8)
beta = stats.beta
hidden_prob = beta.rvs(1,13, size=35)
```

```
print hidden_prob
bandits = Bandits(hidden_prob)
bayesian_strat = BayesianStrategy(bandits)

for j,i in enumerate([100, 200, 500, 1300]):
    plt.subplot(2, 2, j+1)
    bayesian_strat.sample_bandits(i)
    plot_priors(bayesian_strat, hidden_prob, lw = 2, alpha = 0.0,
                plt_vlines=False)
    plt.xlim(0, 0.5)
```

```
[Output]:

[ 0.2411 0.0115 0.0369 0.0279 0.0834 0.0302 0.0073 0.0315 0.0646
  0.0602 0.1448 0.0393 0.0185 0.1107 0.0841 0.3154 0.0139 0.0526
  0.0274 0.0885 0.0148 0.0348 0.0258 0.0119 0.1877 0.0495 0.236
  0.0768 0.0662 0.0016 0.0675 0.027  0.015  0.0531 0.0384]
```

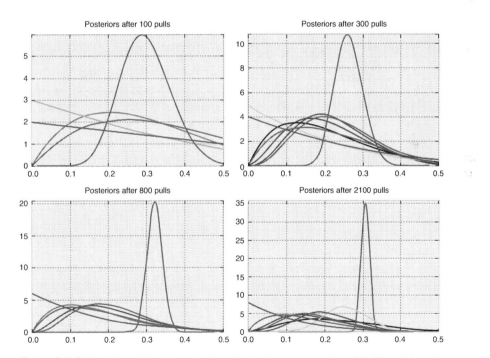

Figure 6.4.5: Evolution of the Bayesian Bandits strategy learning from 35 different bandits

6.5 Eliciting Prior Distributions from Domain Experts

Specifying a subjective prior is how practitioners incorporate domain knowledge about the problem into our mathematical framework. Allowing domain knowledge is useful for many reasons.

- It aids the speed of MCMC convergence. For example, if we know the unknown parameter is strictly positive, then we can restrict our attention there, hence saving time that would otherwise be spent exploring negative values.
- It allows for more accurate inference. By weighing prior values near the true unknown value higher, we are narrowing our eventual inference (by making the posterior tighter around the unknown).
- It expresses our uncertainty better. See the *Price Is Right* problem in Chapter 5.

Of course, practitioners of Bayesian methods are not experts in every field, so we must turn to domain experts to craft our priors. We must be careful with how we elicit these priors, though. Some things to consider:

- From experience, I would avoid introducing Betas, Gammas, and so forth to non-Bayesian practitioners. Furthermore, non-statisticians can get tripped up by how a continuous probability function can have a value exceeding 1.
- Individuals often neglect the rare tail-events and put too much weight around the mean of distribution.
- Individuals will almost always underemphasize the uncertainty in their guesses.

Eliciting priors from non-technical experts is especially difficult. Rather than introducing the notion of probability distributions, priors, and so forth that may scare an expert, the next section introduces a much simpler alternative.

6.5.1 Trial Roulette Method

The trial roulette method[6] focuses on building a prior distribution by placing counters (think casino chips) on what the expert thinks are possible outcomes. The expert is given N counters (say $N = 20$) and is asked to place them on a pre-printed grid, with bins representing intervals. Each column would represent their belief of the probability of getting the corresponding bin result. Each chip would represent a $\frac{1}{N} = 0.05$ increase in the probability of the outcome being in that interval. For example,[7] suppose a student is asked to predict the mark in a future exam. Figure 6.5.1 shows a completed grid for the elicitation of a subjective probability distribution. The horizontal axis of the grid shows the possible bins (or mark intervals) that the student was asked to consider. The numbers in the top row record the number of chips per bin. The completed grid (using a total of 20 chips) shows that the student believes there is a 30% chance that the mark will be between 50 and 59.9.

From this, we can fit a distribution that captures the expert's choice. There are several reasons in favor of using this technique.

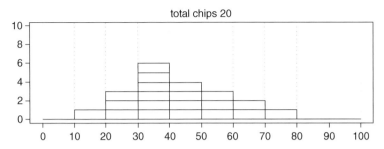

Figure 6.5.1: Trial roulette method of eliciting expert priors (image from [8])

- Many questions about the shape of the expert's subjective probability distribution can be answered without needing to pose a long series of questions to the expert; the statistician can simply read off the density below any given point, or that between any two points.

- During the process of creating the prior distribution, the expert can move around the chips if unsatisfied with the way he or she placed them initially; thus, the expert can be sure of the final result to be submitted.

- It forces the expert to be coherent in the set of probabilities that are provided. If all the chips are used, the probabilities must sum to 1.

- Graphical methods seem to provide more accurate results, especially for participants with modest levels of statistical sophistication.

6.5.2 Example: Stock Returns

Take note, stock brokers: You're doing it wrong. When choosing which stocks to pick, an analyst will often look at the **daily return** of the stock. If S_t is the price of the stock on day t, then the daily return on day t is:

$$r_t = \frac{S_t - S_{t-1}}{S_{t-1}}$$

The **expected daily return** of a stock is denoted $\mu = E[r_t]$. Obviously, stocks with high expected returns are desirable. Unfortunately, stock returns are so filled with noise that it is very hard to estimate this parameter. Furthermore, the parameter might change over time (consider the rises and falls of AAPL—Apple, Inc.—stock), hence it is unwise to use a large historical dataset.

Historically, the expected return has been estimated by using the sample mean. This is a bad idea. As mentioned, the sample mean of a small dataset has enormous potential to be very wrong (see Chapter 4 for full details). Thus, Bayesian inference is a very appropriate procedure here since we are able to see our uncertainty along with probable values.

For this exercise, we will be examining the daily returns of AAPL, GOOG (Google), TSLA (Tesla Motors), and AMZN (Amazon.com, Inc.). These stocks' daily returns are shown in Figures 6.5.3 and 6.5.4. Before we examine the data, suppose we ask our stock fund manager (an expert in finance, but see [9]), "What do you think the return profile looks like for each of these companies?" Our stock broker, without needing to know the language of Normal distributions, or priors, or variances, creates four distributions using the trial roulette method we detailed in the previous section. Suppose they look enough like Normals, so we fit Normals to them. In Figure 6.5.2 are possible priors from our stock broker.

```
figsize(11.0, 5)
colors = ["#348ABD", "#A60628", "#7A68A6", "#467821"]

normal = stats.norm
x = np.linspace(-0.15, 0.15, 100)

expert_prior_params = {"AAPL":(0.05, 0.03),
        "GOOG":(-0.03, 0.04),
        "TSLA": (-0.02, 0.01),
        "AMZN": (0.03, 0.02),
        }

for i, (name, params) in enumerate(expert_prior_params.iteritems()):
  plt.subplot(2,2,i)
  y = normal.pdf( x, params[0], scale=params[1] )
  plt.fill_between(x, 0, y, color=colors[i], linewidth=2,
        edgecolor=colors[i], alpha=0.6)
  plt.title(name + " prior")
  plt.vlines(0, 0, y.max(), "k","--", linewidth=0.5)
  plt.xlim(-0.15, 0.15)
plt.tight_layout()
```

Note that these are subjective priors: the expert has personal opinions on the stock returns of each of these companies and is expressing them in a distribution. This is not wishful thinking; they're introducing domain knowledge.

In order to better model these returns, we should investigate the covariance matrix of the returns. For example, it would be unwise to invest in two stocks that are highly correlated, since they are likely to tank together (a reason why fund managers suggest a diversification strategy). We will use the Wishart distribution for this, introduced in section 6.3.2.

```
import pymc as pm

n_observations = 100 # We will truncate the most recent 100 days.

prior_mu = np.array([x[0] for x in expert_prior_params.values()])
prior_std = np.array([x[1] for x in expert_prior_params.values()])

inv_cov_matrix = pm.Wishart("inv_cov_matrix", n_observations, np.diag
                (prior_std**2))
mu = pm.Normal("returns", prior_mu, 1, size=4)
```

Next, we pull historical data for these stocks.

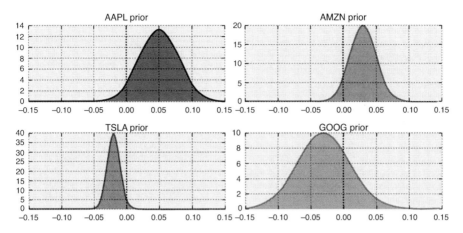

Figure 6.5.2: Prior distributions of the returns of different publically traded stocks

```
import datetime
import ystockquote as ysq

stocks = ["AAPL", "GOOG", "TSLA", "AMZN"]

enddate = datetime.datetime.now().strftime("%Y-%m-%d") # today's date
startdate = "2012-09-01"

stock_closes = {}
stock_returns = {}
CLOSE = 6

for stock in stocks:
  x = np.array(ysq.get_historical_prices(stock, startdate, enddate))
  stock_closes[stock] = x[1:,CLOSE].astype(float)

# create returns

for stock in stocks:
  _previous_day = np.roll(stock_closes[stock], -1)
  stock_returns[stock] = ((stock_closes[stock] - _previous_day)/
                  _previous_day)[:n_observations]

dates = map(lambda x: datetime.datetime.strptime(x, "%Y-%m-%d"),
    x[1:n_observations+1,0])

figsize(12.5, 4)

for _stock, _returns in stock_returns.iteritems():
  p = plt.plot((1+_returns)[::-1].cumprod()-1, '-o', label="%s"%_stock,
      markersize=4, markeredgecolor="none" )
```

(Continues)

(Continued)

```
plt.xticks( np.arange(100)[::-8],
    map(lambda x: datetime.datetime.strftime(x, "%Y-%m-%d"), dates[::8]),
    rotation=60);

plt.legend(loc="upper left")
plt.title("Return space representation of the price of the stocks")
plt.xlabel("Date")
plt.ylabel("Return of $1 on first date, x 100%");
```

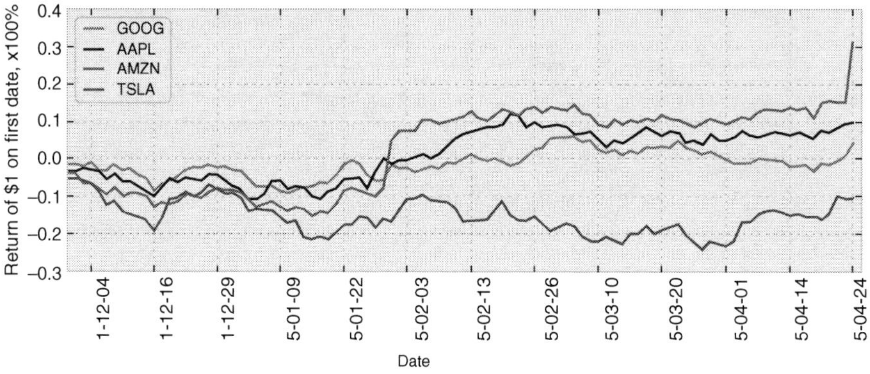

Figure 6.5.3: Return space representation of the price of the stocks

```
figsize(11.0, 5)
returns = np.zeros((n_observations,4))

for i, (_stock,_returns) in enumerate(stock_returns.iteritems()):
    returns[:,i] = _returns
    plt.subplot(2,2,i)
    plt.hist( _returns, bins=20,
            normed=True, histtype="stepfilled",
            color=colors[i], alpha=0.7)
    plt.title(_stock + " returns")
    plt.xlim(-0.15, 0.15)
    plt.xlabel('Value')
    plt.ylabel('Density')

plt.tight_layout()
plt.suptitle("Histogram of daily returns of stocks", size=14);
```

Next, we perform the inference on the posterior mean return and posterior covariance matrix. The resulting posterior distributions are shown in Figure 6.5.5.

```
obs = pm.MvNormal("observed returns", mu, inv_cov_matrix, observed=True,
    value=returns)

model = pm.Model([obs, mu, inv_cov_matrix])
mcmc = pm.MCMC()

mcmc.sample(150000, 100000, 3)
```

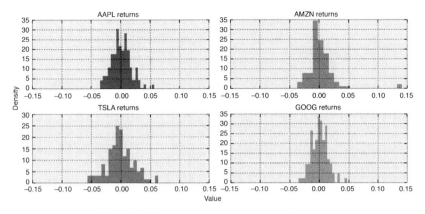

Figure 6.5.4: Histogram of daily returns of stocks

```
[Output]:

[****************100%******************]  150000 of 150000 complete
```

```
figsize(12.5,4)

# examine the mean return first
mu_samples = mcmc.trace("returns")[:]

for i in range(4):
  plt.hist(mu_samples[:,i], alpha = 0.8 - 0.05*i, bins=30,
           histtype="stepfilled", normed=True,
           label="%s"%stock_returns.keys()[i])

plt.vlines(mu_samples.mean(axis=0), 0, 500, linestyle="--", linewidth=.5)

plt.title("Posterior distribution of $\mu$, daily stock returns")
plt.xlabel('Value')
plt.ylabel('Density')
plt.legend();
```

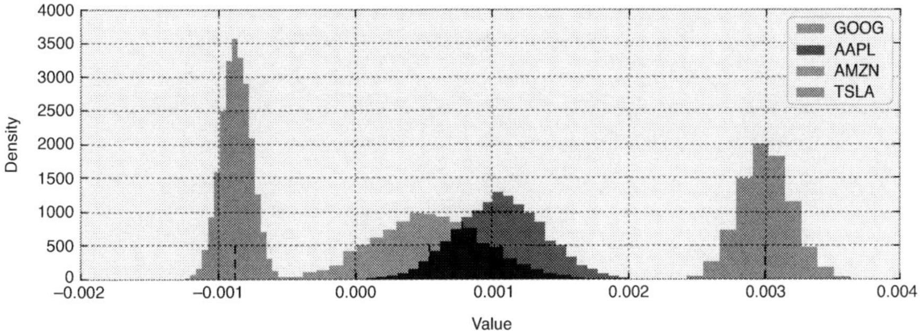

Figure 6.5.5: Posterior distribution of μ, daily stock returns

What can we say about the results? Clearly, TSLA has been a strong performer, and our analysis suggests that it has an almost 1% daily return! Similarly, most of the distribution of AAPL is negative, suggesting that its true daily return is negative.

You may not have immediately noticed, but these variables are a whole order of magnitude less than our priors on them. For example, in Figure 6.5.6, we put these posterior distributions on the same scale as the original prior distributions.

```
figsize(11.0,3)
for i in range(4):
  plt.subplot(2,2,i+1)
  plt.hist(mu_samples[:,i], alpha=0.8 - 0.05*i, bins=30,
           histtype="stepfilled", normed=True, color=colors[i],
           label="%s"%stock_returns.keys()[i])
  plt.title("%s"%stock_returns.keys()[i])
  plt.xlim(-0.15, 0.15)

plt.suptitle("Posterior distribution of daily stock returns")
plt.xlabel('Value')
plt.ylabel('Density')
plt.tight_layout()
```

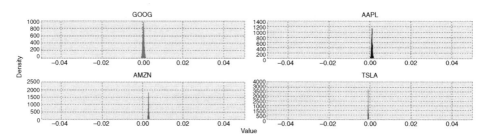

Figure 6.5.6: Posterior distribution of daily stock returns

Why did this occur? Recall that I mentioned that finance has a very very low signal-to-noise ratio. This implies an environment where inference is much more difficult. One should be careful about over-interpreting these results; notice (in Figure 6.5.5) that each distribution is positive at 0, implying that the stock may return nothing. Furthermore, the subjective priors influenced the results. From the fund manager's point of view, this is good, as it reflects his or her updated beliefs about the stocks, whereas from a neutral viewpoint, this result could be too subjective.

In Figure 6.5.7, we show the posterior correlation matrix and posterior standard deviations. An important caveat to know is that the Wishart distribution models the inverse covariance matrix, so we must invert it to get the covariance matrix. We also normalize the matrix to acquire the correlation matrix. Since we cannot plot hundreds of matrices effectively, we settle by summarizing the posterior distribution of correlation matrices by showing the **mean posterior correlation matrix**, or the element-wise expected value of the matrix's posterior distribution. Empirically, this can be computed by averaging over samples from the posterior.

```
inv_cov_samples = mcmc.trace("inv_cov_matrix")[:]
mean_covariance_matrix = np.linalg.inv(inv_cov_samples.mean(axis=0))


def cov2corr(A):
    """
    covariance matrix to correlation matrix
    """
    d = np.sqrt(A.diagonal())
    A = ((A.T/d).T)/d
    return A


plt.subplot(1,2,1)
plt.imshow(cov2corr(mean_covariance_matrix), interpolation="none",
           cmap = plt.cm.hot)
plt.xticks(np.arange(4), stock_returns.keys())
plt.yticks(np.arange(4), stock_returns.keys())
plt.colorbar(orientation="vertical")
plt.title("(Mean posterior) correlation matrix")

plt.subplot(1,2,2)
plt.bar(np.arange(4), np.sqrt(np.diag(mean_covariance_matrix)),
        color="#348ABD", alpha=0.7)
plt.xticks(np.arange(4) + 0.5, stock_returns.keys());
plt.title("(Mean posterior) variances of daily stock returns")
plt.xlabel('Value')
plt.ylabel('Density')

plt.tight_layout();
```

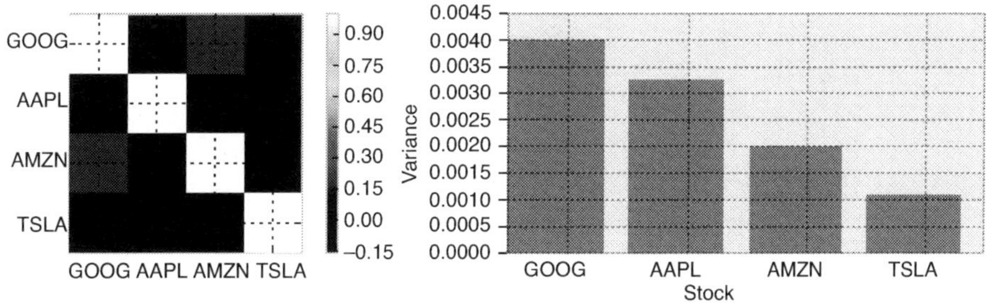

Figure 6.5.7: Left: (Mean posterior) correlation matrix. Right: (Mean posterior) variances of daily stock returns.

Looking at Figure 6.5.7, we can say that it is likely that TSLA has above-average volatility (looking at the return graph, this is quite clear). The correlation matrix shows that there are no strong correlations present, but perhaps GOOG and AMZN express a higher correlation (about 0.30).

With this Bayesian analysis of the stock market, we can throw it into a mean-variance optimizer (I cannot stress this strongly enough: Do *not* use a mean-variance optimizer with frequentist point estimates!) and find the minimum. This optimizer balances the trade-off between a high return and high variance. Denote the optimal weight as w_{opt}, and our maximizing function is

$$w_{opt} = \max_{w} \frac{1}{N} \left(\sum_{i=0}^{N} \mu_i^T w - \frac{\lambda}{2} w^T \Sigma_i w \right)$$

where μ_i and Σ_i are the ith posterior estimate of the mean returns and the covariance matrix. This is another example of loss function optimization.

6.5.3   Pro Tips for the Wishart Distribution

In the previous example, the Wishart distribution behaves pretty nicely. Unfortunately, this is rarely the case. The problem is that estimating an N-by-N covariance matrix involves estimating $\frac{1}{2}N(N-1)$ unknowns. This is a large number even for a modest N. Personally, I've tried performing a simulation similar to the preceding with $N = 23$ stocks, and ended up giving up considering that I was requesting my MCMC simulation to estimate at least $23 * 11 = 253$ additional unknowns (plus the other interesting unknowns in the problem). This is not easy for MCMC. Essentially, you are asking MCMC to traverse a 250-plus-dimensional space. And the problem seemed so innocent initially! Following are some tips.

1. Use *conjugancy* if it applies (see section 6.6).

2. Use a good starting value. What might be a good starting value? Why, the data's sample covariance matrix! Note that this is not empirical Bayes; we are not touching the prior's parameters, but rather are modifying the starting value of the MCMC. Due to numerical instability, it is best to truncate the floats in the sample covariance matrix down a few degrees of precision (instability can cause asymmetrical matrices, which can cause PyMC to cry).

3. Provide as much domain knowledge in the form of priors, if possible. I stress "if possible." It is likely impossible to have an estimate about each $\frac{1}{2}N(N-1)$ unknown. In this case, see tip #4.

4. Use empirical Bayes; that is, use the sample covariance matrix as the prior's parameter.

5. For problems where N is very large, nothing is going to help. Instead, ask yourself, do I really care about *every* correlation? Probably not. Furthermore, ask yourself, do I really, *really* care about correlations? Possibly not. In finance, we can set an informal hierarchy of what we might be interested in the most: first, a good estimate of μ; second, the variances along the diagonal of the covariance matrix; and least

important, the correlations. So, it might be better to ignore the $\frac{1}{2}(N-1)(N-2)$ correlations and instead focus on the more important unknowns.

6.6 Conjugate Priors

Recall that a Beta prior with binomial data implies a Beta posterior. Graphically:

$$\overbrace{\text{Beta}}^{\text{prior}} \cdot \overbrace{\text{Binomial}}^{\text{data}} = \overbrace{\text{Beta}}^{\text{posterior}}$$

Notice the Beta on both sides of this equation—no, you cannot cancel them out; this is not a *real* equation, just a model. This is a really useful property. It allows us to avoid using MCMC, since the posterior is known in closed form. Hence inference and analytics are easy to derive. This shortcut was the heart of the Bayesian Bandits algorithm. Fortunately, there is an entire family of distributions that have similar behavior.

Suppose X comes from, or is believed to come from, a well-known distribution—call it f_α—where α are possibly unknown parameters of f (f could be a Normal distribution, or binomial distribution, etc.). For particular distributions f_α, there may exist a prior distribution p_β such that

$$\overbrace{p_\beta}^{\text{prior}} \cdot \overbrace{f_\alpha(X)}^{\text{data}} = \overbrace{p_{\beta'}}^{\text{posterior}}$$

where β' is a different set of parameters but p is the same distribution as the prior. A prior p that satisfies this relationship is called a *conjugate prior*. As I mentioned, they are useful computationally, as we can avoid approximate inference using MCMC and go directly to the posterior. This sounds great, right?

Unfortunately, not quite. There are a couple issues with conjugate priors.

- The conjugate prior is not objective. Hence it is only useful when a subjective prior is required. It is not guaranteed that the conjugate prior can accommodate the practitioner's subjective opinion.

- There typically exist conjugate priors for simple, one-dimensional problems. For larger problems, involving more complicated structures, hope is lost to find a conjugate prior. For these simpler models, Wikipedia has a nice table of conjugate priors.[10]

Really, conjugate priors are only useful for their mathematical convenience: It is simple to go from prior to posterior. I personally see conjugate priors as only a neat mathematical trick that offers little insight into the problem at hand.

6.7 Jeffreys Priors

Earlier, we talked about objective priors rarely being objective. In part, what we mean by this is that we want a prior that doesn't bias our posterior estimates. The flat prior seems like a reasonable choice, as it assigns equal probability to all values.

But the flat prior is not *transformation-invariant*. What does this mean? Suppose we have a random variable **X** from Bernoulli(θ). We define the prior on $p(\theta) = 1$. This is shown in Figure 6.7.1.

```
figsize(12.5, 5)

x = np.linspace(0.000, 1, 150)
y = np.linspace(1.0, 1.0, 150)
lines = plt.plot(x, y, color="#A60628", lw=3)
plt.fill_between(x, 0, y, alpha=0.2, color=lines[0].get_color())
plt.autoscale(tight=True)
plt.xlabel('Value')
plt.ylabel('Density')
plt.ylim(0, 2);
```

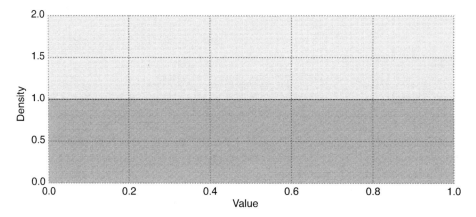

Figure 6.7.1: Prior of θ

Now, let's transform θ with the function $\psi = \log\left(\frac{\theta}{1-\theta}\right)$. This is just a function to stretch θ across the real line. Now how likely are different values of ψ under our transformation?

```
figsize(12.5, 5)

psi = np.linspace(-10, 10, 150)
y = np.exp(psi) / (1 + np.exp(psi))**2
lines = plt.plot(psi, y, color="#A60628", lw = 3)
plt.fill_between(psi, 0, y, alpha = 0.2, color = lines[0].get_color())
plt.autoscale(tight=True)
plt.xlabel('Value')
plt.ylabel('Density')
plt.ylim(0, 1);
```

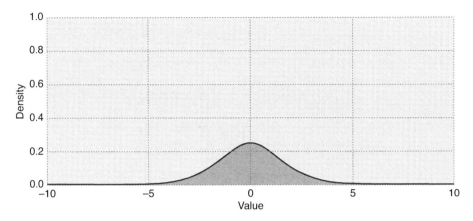

Figure 6.7.2: Prior of $\psi = \log\left(\frac{\theta}{1-\theta}\right)$

As you can see in Figure 6.7.2, it appears that our function is no longer flat! As it turns out, flat priors do carry information in them after all. The point of Jeffreys priors is to create priors that don't accidentally become informative when you transform the variables you originally placed them on. There is lots of literature on Jeffreys priors, but it is beyond the scope of this book.

6.8   Effect of the Prior as *N* Increases

In Chapter 1, I proposed that as the amount of observations, or data, that we possess increases, the less the prior matters. This is intuitive. After all, our prior is based on previous information, and eventually enough new information will overshadow our previous information's value. The smothering of the prior by enough data is also helpful; if our prior is significantly wrong, then the self-correcting nature of the data will present to us a *less wrong*, and eventually *correct*, posterior.

We can see this mathematically. First, recall Bayes' Theorem from Chapter 1 that relates the prior to the posterior.

The posterior distribution for a parameter θ, given a dataset $\mathbf{X}$ can be written as

$$p(\theta|\mathbf{X}) \propto \underbrace{p(\mathbf{X}|\theta)}_{\text{likelihood}} \cdot \overbrace{p(\theta)}^{\text{prior}}$$

or, as is more commonly displayed on the log scale,

$$\log(p(\theta|\mathbf{X})) = c + L(\theta;\mathbf{X}) + \log(p(\theta))$$

The log-likelihood, $L(\theta; \mathbf{X}) = \log\big(p(\mathbf{X}|\theta)\big)$, *scales with the sample size*, since it is a function of the data, while the prior density does not. Therefore, as the sample size increases, the absolute value of $L(\theta; \mathbf{X})$ is getting larger while $\log(p(\theta))$ stays fixed (for a fixed value of θ); thus, the sum $L(\theta; \mathbf{X}) + \log(p(\theta))$ becomes more heavily influenced by $L(\theta; \mathbf{X})$ as the sample size increases.

There is an interesting consequence perhaps not immediately apparent. As the sample size increases, the chosen prior has less influence. Hence inference converges regardless of chosen prior, so long as the areas of non–zero probabilities are the same.

In Figure 6.8.1, we visualize this. We examine the convergence of two posteriors of a binomial's parameter θ, one with a flat prior and the other with a biased prior toward 0. As the sample size increases, the posteriors, and hence the inference, converge.

```
figsize(12.5, 15)

p = 0.6
beta1_params = np.array([1.,1.])
beta2_params = np.array([2,10])
beta = stats.beta

x = np.linspace(0.00, 1, 125)
data = pm.rbernoulli(p, size=500)

plt.figure()
for i,N in enumerate([0, 4, 8, 32, 64, 128, 500]):
  s = data[:N].sum()
  plt.subplot(8, 1, i+1)
  params1 = beta1_params + np.array([s, N-s])
  params2 = beta2_params + np.array([s, N-s])
  y1,y2 = beta.pdf(x, *params1), beta.pdf(x, *params2)
  plt.plot(x, y1, label="flat prior", lw =3)
  plt.plot(x, y2, label="biased prior", lw= 3)
  plt.fill_between(x, 0, y1, color="#348ABD", alpha=0.15)
  plt.fill_between(x, 0, y2, color="#A60628", alpha=0.15)
  plt.legend(title="N=%d"%N)
  plt.vlines(p, 0.0, 7.5, linestyles="--", linewidth=1)
  plt.xlabel('Value')
  plt.ylabel('Density')
  plt.title("Convergence of posterior distributions (with different priors)
            as we observe more and more information")
```

Keep in mind that not all posteriors will "forget" the prior this quickly. This example was just to show that *eventually* the prior is forgotten. The "forgetfulness" of the prior as we become awash in more and more data is the reason why Bayesian and frequentist inference eventually converge as well.

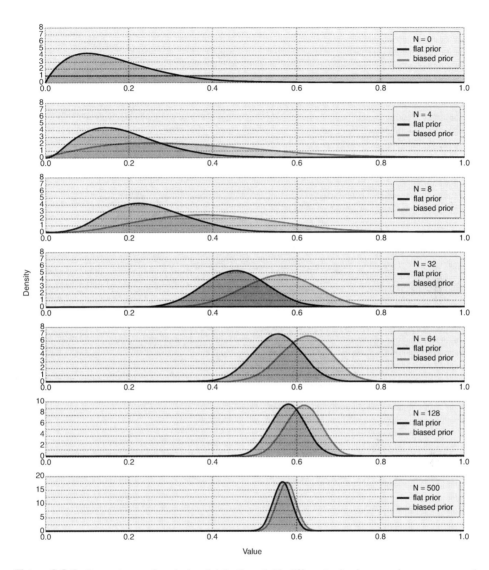

Figure 6.8.1: Convergence of posterior distributions (with different priors) as we observe more and more information

6.9   Conclusion

This chapter has reevaluated our use of priors; a prior becomes another object to add to our model, and one that should be chosen with great care. Often, the prior is seen as both the weakest and the strongest point of Bayesian inference—the former because the idea of choosing a prior invokes subjectivity and opinions, and the latter because it allows very flexible models, for any data.

Hundreds of papers have been written on the subject of priors, and research in this area has expanded the breadth of Bayesian analysis. Its importance should not be understated—including in practice. I hope that this chapter has given you some heuristics for choosing well-behaving priors.

6.10   Appendix

6.10.1   Bayesian Perspective of Penalized Linear Regressions

There is a very interesting relationship between a penalized least-squares regression and Bayesian priors. A penalized linear regression is an optimization problem of the form

$$\text{argmin}_\beta \ (Y - X\beta)^T(Y - X\beta) + f(\beta)$$

for some function f, typically a norm like $||\cdot||_p^p$. For $p = 1$, we recover the LASSO model, which penalizes the absolute value of the coefficients in β. For $p = 2$, we recover ridge regression, which penalizes the square of the coefficients in β.

We will first describe the probabilistic interpretation of least-squares linear regression. Denote our response variable Y, and features are contained in the data matrix X. The standard linear model is

$$Y = X\beta + \epsilon$$

where $\epsilon \sim \text{Normal}(\mathbf{0}, \sigma \mathbf{I})$, $\mathbf{0}$ is the vector of all zeros, and $\mathbf{I}$ is the identity matrix. Simply, the observed Y is a linear function of X (with coefficients β) plus some noise term. Our unknown to be determined is β. We use the property of Normal random variables

$$\mu' + \text{Normal}(\mu, \sigma) \sim \text{Normal}(\mu' + \mu, \sigma)$$

to rewrite the linear model as

$$Y = X\beta + \text{Normal}(\mathbf{0}, \sigma \mathbf{I})$$
$$Y = \text{Normal}(X\beta, \sigma \mathbf{I})$$

In probabilistic notation, denote the probability distribution of Y as $f_Y(y \mid \beta)$, and recall the density function for a Normal random variable (see [11]):

$$f_Y(Y \mid \beta, X) = \text{Likelihood}(\beta \mid X, Y) = \frac{1}{\sqrt{2\pi}\sigma} \exp\left(\frac{1}{2\sigma^2}(Y - X\beta)^T(Y - X\beta)\right)$$

This is the likelihood function for β. We take the log

$$\ell(\beta) = K - c(Y - X\beta)^T(Y - X\beta)$$

where K and $c > 0$ are constants. Maximum likelihood techniques wish to maximize this for β,

$$\hat{\beta} = \text{argmax}_\beta \; -(Y - X\beta)^T(Y - X\beta)$$

Equivalently, we can *minimize the negative* of this:

$$\hat{\beta} = \text{argmin}_\beta \; (Y - X\beta)^T(Y - X\beta)$$

This is the familiar least-squares linear regression equation. Therefore, we showed that the solution to a linear least-squares is the same as the maximum likelihood assuming Normal noise. Next we extend this to show how we can arrive at penalized linear regression by a suitable choice of prior on β.

In the preceding, once we have the likelihood, we can include a prior distribution on β to derive the equation for the posterior distribution

$$P(\beta | Y, X) = \text{Likelihood}(\beta | X, Y)p(\beta)$$

where $p(\beta)$ is a prior on the elements of β. What are some interesting priors?

1. If we include no explicit prior term, we are actually including an uninformative prior, $P(\beta) \propto 1$. Think of it as uniform over all numbers.

2. If we have reason to believe the elements of β are not too large, we can suppose that

$$\beta \sim \text{Normal}(\mathbf{0}, \lambda\mathbf{I})$$

The resulting posterior density function for β is *proportional to*

$$\exp\left(\frac{1}{2\sigma^2}(Y - X\beta)^T(Y - X\beta)\right)\exp\left(\frac{1}{2\lambda^2}\beta^T\beta\right)$$

and taking the log of this, and combining and redefining constants, we arrive at

$$\ell(\beta) \propto K - (Y - X\beta)^T(Y - X\beta) - \alpha\beta^T\beta$$

We arrive at the function we wish to maximize (recall the point that maximizes the posterior distribution is the MAP, or maximum a posterior):

$$\hat{\beta} = \text{argmax}_\beta \; -(Y - X\beta)^T(Y - X\beta) - \alpha\,\beta^T\beta$$

Equivalently, we can minimize the negative of this, and rewriting $\beta^T\beta = ||\beta||_2^2$,

$$\hat{\beta} = \text{argmin}_\beta \; (Y - X\beta)^T(Y - X\beta) + \alpha\,||\beta||_2^2$$

This term is exactly ridge regression. Thus we can see that ridge regression corresponds to the MAP of a linear model with Normal errors and a Normal prior on β.

3. Similarly, if we assume a prior from a Laplace distribution for β,

$$f_\beta(\beta) \propto \exp\left(-\lambda||\beta||_1\right)$$

and following the same steps as before, we recover:

$$\hat{\beta} = \text{argmin}_\beta \ (Y - X\beta)^T(Y - X\beta) + \alpha \ ||\beta||_1$$

which is LASSO regression. Some important notes about this equivalence: The sparsity that is a result of using a LASSO regularization is not a result of the prior assigning high probability to values of 0; quite the opposite, actually. It is the combination of the $||\cdot||_1$ function and using the MAP that creates sparsity on β. The prior does contribute to an overall shrinking of the coefficients toward 0, though. An interesting discussion of this can be found in [12].

For an example of Bayesian linear regression, see Chapter 5's example on financial losses.

6.10.2 Picking a Degenerate Prior

So long as the prior has non-zero probability in an area, the posterior can assign any amount of probability there. What happens when we assign 0 prior probability to an area that the true value does indeed belong to? We'll perform a small experiment to demonstrate just that. Suppose we observe Bernoulli data, and we wish to estimate the value of p (the probability of a success).

```
p_actual = 0.35
x = np.random.binomial(1, p_actual, size=100)
print x[:10]
```

```
[Output]:

[0 0 0 0 1 0 0 0 1 1]
```

We are going to pick a bad prior for p; let's choose Uniform(0.5, 1). This prior has assigned 0 probability to the true value of 0.35. Let's see what happens to our inference:

```
import pymc as pm

p = pm.Uniform('p', 0.5, 1)
obs = pm.Bernoulli('obs', p, value=x, observed=True)

mcmc = pm.MCMC([p, obs])
mcmc.sample(10000, 2000)
```

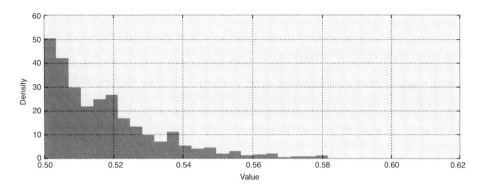

Figure 6.10.1: Posterior distribution of unknown *p* with a Uniform (0.5, 1) prior

```
[Output]:

[------------------100%------------------] 10000 of 10000 complete in 0.7 sec
```

```
p_trace = mcmc.trace('p')[:]
plt.xlabel('Value')
plt.ylabel('Density')
plt.hist(p_trace, bins=30, histtype='stepfilled', normed=True);
```

In Figure 6.10.1, we can see that the posterior distribution smashes up against the lower bound of the prior. This suggests that the true value is likely below 0.5. Seeing this behavior in posteriors is a good indicator that your prior assumptions are incorrect.

6.11 References

1. Gelman, Andrew and Cosma Rohilla Shalizi. "Philosophy and the Practice of Bayesian Statistics," *British Journal of Mathematical and Statistical Psychology* 66 (2013): 8–38.

2. Gelman, Andrew. "Prior Distributions for Variance Parameters in Hierarchical Models," *Bayesian Analysis* 1, no. 3 (2006): 515–34.

3. Scott, Steven L. "A Modern Bayesian Look at the Multi-Armed Bandit," *Applied Stochastic Models in Business and Industry* 26 (2010): 639–58.

4. Kuleshov, Volodymyr, and Doina Precup. "Algorithms for the Multi-Armed Bandit Problem," *Journal of Machine Learning Research* 1 (2000): 1–48.

5. Neufeld, James. "Reddit's 'Best' Comment Scoring Algorithm as a Multi-Armed Bandit Task," Simple ML Hacks, posted April 9, 2013, accessed April 25, 2013, `http://simplemlhacks.blogspot.com/2013/04/reddits-best-comment-scoring-algorithm.html`.

6. Oakley, Jeremy E., Alireza Daneshkhah, and Anthony O'Hagan. "Nonparametric Elicitation Using the Roulette Method," unpublished paper, accessed June 2, 2015, `http://www.tonyohagan.co.uk/academic/pdf/`

    `elic-roulette.pdf.`

7. "Eliciting Priors from Experts," Cross Validated, accessed May 1, 2013, `http://stats.stackexchange.com/questions/1/` `eliciting-priors-from-experts.`

8. Oakley, Jeremy E. "Eliciting Univariate Probability Distributions," unpublished paper, last modified September 10, 2010, accessed November 29, 2014, `http://www.jeremy-oakley.staff.shef.ac.uk/` `Oakley_elicitation.pdf.`

9. Taleb, Nassim Nicholas. *The Black Swan: The Impact of the Highly Improbable.* New York: Random House, 2007.

10. "Conjugate Prior," Wikipedia, The Free Encyclopedia, last modified June 6, 2015, 10:23 PM EST, accessed June 10, 2015, `https://en.wikipedia.org/wiki/Conjugate_prior.`

11. "Normal Distribution," Wikipedia, The Free Encyclopedia, last modified June 1, 2015, 12:38 AM EST, accessed June 10, 2015, `https://en.wikipedia.org/wiki/Normal_distribution.`

12. Starck, J.-L., D. L. Donoho, M. J. Fadili, and A. Rassat. "Sparsity and the Bayesian Perspective," *Astronomy and Astrophysics* (February 18, 2013): n. page.

7

Bayesian A/B Testing

7.1   Introduction

Part of a statistician's or data scientist's goal is to be a champion of experiments, and one of the best tools for a data scientist is a well-designed split-test experiment. We've seen split-tests previously. In Chapter 2, we introduced Bayesian analysis of an A/B test on conversion rates for a Web site. This chapter will extend that analysis to new areas.

7.2   Conversion Testing Recap

The fundamental idea in an A/B test is that we consider a perfect counterfactual universe, where the population under study is identical but subject to some treatment, then any differences between the populations after the study must be attributed to the treatment. In practice, we can't spin up other universes, so we rely on using large enough samples in two groups that *approximate* a counterfactual.

Let's recall our example from Chapter 2: we have two Web site designs, called *A* and *B*. When a user lands on our Web site, we randomly show them design *A* or *B*, and record this assignment. After enough visitors have done this, we join this dataset against some metric of interest (typically, for Web sites, we are interested in a purchase or signup). For example, consider the following numbers:

```
visitors_to_A = 1300
visitors_to_B = 1275

conversions_from_A = 120
conversions_from_B = 125
```

What we are really interested in is the probability of conversion, given site *A* or *B*. As a business, we want this probability to be as high possible. So our goal is to determine which site, *A* or *B*, has a high probability of conversion.

To do this, we'll model the probability of conversion given site *A*, or site *B*. Since we are modeling a probability, a good choice for a prior distribution is the Beta distribution. (Why? It is restricted to values between 0 and 1, identical to the range that probabilities can take on.) Our number of visitors and conversion data are binomial: for site A, out of 1,300 *trials*, we had 120 *successes*. You'll recall from Chapter 6 that a Beta prior and binomial observations have a conjugate relationship; this means we don't need to perform any MCMC!

If my prior is Beta(α_0, β_0), and I observe N trials and X successes, then my posterior is Beta($\alpha_0 + X, \beta_0 + N - X$). Using the built in beta function from SciPy, we can directly sample from the posterior.

Let's suppose our prior is a Beta(1, 1); recall that this is identical to a uniform distribution on [0, 1].

```
from scipy.stats import beta
alpha_prior = 1
beta_prior = 1

posterior_A = beta(alpha_prior + conversions_from_A,
                   beta_prior + visitors_to_A - conversions_from_A)

posterior_B = beta(alpha_prior + conversions_from_B,
                   beta_prior + visitors_to_B - conversions_from_B)
```

Next, we'd like to determine which group has a large probability of conversion. To do this, similar to MCMC, we use samples from the posterior and compare the probability that samples from the posterior of A are larger than samples from the posterior of B. We use the rvs method to generate samples.

```
samples = 20000 # We want this to be large to get a better approximation.
samples_posterior_A = posterior_A.rvs(samples)
samples_posterior_B = posterior_B.rvs(samples)

print (samples_posterior_A > samples_posterior_B).mean()
```

```
[Output]:

0.31355
```

So we can see here that there is a 31% chance that site A converts better than site B. (Conversely, there is a 69% chance that site B converts better than A.) This is not very significant; consider that if we reran this experiment with identical pages, it would return a probability close to 50%.

We can visualize the posterior, too, without using histograms. This is done by using the pdf method. Figure 7.2.1 shows the conversion posteriors of sites A and B.

```
%matplotlib inline
from IPython.core.pylabtools import figsize
from matplotlib import pyplot as plt
figsize(12.5, 4)
plt.rcParams['savefig.dpi'] = 300
plt.rcParams['figure.dpi'] = 300
```

```
x = np.linspace(0,1, 500)
plt.plot(x, posterior_A.pdf(x), label='posterior of A')
plt.plot(x, posterior_B.pdf(x), label='posterior of B')
plt.xlabel('Value')
plt.ylabel('Density')
plt.title("Posterior distributions of the conversion
          rates of Web pages $A$ and $B$")
plt.legend();
```

In Figure 7.2.2, we zoom in closer to the area of interest.

```
plt.plot(x, posterior_A.pdf(x), label='posterior of A')
plt.plot(x, posterior_B.pdf(x), label='posterior of B')
plt.xlim(0.05, 0.15)
plt.xlabel('Value')
plt.ylabel('Density')
plt.title("Zoomed-in posterior distributions of the conversion\
          rates of Web pages $A$ and $B$")
plt.legend();
```

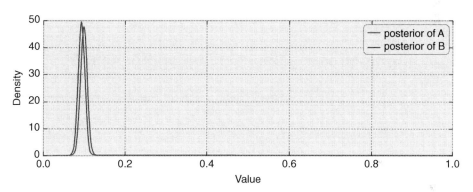

Figure 7.2.1: Posterior distributions of the conversion rates of Web pages *A* and *B*

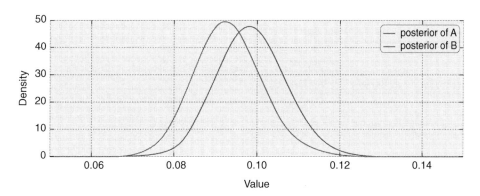

Figure 7.2.2: Zoomed-in posterior distributions of the conversion rates of Web pages *A* and *B*

Conversion tests are popular because of their simplicity: The observable is binary and the analysis is straightforward. What happens when you have multiple paths a user could take, and there are business implications for each path? We'll explore this next.

7.3 Adding a Linear Loss Function

A common goal of Internet companies is not only to gain signups, but also to optimize which signup plan the user might select. For example, a business might want new customers to choose a higher-priced plan if presented with two or more plan options.

Suppose users are shown two different versions of this pricing page, and we'd like to determine the *expected revenue* we receive per impression. Our previous A/B test analysis was only concerned with whether the user signed up or not; now, we want to know what the expected revenue to be earned is.

7.3.1 Expected Revenue Analysis

For the moment, ignore the A/B test and consider the analysis for a single Web page style. In a completely transparent world, where we knew everything, we could calculate this expected value for this fictional company:

$$E[R] = 79p_{79} + 49p_{49} + 25p_{25} + 0p_0$$

where p_{79} is the probability of selecting the \$79 pricing plan, and so on. I've also included a fictional \$0 pricing plan for someone who *doesn't* pick a plan. This is added so that the probabilities sum to 1.

$$p_{79} + p_{49} + p_{25} + p_0 = 1$$

The next step is to estimate these probabilities. We can't use a Beta/binomial model for each probability, as the probabilities are correlated; they must sum to 1. For example, if p_{79} is high, then the other probabilities must be low. We need to model all the probabilities together.

There is a generalization of the binomial distribution called the multinomial distribution. It's available in both PyMC and NumPy, but I'll use the latter. In the following code, I set a probability vector, denoted by P, that specifies what the probability is that an individual would fall into that bucket. If we set the length of P to 2 (and make sure the values inside sum to 1), then we recover the familiar binomial distribution

```
from numpy.random import multinomial
P = [0.5, 0.2, 0.3]
N = 1
print multinomial(N, P)
```

```
[Output]:

[1 0 0]
```

```
N = 10
print multinomial(N, P)
```

```
[Output]:

[4 3 3]
```

For our signup page, our observables follow a multinomial distribution, where we do not know the values of the probability vector P.

There is a generalization of the Beta distribution as well. It is called the *Dirichlet distribution*. It returns a vector of positive values that sum to 1. The length of this vector is determined by the length of an input vector, and this input vector's values are analogous to a parameter in a prior.

```
from numpy.random import dirichlet
sample = dirichlet([1,1]) # [1,1] is equivalent to a Beta(1,1)
# distribution.
print sample
print sample.sum()
```

```
[Output]:

[ 0.3591  0.6409]
1.0
```

```
sample = dirichlet([1,1,1,1])
print sample
print sample.sum()
```

```
[Output]:

[ 1.5935e-01  6.1971e-01  2.2033e-01  6.0750e-04]
1.0
```

Luckily, we have a relationship between the Dirichlet and multinomial distributions similar to that between the Beta and the binomial distributions. The Dirichlet distribution is a conjugate prior to the multinomial distribution! This means we have exact formulas for the posteriors of the unknown probabilities. If our prior is Dirichlet$(1, 1, \ldots, 1)$, and our observables are $N_1, N_2, \ldots, N_m$, then our posterior is

$$\text{Dirichlet}(1 + N_1, 1 + N_2, ..., 1 + N_m)$$

Samples from this posterior will always sum to 1, so we can use these samples in the expected value formula from 7.3.1. Let's try this with some sample data. Suppose 1,000 people view the page, and we have the following signups.

```
N    = 1000
N_79 = 10
N_49 = 46
N_25 = 80
N_0  = N - (N_79 + N_49 + N_49)

observations = np.array([N_79, N_49, N_25, N_0])

prior_parameters = np.array([1,1,1,1])
posterior_samples = dirichlet(prior_parameters + observations,
                              size=10000)

print "Two random samples from the posterior:"
print posterior_samples[0]
print posterior_samples[1]
```

```
[Output]:

Two random samples from the posterior:
[ 0.0165  0.0497  0.0638  0.8701]
[ 0.0123  0.0404  0.0694  0.878 ]
```

We can plot the probability density function of this posterior, too:

```
for i, label in enumerate(['p_79', 'p_49', 'p_25', 'p_0']):
    ax = plt.hist(posterior_samples[:,i], bins=50,
                  label=label, histtype='stepfilled')

plt.xlabel('Value')
plt.ylabel('Density')
plt.title("Posterior distributions of the probability of\
          selecting different prices")
plt.legend();
```

As you can see in Figure 7.3.1, there is still uncertainty in what we think the probabilities might be, so there will also be uncertainty in our expected value. That's okay; what we get is a posterior of our expected value. We do this by passing each sample from the Dirichlet posterior through the following expected_revenue function.

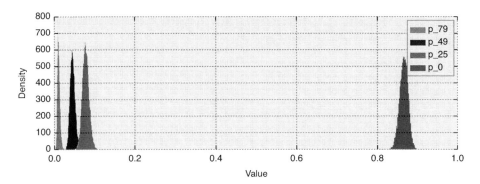

Figure 7.3.1: Posterior distributions of the probability of selecting different prices

This approach should feel a lot like using a loss function, as that is essentially what we are doing: We are estimating parameters, then passing them through a loss function to relate them back to the real world.

```
def expected_revenue(P):
    return 79*P[:,0] + 49*P[:,1] + 25*P[:,2] + 0*P[:,3]

posterior_expected_revenue = expected_value(posterior_samples)
plt.hist(posterior_expected_revenue, histtype='stepfilled',
        label='expected revenue', bins=50)
plt.xlabel('Value')
plt.ylabel('Density')
plt.title("Posterior distributions of the expected revenue")
plt.legend();
```

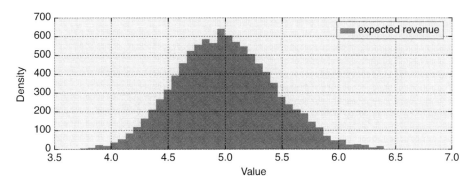

Figure 7.3.2: Posterior distributions of the expected revenue

We can see from Figure 7.3.2 that the expected revenue is likely between \$4 and \$6, and unlikely to be outside this range.

7.3.2   Extending to an A/B Experiment

Let's try this analysis with two different Web pages, denoted site *A* and *B*, for which I've created some artificial data:

```
N_A     = 1000
N_A_79 = 10
N_A_49 = 46
N_A_25 = 80
N_A_0   = N_A - (N_A_79 + N_A_49 + N_A_49)
observations_A = np.array([N_A_79, N_A_49, N_A_25, N_A_0])


N_B     = 2000
N_B_79 = 45

N_B_49 = 84
N_B_25 = 200
N_B_0   = N_B - (N_B_79 + N_B_49 + N_B_49)
observations_B = np.array([N_B_79, N_B_49, N_B_25, N_B_0])


prior_parameters = np.array([1,1,1,1])

posterior_samples_A = dirichlet(prior_parameters + observations_A,
                                size=10000)
posterior_samples_B = dirichlet(prior_parameters + observations_B,
                                size=10000)

posterior_expected_revenue_A = expected_value(posterior_samples_A)
posterior_expected_revenue_B = expected_value(posterior_samples_B)

plt.hist(posterior_expected_revenue_A, histtype='stepfilled',
         label='expected revenue of A', bins=50)
plt.hist(posterior_expected_revenue_B, histtype='stepfilled',
         label='expected revenue of B', bins=50, alpha=0.8)
plt.xlabel('Value')
plt.ylabel('Density')
plt.title("Posterior distribution of the expected revenue\
          between pages $A$ and $B$")
plt.legend();
```

In Figure 7.3.3, notice how far apart the two posteriors are, suggesting a significant difference in the Web pages' performances. The average expected revenue for page *A* is about \$1 less than page *B*'s. (That might not seem like much, but this is *per page view*, which can really add up.) To confirm this difference exists, we can look at the probability that the revenue for page *B* is larger than page *A*'s, similar to what we performed in the previous conversion analysis.

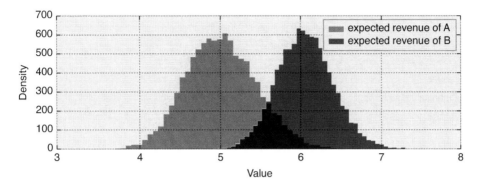

Figure 7.3.3: Posterior distribution of the expected revenue between pages *A* and *B*

```
p = (posterior_expected_revenue_B > posterior_expected_revenue_A).mean()
print "Probability that page B has a higher revenue than page A: %.3f"%p
```

```
[Output]:

Probability that page B has a higher revenue than page A: 0.965
```

This value, 96%, is high enough to be significant, so the business should choose page *B* going forward.

Another interesting plot to look at is the posterior difference in revenue between the pages, shown in Figure 7.3.4. We get this for free since we are using Bayesian analysis; we simply look at the histogram of the difference of the two expected revenue posteriors.

```
posterior_diff = posterior_expected_revenue_B -
                 posterior_expected_revenue_A

plt.hist(posterior_diff, histtype='stepfilled', color='#7A68A6',
         label='difference in revenue between B and A', bins=50)
plt.vlines(0, 0, 700, linestyles='--')
plt.xlabel('Value')
plt.ylabel('Density')
plt.title("Posterior distribution of the delta between expected\
          revenues of pages $A$ and $B$")
plt.legend();
```

Looking at this posterior, we see that there is about a 50% chance that the difference is *more* than $1, and possibly even larger than $2. And if we are wrong about our choice of *B* (which is possible), we probably won't lose much: The distribution doesn't extend much past −$0.50.

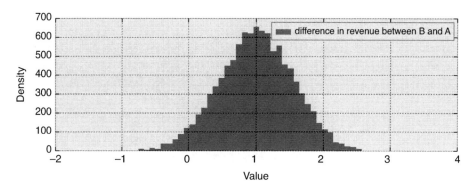

Figure 7.3.4: Posterior distribution of the delta between expected revenues of pages *A* and *B*

7.4 Going Beyond Conversions: t-test

Probably the most taught statistical test in classrooms is the **t-test**. The traditional t-test is a frequentist test to determine if a sample average deviates far from a predetermined value. There is a Bayesian version of the t-test, popularized by John K. Kruschke, that will be used here. This model is called BEST, for *Bayesian Estimation Supersedes the t-test*. The original paper by Kruschke[1] is very accessible, and I highly recommend reading it.

7.4.1 The Setup of the t-test

Following our A/B testing theme, suppose we have data about the length of time a user is on a test page. This data is not binary; it's continuous. For example, we'll create some artificial data with the following code:

```
N = 250
mu_A, std_A = 30, 4
mu_B, std_B = 26, 7

# create durations (seconds) users are on the pages for
durations_A = np.random.normal(mu_A, std_A, size=N)
durations_B = np.random.normal(mu_B, std_B, size=N)
```

Keep in mind that in real life, we do not see the parameters in the previous block of code; we just see the output:

```
print durations_A[:8]
print durations_B[:8]
```

```
[Output]:

[34.2695  28.4035  22.5516  34.1591  31.1951  27.9881  30.0798  30.6869]
[36.1196  19.1633  32.6542  19.7711  27.5813  34.4942  34.1319  25.6773]
```

Our task is to determine on which page, *A* or *B*, users stay longer. We have five unknowns for this model, two mean parameters (denoted by μ), two standard deviation parameters (denoted σ), and one additional model unique to t-tests: ν (pronounced "nu"). The ν parameter sets how likely we are to see large outliers in our data. According to the BEST model, our priors for the unknowns are as follows.

1. μ_A and μ_B come from a Normal distribution with prior mean equal to the pooled mean of data from *A* and *B*, and prior standard deviation equal to 1,000 times the pooled standard deviation. (This is a very wide, uninformative prior.)

```
import pymc as pm

pooled_mean = np.r_[durations_A, durations_B].mean()
pooled_std = np.r_[durations_A, durations_B].std()
tau = 1./np.sqrt(1000.*pooled_std) # PyMC uses a precision
                                   # parameter, 1/sigma**2

mu_A = pm.Normal("mu_A", pooled_mean, tau)
mu_B = pm.Normal("mu_B", pooled_mean, tau)
```

2. σ_A and σ_B come from a uniform distribution, restricted to one one-thousandths of the pooled standard deviation, to 1000 times the standard deviation. (Again, a very wide uninformative prior).

```
std_A = pm.Uniform("std_A", pooled_std/1000., 1000.*pooled_std)
std_B = pm.Uniform("std_B", pooled_std/1000., 1000.*pooled_std)
```

3. Finally, ν is estimated from a shifted exponential distribution with parameter equal to 29. For more details about why this was chosen, it is detailed in Appendix A of [1]. One interesting detail of BEST is that ν is shared between the two groups. This will be clearer in the following diagram.

```
nu_minus_1 = pm.Exponential("nu-1", 1./29)
```

All together, our model looks like Figure 7.4.1 (from [2]).
Let's finish putting the pieces model of the model together:

```
obs_A = pm.NoncentralT("obs_A", mu_A, 1.0/std_A**2, nu_minus_1 + 1,
                       observed=True, value=durations_A)
obs_B = pm.NoncentralT("obs_B", mu_B, 1.0/std_B**2, nu_minus_1 + 1,
                       observed=True, value=durations_B)

mcmc = pm.MCMC([obs_A, obs_B, mu_A, mu_B, std_A, std_B, nu_minus_1])
mcmc.sample(25000,10000)
```

```
[Output]:

[------------------100%-----------------] 25000 of 25000 complete
 in 16.6 sec
```

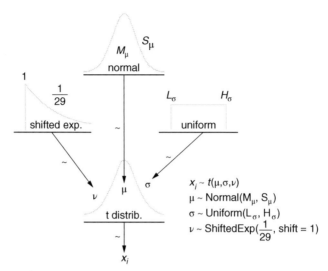

Figure 7.4.1: Graphical representation of the BEST model[2]

```
mu_A_trace, mu_B_trace = mcmc.trace('mu_A')[:], mcmc.trace('mu_B')[:]
std_A_trace, std_B_trace = mcmc.trace('std_A')[:], mcmc.trace('std_B')[:]
nu_trace = mcmc.trace("nu-1")[:] + 1

figsize(12,8)
def _hist(data, label, **kwargs):
    return plt.hist(data, bins=40, histtype='stepfilled',
                    alpha=.95, label=label, **kwargs)

ax = plt.subplot(3,1,1)
_hist(mu_A_trace,'A')
_hist(mu_B_trace,'B')
plt.legend()
plt.title('Posterior distributions of $\mu$')

ax = plt.subplot(3,1,2)
_hist(std_A_trace, 'A')
_hist(std_B_trace, 'B')
plt.legend()
plt.title('Posterior distributions of $\sigma$')

ax = plt.subplot(3,1,3)
_hist(nu_trace,'', color='#7A68A6')
plt.title(r'Posterior distribution of $\nu$')
plt.xlabel('Value')
plt.ylabel('Density')
plt.tight_layout();
```

From Figure 7.4.2, we can see that there is a clear difference between these two groups (by construction, of course). In the top plot of Figure 7.4.2, we've plotted the posteriors

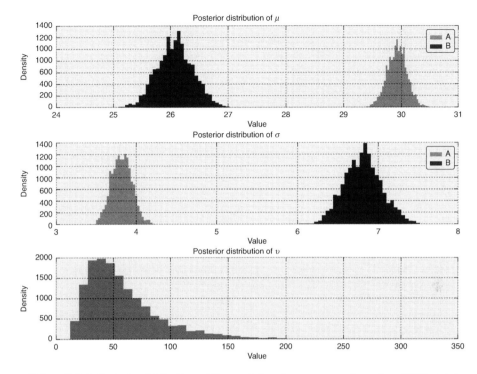

Figure 7.4.2: Posterior distributions of the model's unknown parameters of our BEST model

of the μ_1 and μ_2 unknowns. The second plot is a plot of σ_1 and σ_2. We can see that not only does page A have a higher average duration of time spent on the page, but the volatility of each page view is lower (as page A's standard deviation is lower). Furthermore, with these posteriors, we can calculate differences between groups, effect sizes, and so on.

One nice feature about the BEST model is that it is opinionated enough that it could be wrapped up into a nice function, with few modifications after that.

7.5   Estimating the Increase

Decision makers, after an A/B test, are often interested in the *size* of the increase. This is wrong, and I label this confusing the **continuous problem** with the **binary problem**. The continuous problem is trying to measure *how much better* one is (a continuous range of possible values), and the binary problem is trying to determine *which is better* (only two possible values). The problem is that answering the continuous problem requires orders of magnitude more data than answering the binary problem, but businesses want to use the binary problem's answer to answer the continuous problem. In fact, the most common statistical tests attempt only to answer the binary problem, which is what we have done in the preceding sections.

Regardless, business units still want to see both questions answered. Let's first look at what *not* to do. Suppose you estimate the conversion rates of both groups using the methods we've discussed so far. The business would like to know the relative increase of the result, sometimes called the *lift* of the experiment. One idea is to naively take the mean of both posteriors and compute the relative increase:

$$\frac{\hat{p}_A - \hat{p}_B}{\hat{p}_B}$$

This can lead to some serious errors. The first is that we have swept all uncertainty about the true values of p_A and p_B under the rug. By measuring lift using the previous equation, we've assumed we exactly know these values. This almost always grossly overestimates the value, especially when p_A and p_B are close to 0. This is why you see ridiculous headlines like "How a Single A/B Test Increased Conversions by 336%"[3] (that's a real headline, too!).

The problem is that we want to preserve uncertainty; statistics is about modeling uncertainty, after all! To do this, we just pass our posteriors through a function, and output a new posterior. Let's try this on a conclusive A/B test. The posterior distributions are presented in Figure 7.5.1.

```
figsize(12,4)

visitors_to_A = 1275
visitors_to_B = 1300

conversions_from_A = 22
conversions_from_B = 12

alpha_prior = 1
beta_prior = 1

posterior_A = beta(alpha_prior + conversions_from_A,
                   beta_prior + visitors_to_A - conversions_from_A)

posterior_B = beta(alpha_prior + conversions_from_B,
                   beta_prior + visitors_to_B - conversions_from_B)


samples = 20000
samples_posterior_A = posterior_A.rvs(samples)
samples_posterior_B = posterior_B.rvs(samples)

_hist(samples_posterior_A, 'A')
_hist(samples_posterior_B, 'B')
plt.xlabel('Value')
plt.ylabel('Density')
plt.title("Posterior distributions of the conversion\
          rates of Web pages $A$ and $B$")
plt.legend();
```

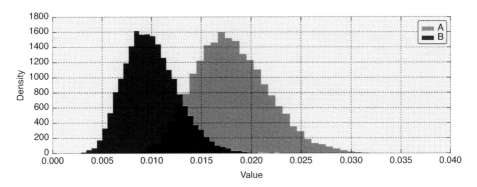

Figure 7.5.1: Posterior distributions of the conversion rates of Web pages *A* and *B*

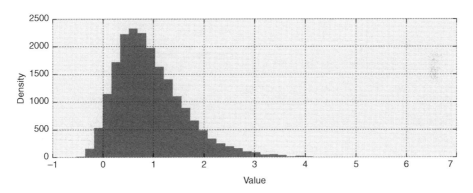

Figure 7.5.2: Posterior distribution of the relative lift of Web page *A*'s conversion rate over Web page *B*'s conversion rate

We'll pass the posteriors through a function that computes the relative increase pairwise. The resulting posterior is shown in Figure 7.5.2.

```
def relative_increase(a,b):
    return (a-b)/b

posterior_rel_increase = relative_increase(samples_posterior_A,
    samples_posterior_B)
plt.xlabel('Value')
plt.ylabel('Density')
plt.title("Posterior distribution of the relative lift of Web page\
        $A$'s conversion rate over Web page $B$'s conversion rate")

_hist(posterior_rel_increase, 'relative increase', color='#7A68A6');
```

From Figure 7.5.2 and the next calculation, we can see that there is an 89% chance that the relative increase is 20% or more. Furthermore, there is a 72% chance that the increase is as great as 50%.

```
print (posterior_rel_increase > 0.2).mean()
print (posterior_rel_increase > 0.5).mean()
```

```
[Output]:

0.89275
0.72155
```

If we were to naively use the point estimates, which would be

$$\hat{p}_A = \frac{22}{1275} = 0.017$$

$$\hat{p}_B = \frac{12}{1300} = 0.009$$

then our estimate of the relative increase would be 87%—probably too high of a value.

7.5.1   Creating Point Estimates

As I've said before, it is rude to hand over a distribution to someone, especially to a business unit who is expecting a single number. So what do you do? There are three options as I see it:

1. Return the mean of the posterior relative increase distribution. I actually don't like this suggestion, and I left it in to explain why. Looking at Figure 7.5.2, we can see a long right tail of possible values. This implies a **skewed** distribution. When we have a skewed distribution, a summary statistic like the mean is overly influenced by the tail, hence we would be overrepresenting the tail and overestimating the *true* relative increase.

2. Return the median of the posterior relative increase distribution. In light of the previous discussion, the median is a more appropriate choice. The median is more robust to skewed distributions. In practice, though, I've found the median to still give an overly inflated value.

3. Return a percentile (less than 50%) of the posterior relative increase distribution. For example, return the 30th percentile of the distribution. This has two desirable properties. The first is that it is mathematically equivalent to applying a loss function on top of the relative increase posterior that penalizes overestimates more than underestimates, hence this value is a conservative estimate. Secondly, as we get more and more data from our experiment, the relative increase posterior distribution gets skinnier and skinnier, meaning any percentiles eventually converge to the same point.

In Figure 7.5.3, I've plotted the three summary statistics:

```
mean = posterior_rel_increase.mean()
median = np.percentile(posterior_rel_increase, 50)
conservative_percentile = np.percentile(posterior_rel_increase, 30)

_hist(posterior_rel_increase,'', color='#7A68A6');
plt.vlines(mean, 0, 2500, linestyles='-.', label='mean')
plt.vlines(median, 0, 2500, linestyles=':', label='median', lw=3)
plt.vlines(conservative_percentile, 0, 2500, linestyles='--',
           label='30th percentile')
plt.xlabel('Value')
plt.ylabel('Density')
plt.title("Different summary statistics of the posterior distribution
           of the relative increase")

plt.legend();
```

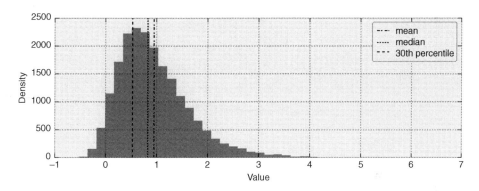

Figure 7.5.3: Different summary statistics of the posterior distribution of the relative increase

7.6 Conclusion

In this chapter, we have discussed what Bayesian A/B testing looks like. The two largest benefits of Bayesian A/B testing over traditional methods are:

1. Interpretable probabilities: In Bayesian analysis, you can directly answer the question *What is the probability that we are wrong?* In a frequentist setting, this is difficult or impossible to answer.

2. Easy application of loss functions: We saw in Chapter 5 how loss functions can connect abstract models of probability distributions to real-world problems. In this chapter, we applied a linear loss function to determine the expected revenue of a page view, and another loss function to determine an appropriate point estimate.

Like in other applications, Bayesian analysis is more flexible and interpretable than other methods, and comes at only moderate computational cost for the more complex models. I predict that Bayesian A/B testing will become more common than traditional methods very soon.

7.7   References

1. Kruschke, John K. "Bayesian Estimation Supersedes the *t* test," *Journal of Experimental Psychology: General,* 142, no. 2 (2013): 573–603.

2. Graphical representation of the BEST model by Rasmus Bååth, licensed under CC BY 4.0. `http://www.sumsar.net/blog/2014/02/bayesian-first-aid-one-sample-t-test/`.

3. Sparks, Dustin. "How a Single A/B Test Increased Conversions by 336% [Case Study]," unbounce.com, accessed June 2, 2015, `http://unbounce.com/a-b-testing/how-a-single-a-b-test-increased-conversions/`.

Glossary

95% credible interval	the interval in the domain of a posterior probability that contains 95% of the distribution.
95% least plausible value	the lower bound of the 95% credible interval.
absolute-loss function	a type of loss function that increases linearly with the difference, often used in machine learning and robust statistics. See also *loss function*.
autocorrelation	a measure of how related a series of numbers is to itself, ranging from 1 (perfect positive autocorrelation) to 0 (no autocorrelation) to −1 (perfect negative correlation).
Bayesian point estimate	the output of a function that summarizes the posterior distribution.
Bayesian p-values	a statistical summary of a model, analogous to frequentist p-values.
Bayesianism	a statistical paradigm that defines a probability as the measure of belief, or confidence, in an event occurring.
Bernoulli distribution	a binary random variable that can only take the value of 0 or 1.
Beta distribution	a distribution that defines random variables between 0 and 1, making it a popular choice for modeling probabilities and proportions.
binary problem	measuring *which is better* (from only two possible values). Contrast *continuous problem*.
child variable	a variable that is affected by another variable. Contrast *parent variable*.
continuous problem	measuring *how much better* (from a continuous range of possible values) one thing is than another. Contrast *binary problem*.
continuous random variable	a variable that can take on arbitrarily exact values, such as temperature or speed. Contrast *discrete random variable* and *mixed random variable*.

daily return	the relative change in an investment over one trading day.
deterministic variable	a variable that is not random if the variable's parents' values are known. Contrast *stochastic variable*.
discrete random variable	a variable that may only assume values on a specified list, such as a movie rating. Contrast *continuous random variable* and *mixed random variable*.
Empirical Bayes	a trick that combines frequentist and Bayesian inference by using frequentist methods to select the hyperparameters and then proceeding to use Bayesian methods on the original problem.
expected daily return	the expected relative change in an investment over one trading day.
expected total regret	over many trials, what the average total regret may be for a multi-armed bandit problem. This can be calculated by averaging over many runs of a multi-armed bandit algorithm.
flat prior	a uniform distribution over the entire range of the unknown, implying that each possible value should be assigned an equal weighting.
frequentism	the classical paradigm of statistics in which probability is defined as the long-run frequency of events.
goodness of fit	the measure of how well a statistical model fits the observed data.
loss function	a function of the true parameter that measures how bad the current estimate is.
mean posterior correlation matrix	the element-wise expected value of the matrix's posterior distribution, which can be computed empirically by averaging over samples from the posterior.
mixed random variable	a variable that assigns probabilities to both discrete and continuous random variables; a combination of these two variable types. See also *continuous random variable* and *discrete random variable*.
objective prior	a prior that aims to allow the data to influence the posterior the most. See also *flat prior*; contrast *subjective prior*.
parent variable	a variable that influences another variable. Contrast *child variable*.
posterior probability	an updated belief about event A given evidence X, denoted $P(A|X)$. See *prior probability*.

Principle of Indifference	the idea that if an individual is choosing among n items, and each item is indistinguishable from the others, then each item should be chosen with probability $1/n$.
prior probability	a belief about event A, denoted $P(A)$, prior to incorporating evidence about the event. See *posterior probability*.
separation plot	a data-visualization approach to allow the graphical comparison of alternate models against one another.
sparse prediction	a Bayesian point estimate that is shrunk toward 0.
squared-error loss function	a type of loss function that increases quadratically with the difference, used in estimators like linear regression, calculation of unbiased statistics, and many areas of machine learning. See also *loss function*.
stochastic variable	a variable whose value is still random even if its parent variables' values are known. Contrast *deterministic variable*.
subjective prior	a prior that allows the practitioner to express his or her views. Contrast *objective prior*.
traces	samples returned from the posterior distribution by MCMC (Markov Chain Monte Carlo).
t-test	a frequentist test to determine if a sample average deviates far from a predetermined value.
Wishart distribution	a distribution over all positive semi-definite matrices.

Index

M

Made in the USA
Monee, IL
01 October 2020